Parricide in the United States, 1840–1899

Parricide in the United States, 1840–1899

KERRY SEGRAVE

McFarland & Company, Inc., Publishers
Jefferson, North Carolina, and London

LIBRARY OF CONGRESS CATALOGUING-IN-PUBLICATION DATA

Segrave, Kerry, 1944–
    Parricide in the United States, 1840–1899 / Kerry Segrave.
        p.   cm.
    Includes bibliographical references and index.

    ISBN 978-0-7864-4523-3
    softcover : 50# alkaline paper ∞

    1. Parricide—United States—History—19th century.   I. Title.
HV6542.S44   2009
364.152'3—dc22   2009017957

British Library cataloguing data are available

On the cover: family photo ©2009 eclecticollections; shadow and
background ©2009 Shutterstock

Manufactured in the United States of America

*McFarland & Company, Inc., Publishers
    Box 611, Jefferson, North Carolina 28640
    www.mcfarlandpub.com*

Table of Contents

Preface

Parricide, for the purpose of this book, is defined as the killing of a parent, either a mother or a father—matricide or patricide. Profiled herein are selected individual cases of parricide that occurred in the United States during the period 1840 to 1899. Most of the cases involve children convicted of the crime of patricide or matricide, although a few cases are included wherein the accused was found not guilty. As well, a few suspects were apparently successful in escaping capture and were never found and brought to justice. In a few instances the final outcome of the case was never reported in the press.

For current times, the crime of parricide is estimated to be around 2 percent of total homicides with that total split between matricide and patricide roughly equally. No such statistics are available for the last half of the 19th century but nothing suggests the percentage would differ greatly from current estimates. Over time in America women have made up, roughly, 10 percent of all the murderers. And that is roughly the percentage of females profiled in this book.

Chapter 1 looks at sons charged with killing their fathers in situations where family abuse seemed to be the motivating factor for the murders. In chapter 2 are profiled sons charged with killing fathers in circumstances in which alcohol played a prominent role. Chapter 3 looks at sons murdering fathers wherein financial gain was the apparent major reason for the crime, while chapter four outlines the stories of sons charged with killing fathers for various other reasons. Chapters 5, 6, and 7 are similar to chapters two, three, and four, except the victims in the former chapters are all mothers. In chapter 8 are profiled daughters who were charged with killing a parent. Chapter 9 is devoted to multiple killers and a single victim. That is, two or more siblings were charged with killing a mother or a father. Lastly, chapter 10 profiles murderers who each claimed multiple victims. That is, he or she killed at least one parent and mur-

dered, or attempted to murder at the same time, one or more other people, although the other victim or victims did not have to be related.

Included in the last chapter is America's most infamous parricide—
Lizzie Borden. She is still remembered today—although she was found not
guilty—while none of the other parricides featured in this book have
remained current in the American memory, although many achieved much
media notoriety at the time of their crime. America's justice system was
in a fairly rudimentary condition in the time period covered and items
such as separate treatment for juveniles and the idea that a criminal did
not profit from his crime were not yet in place. Some of the cases in this
book helped to move that system along. But at the time, young teenaged
parricides were treated and incarcerated as if they were adults and several
people profiled in this book had high-priced legal help to defend them at
their murder trials only because they paid such people out of the money
they inherited from a parent after killing that parent. Within the category
of homicide the act of parricide was always considered more extreme,
repugnant, and revolting than an "ordinary" murder. The act of killing
the one who gave a person life always struck an extra raw nerve. Those
featured in this book range from youngsters lashing out after receiving one
too many beatings from a father to a callous plan by a child to kill a parent for money. They range from a precocious, and lethal, 12-year-old to
middle-aged children who today would likely be defined as completely mad
and institutionalized, thus preventing a crime. Punishment for those convicted of parricide ranged from a short stint in jail to execution.

1

Sons, Fathers, and Family Abuse

John Rose

In the words of one newsman, "one of the most horrible and unnatural murders" ever committed took place on Thursday, October 4, 1866, about five miles east of Carthage, Illinois. Jesse Rose was the victim, murdered by his own son while a second son stood by as an accessory to the act. Jesse was a farmer who had purchased a small place about six miles east of Carthage and moved his family onto the place two years earlier after buying the farm. "He is represented to have been a man of very ordinary mortal acquirements; not a good manager; rather shiftless, and withal a poor provider for his family," said a reporter. "His domestic relations with his family have been at times turbulent, and it is said he sometimes, in a fit of passion, beat and abused his wife terribly. He was not a dissipated man in the full acceptance of the term; but he sometimes came home full of liquor." Three days after the murder a reporter with the *Carthage Republican* called on the widow and was granted an interview. Cena Rose, daughter of John Long, had been born in the county and had been married to Jesse for 19 years. The couple had eight children, five of whom were still alive: John, 18; Berry, 16; Charles, 10; Willie, five; and Thomas, two. Cena's three daughters were all dead. The family had lived in various places in the area over the years before settling on the farm near Carthage. Jesse was not a good provider, explained his widow: "He often let us go for weeks and weeks without anything but bread and molasses, and sometimes not enough of that. He was not kind to me. He was apt to get fretted about little things, and then he was very angry and abusive. If we didn't do exactly as he wanted us to do he would scold and storm at us. In these disputes the children took my part. My oldest boy John would get very angry and tell his father that he must not abuse mother so."[1]

On that fateful Thursday, Jesse went to Carthage and did not return home until after dark. Cena went to bed at 8:00 P.M. and the boys followed suit at various later hours. In the morning Jesse still was not home. Breakfast was being prepared and Charles was sent out on an errand to fetch some milk from a neighbor. But soon he came racing back, crying, and saying his father was dead in the road. Cena went out and found her husband's body in a field about 200 yards from the house. Neighbors were called and soon gathered; then the authorities arrived. Throughout all of that John did not tell his mother he had killed his father; John confessed to a reporter. According to John's account, Jesse returned from Carthage after sundown but did not stay for supper or even go into the house, as he planned to go to the local schoolhouse for a writing class that evening. During that time, John and Berry went to the field to tend the cattle, with John thinking all the while about killing his father. Telling his brother Berry that he had made up his mind to kill Jesse, John waited around outside the house for his father's return. Jesse got back from the schoolhouse around 10:00 P.M., at which time John attacked him and struck him several blows with an axe. John said Berry didn't say much about his plan; but he did not oppose it. "I killed him because he abused mother; he whipped and kicked her often; he wouldn't provide things for us to eat, he was abusive to all but the little children; I never went to school but very little; I cannot read or write; none of us can read or write except father; mother reads a little; I never went to Sunday-school," went John's confession.[2]

A grand jury met on Monday, October 8, and indicted John Rose for the murder of Jesse Rose and acquitted Berry and Cena. On Tuesday morning John was taken to court, where he pled not guilty and was assigned a lawyer. On Tuesday afternoon the trial was held and neighbors of the accused testified to his lack of "ordinary sense or knowledge of human responsibility; that he was, in fact, but little removed from an idiot." Therefore it was agreed by both sides in the case that John should enter a plea of guilty to manslaughter, which was done. Still on Tuesday, the court sentenced John Rose to the state penitentiary for life.[3]

Frank Walworth

One of the most notorious and well publicized cases of a child killing a parent in the time period covered by this book was the case involving the Walworth family. Frank Walworth, 19, shot and killed his father,

Mansfield Walworth, on the morning of June 3, 1873, in New York City, in a prominent Broadway hotel—Sturtevant House. Mansfield was a well known author and lived apart from his family, having separated from them. Domestic trouble was listed as the cause of the murderous tragedy. Frank, who lived with his mother and sisters in Saratoga, New York, went to the nearest police precinct after the shooting and surrendered. He told the police briefly of the family separation, of some years standing, that he was studying law and that his father was about 41 years old; but Frank did not know where his father was born. Mansfield had not lived with his wife since she and Frank and his daughters left New York City about three years earlier to live in Saratoga. However, continued the young man, over that period he had repeatedly sent "insulting and threatening" letters to them at their new home. Also, he said, Mansfield had recently threatened to shoot both his wife and son and "I shot him because of this." Shortly before the killing Frank had met his father in the streets of Saratoga and told him if he did not keep away from him and his mother and if he did not refrain from insulting his mother then he would shoot him. On the day before the murder Frank went to New York City and checked into the hotel and left a note for his father to call on him. Mansfield went to his son's room the following morning. When the father went into the room the son drew a gun and told him to promise he would not threaten or insult his mother and him any more, which Mansfield promised. Shortly after that climax the two men began to discuss family matters and, said Frank, continuing his story, Mansfield used some "very insulting language" while at the same time putting his hand in his pocket as though he was going to draw a gun. In response Frank shot him. When the first shot did not topple Mansfield, who kept coming towards his son, Frank fired three more shots at his father. And that was the story that Frank told the police. The Walworth family was very prominent socially. Mansfield was a nephew of New York State Chief Justice Barbour and the son of the late New York State Chancellor Reuben Walworth, one of the most distinguished citizens in New York State and a man identified with the great temperance, tract, and Bible societies. A brother of the deceased was a popular and eloquent mission preacher. "The family has been largely identified with the most prominent interests in this State," said a reporter. At the time of Mansfield's death the *New York Weekly* was publishing a Mansfield serial story and he had another novel being published.[4]

The day of the murder, one reporter commented, "So far, the case is one of unusual repulsiveness: a father in the prime of life ruthlessly shot dead by his son, only nineteen years old." Frank was descended from the Walworth family of New York State and on his mother's side from the Hardin family of Illinois, "thus uniting the purest blood in the country." Mansfield Tracy Walworth was the eldest son, by a first wife, of the late Reuben Hyde Walworth, ex–Chancellor of the State of New York, and nephew of Chief Justice Barbour of the Supreme Court of New York State who, on hearing of the tragedy, adjourned the court, in which he was sitting at the time. Chancellor Walworth had also been Grand Master for the State of New York in the Masonic Order. He had died in 1867 at the age of 80. Mansfield was born in 1830 at Albany, New York. He studied law and was admitted to the bar, but eventually he abandoned the practice of the law for literature and began his writing career by contributing short sketches to the *Home Journal*. In 1853 his first novel, *The Mission of Death*, was published and had since gone through 12 editions. His next novel, *Lulu, a Tale of the National Hotel Poisoning*, was published with several editions issued. Mansfield's third novel, *Hotspur*, came out in 1864 and was followed by his fourth, *Stormcliff*, in 1866. *Warwick, or The Lost Nationalities of America*, a novel focusing on the Roman Catholic faith, came out in 1869. His brother Charles Walworth soon after converted to Roman Catholicism and was then a Paulist priest. Two more novels were published before Mansfield's death, *Delaplaine* and *Beverly* (his last novel), along with a nonfiction work, *The Chancellors of New York*. His serialized work, *Married in Mask*, was running in a New York City weekly publication at the time of his murder. One of the characters in the latter was said to be a satirical depiction of his wife. Also, Mansfield had published numerous short stories in magazines and was active on the lecture circuit in New York City. In the view of the reporter who summarized the murder victim's literary career, Mansfield's literary works were more descriptive than driven by plot or character: "His works were only intended for and only bought by the numerous class of persons who admire glittering and gaudy description and sentimental story-telling. In this respect they were admirably successful and netted the author a fair income."[5]

Mansfield's wife, Nellie Hardin, was the daughter of the famous Colonel John J. Hardin of Illinois. Colonel Hardin was said to have been one of the most distinguished lawyers in the state and a formidable rival of Senator Stephen A. Douglas, so much so that Douglas on one occasion declared Hardin to be the only man in Illinois he feared to meet in debate. Hardin had served as a member of the Illinois legislature and as a representative from Illinois in the United States Congress. He died in battle in 1847 in the Mexican War, during which he gained a reputation as a great solider. The widow, Mrs. Hardin, then moved with her daughter to New York State and met Chancellor Walworth, then a widower, and his son Mansfield. The elder couple married, making young Mansfield Walworth and Nellie Hardin step-siblings. A brief courtship followed and the younger pair were married. By that marriage Mansfield and Nellie had three children, Frank and two daughters, aged 14 and 15 at the time of the murder. On the occasion of his son's marriage, Chancellor Walworth settled on his daughter-in-law the property at Saratoga, New York, where she then resided with the children.[6]

Nellie and Mansfield were apparently happy for the first few years of their married life, but, said a journalist, after that it "was a continual quarrel, not on her part, but on his. Her children were treated by Walworth, not as a father should treat his children, and she was regarded by her husband not as a man should respect and love his wife." From quarrels they moved on to violence and Mansfield reportedly struck Nellie on occasion. As Frank grew and matured he tried to protect his mother and became himself another target for the father's innuendoes and insults. When such insults and ill treatment became unbearable—three years earlier—Nellie separated from her husband and took the children with her to live on the Saratoga property, where she also established and ran successfully a ladies' boarding school. Mansfield remained in New York City where he continued his literary endeavors. As well, he wrote letters to Nellie and Frank at Saratoga. Mrs. Walworth still had some of those letters, of which it was said, "They teem with insults, one of them threatening to break up her school by making charges against her character. In others of the letters are threats to shoot her and her son Frank." Several letters containing similar threats were mailed from Mansfield directly to Frank at Saratoga. Such letters continued to come and finally Frank determined that they should end. On a Monday morning an angry Frank packed a bag and left Saratoga without bidding his mother and sisters good-bye. He went to New York City and checked into Sturtevant House at 3:00 P.M. on Tuesday and was given room 267. He took a bath and left the hotel, proceeding to his father's residence only to find him out. Leaving a note, Frank asked his father to come and see him at the hotel in an hour or two, to settle some family matters. For the rest of the day Frank waited at the hotel, expecting his father, who never came. At 6:15 the next morning Mansfield showed up at the hotel. After the clerk checked with Frank and Frank agreed,

Mansfield went upstairs and entered room 267. Some minutes after that, four shots rang out. Frank was soon observed calmly leaving the room and exiting the hotel. Sources in Saratoga reported, "[I]t appears that Mrs. Walworth and her son have the entire sympathy of the community resident there, young Walworth sustaining a high character, while his father bore a reputation directly the reverse."[7]

Reverend Father Preston, said to be an intimate of Mansfield and one who enjoyed his greatest confidence, stated a few days after the murder that the obscene letters referred to by the parricide and his friends as having been the cause of the murder contained accusations against Nellie of indiscriminate infidelity and assertions that Frank was a bastard. Mansfield's friends declared that ample proof would be brought forward at the trial, if necessary, to establish the fact that Mansfield had lots of grounds for his charges against his wife. They added that the deceased himself had "improper relations" with her six months before their marriage and that only because of that circumstance would their parents consent to their marriage. That latter fact was said to be the basis of the slur upon Frank's birth, which spurred the young man to take vengeance. Early in January 1871 Nellie's action for a separation began. Relief asked for was a divorce on the ground of cruel and inhumane treatment. Adultery was not charged in the papers filed nor was there any plea for an absolute divorce. Legal papers were served on Mansfield on January 27, 1871, but he took no notice and he allowed the matter to go by default. Shortly thereafter the decree was confirmed, with the divorce containing a clause compelling Mansfield to pay his wife a certain sum of money for her support and a sum of money for the support of the children. At that point Mansfield disputed the action. After exchanges between lawyers a compromise was reached wherein the clause in the decree granting alimony to the wife was struck out. In all other respects the decree was allowed to stand.[8]

With respect to the Walworth murder, a newspaper editorial declared, one month after the killing, "The case presents points that are calculated to confuse the moral casuists as well as confound the philosophers of the law. It presents the anomaly of a bad man killed by a good man ... and this crime, so horrible that the Romans gave it no name in their law, committed from the best of motives. To add to the dramatic interest of the affair, all the personages concerned are of the first blood, not only of New York, but of the country." The editor added, "There can be no doubt but he killed his father, as he supposed, in defense of the dignity and honor and life of his mother. It is a sad case; as we have said, the worst of crimes, committed from the best of motives."[9]

Frank's trial took place in July 1873 with Charles O'Connor, described as one of the most prominent lawyers in the United States, being one of four representing the defendant. In the view of a *New York Times* editor, "[W]e all look to Mr. O'Connor for something very much better than we ordinarily get from some of the ill-trained and ill-educated members of his profession." Still, the editor was not happy with some of O'Connor's tactics: "he seems to have found it necessary to heap every kind of condemnation upon the father," portraying him as a "shameless monster of impiety and wickedness." And he was unhappy that a friend of the family had described the victim, in court, in such fashion as to make it "seem as if some evil genius had collected all wickedness and scandalous false pretense in one vessel, and poured it in at the creation of this Mansfield Tracy Walworth." Also, the editor did not like O'Connor's implication at the trial that if a son murdered a father whose life was not that of a good man, he had committed no crime either against God or against man. Pointedly, the editor wondered why, if Frank and Nellie feared for their lives from Mansfield as it was strongly argued at the trial, the pair did not seek help and protection in other ways. Why had they never gone to the authorities? Why had they not gone to a high-priced lawyer such as O'Connor, who surely could have pointed out to them a less drastic solution?[10]

In July 1873 Frank was convicted of murder in the second degree and sentenced to life imprisonment. On July 10 he was sent to Sing Sing penitentiary. About one year later he was transferred to the asylum for insane prisoners at Auburn State Prison in New York. Reportedly there was then a movement afoot to procure a pardon for Frank because, it was argued, he had a tendency to epilepsy and insanity. When a reporter went to Auburn to visit him the inmate went into his routine. As soon as the prisoner saw the newsman he threw himself onto a cot behind a screen and turned to face the wall. From the keeper the reporter learned that Frank had avoided looking at any of his visitors except his mother and grandmother ever since he had been there. Since that visit he had been taken to the asylum to be assessed for insanity. It was reported to be the intention of New York State governor Dix to visit him at Auburn to see him before the decided whether or not to issue a pardon.[11]

About one year after that, in September 1875, another reporter was given a tour of the lunatic asylum for insane convicts, a separate part of the Auburn State Prison complex, to see the notable lunatics. The first such he saw was Frank Walworth. That journalist asked his doctor guide in the facility if the prisoner was really crazy or if his incarceration there simply been arranged through the wealth of his family. The physician "guardedly" replied, "He is an epileptic and medical authorities do not deem epileptics at all times responsibly sane." Governor Robinson of New York State issued a pardon freeing Frank Walworth on August 1, 1877.[12]

A report in August 1879 noted that Frank was then back at the Walworth family home in Saratoga. "He has not a single feature or trait of character that would indicate he is a parricide. His health is poor, but he is reading law," commented a reporter. "He is tall, fair and manly in his bearing, but he has an inexpressibly sad, pre-occupied expression. He is of course isolated from society. On his exit from prison his former friends cut him, and his proud spirit felt it heavily." His mother, Nellie, was said to have the respect and sympathy of the entire community. She was then on the brink of turning 50 years of age but was said to look 10 years younger. It was presumed that the old homestead would be sold and she, with Frank, would sail for the Old World to join her other children, who were already residing there.[13]

James L. Bailey

A young man named James L. Bailey shot and killed his father in New York City on the afternoon of July 18, 1875. After the crime he walked out of the family home and gave himself up to a passing policeman to whom he confessed the deed. Witness to the murder was the Bailey wife and mother. The Bailey family resided at 424 West 49th Street in a three-storey brick building, one of a group of eight identical houses on the block. On the top floor resided the Baileys—James, 50, a blacksmith; Ann, the wife; and sons James L. Bailey, a 22-year-old printer, and 18-year-old Robert. Of the father little was known by the neighbors as he was away a lot and being a retiring man he made few acquaintances when he was home. It was known that he was an Englishman who had brought his family to America around 12 years earlier and who worked at his trade part of the time but was out of work at other times. The rest of the family were known to the neighbors as quiet, industrious people of frugal habits who were able to live in comfort and in a respectable manner on the wages earned by the two sons. Rumors circulated that there was a scandal in the

Bailey household and that the father was not a good husband or a faithful husband and it was believed he was at times destitute when not living at home, while his family was living in comfort. But the family never spoke of their troubles, so the truth of the rumors was unknown. In the weeks leading up to the murder the deceased had continued to live in that irregular manner. On Saturday night, July 17, Bailey slept at home and he went out the next morning to walk and talk with friends, read the papers, and so forth. Around 2:00 P.M. he arrived home, finding his wife and eldest son to be there. He was not seen alive again and the only story of the ensuing 30 minutes or so came from Ann in her statement to the police. Around 2:30 P.M. neighbors heard cries and the sounds of a struggle in the Bailey rooms, then a pistol shot. Before the neighbors could respond to the situation both mother and son left their apartment, went into the street and found a police officer. "I have shot my father, and I want to give myself up," declared the son. Police took the gun and a letter, said to be the cause of the dispute. James L. told the police he had found the letter—from his father to a woman named Sarah Richards. He declared that his father had been intimate with Richards and had neglected his wife. An altercation in the apartment between them over that fact had led to blows, causing the mother to try and separate them. When his father turned to attack his mother, James L. shot him, in her defense.[14]

In that letter James told Sarah he would see her the following night and help her to pay her rent. James also told Sarah to send her son to a specific location so James could get him some wood for cooking to take back to Sarah. When Ann testified at the coroner's inquest, she said she and James had lived very unhappily together and he had left her about 18 months earlier and had gone to England, unbeknownst to her. Before he left, though, she said he stole $200 from the family home that belonged to her and James L. Six months after he left for England he was back in New York City, returning in August 1874. With him were a widow and her four children—the Sarah Richards family—with whom he had lived during his stay in England. Ann came to know of the situation from information given to her by her sister-in-law. James soon called upon Ann, only to have his wife tell him what she had learned; he denied everything. She was not satisfied with the denial and a few days after he turned up she went to a boardinghouse in the city and found him staying there with Richards. When Ann asked him what he intended to do, James told her to go away and leave him alone. Richards told Ann there was nothing between them and that James resided in her flat only as a lodger. Feeling sorry for her husband because he was so obviously poor, she took him back. But James often slipped out of the house and went to be with Richards; he was seen with her by Ann's son, her nephew, and others. After the landlady of Richards learned of the nature of the relationship between James and Sarah, she banned James from the Richards flat. Another brief period occurred when James left Ann, but she took him back when he again promised to give up Sarah. But he continued to sneak out to see her. Even when Ann told him to leave for good, and he apparently had done so, James sometimes turned up at night sleeping in the hallway by his wife's rooms or any other place in the building he could find if she would not admit him to the flat. Sometimes James would come for meals when his sons were absent, as they very much resented his treatment of their mother. On the night of Saturday, July 17, he showed up at the family home a little drunk. He went to lie down in the hallway but Ann told him to get up and she let him into the apartment to sleep on the kitchen floor for the night. She told him on the Sunday morning as he was going out not to come back to the house that day, but he returned at 2:00 P.M., whereupon Ann and James L. confronted him with the newly discovered letter. James got angry, cursed, and threw a plate at his wife. He grabbed Ann by the head and was trying to shove her out the window. As well, he hit James L. repeatedly with the stove lifter. Then a shot rang out.[15]

Musing on the Bailey case, an editor with the *Brooklyn Eagle* first summarized the case and then said, "Accepting the story [of self defense] of mother and son to be true, the moralist is left to decide whether a son has a right to select which of his parents a child may protect against the other, unto death. The Roman once thought the crime of parricide so utterly inhuman, that he made no law against it, refusing, by the enacting of a law, to recognize the possibility of such an act being perpetrated by a Roman. When finally forced to recognize it, he punished it with extra severity." Also pointed out was that in France at one time in the past the law severed the right hand of the parricide from his wrist just before it inflicted death for the crime. And throughout central Germany, a similar law was said to have existed for quite a long time; "and in all civilizations there has always existed a real or feigned horror and belief that the murder of a father by a son has in it an element of the devilish which forms no part of other murders." Believing that family difficulties and spousal violence and murders were increasing, the editor asserted the consideration of what a son was to do with respect to a bad father and a good mother, or a bad mother and a good father, was "fast becoming a duty" and "some guide to action is needed by the children of parents subject to this row-creating weakness" and the resulting divided loyalties and duties. "The superior veneration in which motherhood is entertained in France would secure the son's acquittal," thought the editor. "In England it would probably be held that he had no right to interfere. It remains to be seen by the law's treatment of Bailey how the matter will be looked on here." If the story told by Ann and James L. was true, concluded the editor, "it is very doubtful that the extreme, or indeed any, punishment by the law will be inflicted upon young Bailey. The question to be answered is whether any ought to be."[16]

A coroner's inquest into the Bailey death was held on July 21. Several independent witnesses living in houses on the opposite of the street testified to seeing James trying to throw his wife out of the window. When the jury returned its verdict it declared James L. Bailey had fired the fatal shot in defense of his own life and the life of his mother. Coroner Woltman said he should hold the accused for trial but would allow him bail in the amount of $2,000, which was immediately posted and the prisoner discharged. Apparently no further action was taken in the Bailey case.[17]

Sidney Pickering

A tragedy took place in August 1879 in Piute County, Utah, near Marshall's Ranch on the Sevier River. John Pickering whipped his 12-year-old son, Sidney Pickering, according to a report, "most unmercifully" and for "some trivial reason." As well, John told his son that if he allowed the sheep to get into the meadow he would "cut him into little pieces." On the morning following the day of the beating, Sidney took a pistol, rested it on a chair to steady his aim, and fired a shot at his father. The ball entered John's chest and killed him instantly. Sidney then went out and milked the cows as he usually did each morning. After that chore was completed he went and told some neighbors that his father had been killed by a man. But he told several conflicting stories and finally broke down and confessed to having committed the murder himself. Sidney showed no remorse or regret over his act, nor did he shed a tear. It was also reported the lad "narrowly escaped lynching at the hands of the exasperated citizens when he confessed and was arrested."[18]

A later report said that when he had received the whipping at the hands of John he told his father that was the last time he would submit to such treatment and then threatened to leave home and never return. When Sidney got up the next morning his father was still asleep; he put on his father's shoes and walked out into the road through the dust, so as to make a man's tracks. Then he went back to the house and shot John while the latter was still asleep in bed. After the shooting Sidney went to Jim Marshall's ranch five miles distant and told Marshall that John T. Mathias, the stage driver, had shot and killed his father.[19]

Sidney Pickering pled guilty in court to manslaughter and was sentenced to two years imprisonment.[20]

Guy Smith

Milton Smith, who lived one mile south of Kirkwood, Missouri, was shot and mortally wounded on July 7, 1882, by his son Guy Smith, 13, whom he had just punished for fighting with the lad's brother.[21]

A different account called Guy "a wild lad." About three weeks earlier Milton had whipped him, and Guy openly boasted that he would be avenged. When asked what he would do Guy replied, "I'll kill him. I'll have his life." No attention was paid to such remarks. On the morning of July 7 Milton, his sister Mrs. Eads, Guy, and the boy's grandfather had their breakfast and went out to do the chores. When Guy came in he was in a bad mood and began to smash the china and throw things around generally. His grandmother went out and called Milton to come into the house and quiet him down. When Milton came into the house he seized the boy and gave him a "good thrashing." Having finished administering the punishment he left the room and walked out of the house. Guy remained in the room for a minute but then went outside with a shotgun in his hands. Approaching Milton, Guy shot him, killing him almost instantly. Sinking to the ground, Milton cried out, "I am killed! Send for the doctor!" and never spoke again. Guy dropped the gun and tried to run away but was seized and held by members of the family until the police arrived.[22]

Still another early account gave a slightly different version. In this one, Guy was described as a "mischievous, wild child" who was fond of practical jokes. He had frightened a younger brother by a trick he had played on him, and the younger boy went and told their father. Milton listened to the boys, determined Guy had done wrong and punished him.

In a fit of rage, because of the punishment, Guy seized a pistol and shot his father.[23]

Yet another version of the story appeared in the press near the end of July. In that account Guy was said to be 12 years old. Reportedly, Guy had quarreled with his brother Louis, and Milton had given both of them a whipping. At the time, the boys were milking the cows and after finishing that chore Guy went into the kitchen, washed his hands, then went to his grandmother's room and got a shotgun that was kept there. He returned to the kitchen, where Milton was, and fired one of the barrels into his father's body. On July 29 Guy Smith went on trial for murder in the first degree at Clayton, Missouri, the county seat. On the evening of July 29 the jury returned a verdict of guilty and, said a reporter, "[T]he child will probably be sentenced to be hung." Also noted by the journalist was that Guy "has been a strange child since birth. His head is abnormally large and high and runs almost to a point like a cone. He has a quick, strong temper and physicians say has always been liable to water on the brain." On the witness stand Guy acknowledged he meant to shoot his father and to hurt him as badly as his father had hurt him, but did not intend to kill him.[24]

Early in August it was reported that Guy Smith had been sentenced to be executed by hanging. However, legal appeals apparently averted that fate, because a short item published on November 24, 1882, announced that Guy Smith had been sentenced to the county jail for one year.[25]

John Porter

Mrs. Elizabeth Porter, about 55, had been married nearly 30 years and was the mother of eight children by February 1883. The family resided near Nevada, Iowa, and at that time she and her son John Porter went on trial for the murder of Mr. Porter, the father and husband of the accused pair. At the trial Elizabeth testified to the severe acts of cruelty on the part of her husband, as did other members of the family. She said there were so many acts of violence toward herself and her children that she could not remember them all. When asked why she did not tell about the killing of her husband at the time it happened, but participated in a cover-up of the crime, she said her son John had persuaded her not to tell. She first told neighbors that John had killed his father. Elizabeth added that she had nothing to do with the disposition of the body and knew nothing about its whereabouts until the corpse was found. Mrs. Porter did not know the exact ages of her children as the leaf in the Bible containing that information had been torn out and gone missing. While talk of divorce had taken place between the couple, no action had ever occurred. John Porter made a statement at the trial in which he said he was about 14 years old; on the day his father was killed he and his brother George went out into the field to husk corn. Mr. Porter was in the field plowing and when his father called to him, John replaced him and plowed the field for the rest of the day. In the evening John put up the team in the barn, went into the house and loaded the gun, after which he went out to shoot some quail. However, it was a fruitless quest and he returned home with no quail. As he entered the house he heard a fuss in the kitchen. When he went to that room John saw his father grab and beat his mother, knocking her down. She called for John to pull his father off her. All three ended up outside and as his father was about to strike his mother with a club, John shot him in the back with the gun he was still carrying. After the first shot, Mr. Porter turned and advanced toward his son. John shot him again. Elizabeth retreated into the house. John dragged the body to one of the outbuildings on the farm and covered it up to conceal it for the time being. On the following morning he took the body to a field and buried it there. A day or so later he dug it up and took the body to another area where, in his view, he fixed it so as to make people think his father had committed suicide. At the conclusion of the trial John and Elizabeth were both found guilty of murder and each received a sentence of 21 years confinement in the Fort Madison penitentiary. At the time of sentencing, said a reporter, "[I]t was a scene sad beyond expression—a woman broken with more than a half century of years, the troubles of motherhood, and many other troubles, self-invited or otherwise, and a boy with the curse of an unfortunate organization stamped upon his expressionless face.... May Story County never witness the like again."[26]

Jacob Byers

John S. Byers was murdered by his son Jacob U. Byers on Saturday, August 20, 1887, at a farmhouse in East Mahoning Township, about two miles from the village of Richmond, Pennsylvania. It appeared the pair had been attending the reunion of Company A, 61st Regiment, at Richmond on Friday. When it came time to go home the father could not find his son and went home alone. It was about 3:00 A.M. when Jacob got home. Just two hours later, at 5:00 A.M., John called him to get up. Jacob was in the process of getting dressed in his work clothes and putting his revolver away in his valise when his father came into his son's room carrying in his hand the iron rod from the end gate of a wagon. As soon as Jacob saw his father he knew the old man was angry. John entered the room and struck his son, who then jumped back and told him to leave him alone. John got angrier and advanced on his son and stabbed him in the arm. Frightened and in pain, Jacob raised his revolver and shot his father in the chest. Jacob ran from the room; John took a few steps but then fell to the floor dead. Jacob made no attempt to escape but was not arrested until about 2:00 that afternoon. According to an article, "Jacob Byers, the parricide, is a boy just past eighteen years of age and not very bright, never having had any education." John was about 50 years old and considered by his neighbors to be a good citizen, except when he was excited, at which time he was "most violent in his manner." He had been a soldier in the Civil War and had been wounded in the head. Speculation was that his injury was responsible for John's "passionate outbursts when disputing with anyone or when anyone held views different from his." Often when the two of them were working on the farm, John would be dissatisfied with the manner in which his son was doing work. Instead of telling the boy about it he would be so enraged that he would throw stones or clubs at him. Most people in the area were said to be of the opinion the shooting was justified.[27]

Jacob Byers was brought to trial in September 1887 on a charge of murdering his father. It was a trial that lasted 2 1/2 days and at which Jacob testified how he had often been abused by his father, how John often hit him, knocking him down, kicking him, and so forth. Jacob's mother and John's wife, Sarah Byers, also told of her husband's fits of anger. She had given birth to 10 children, three of which had died. Percy Byers, the 14-year-old brother of Jacob, also told of being beaten by the father. After deliberating for 4 1/2 hours, the jury returned with a verdict of not guilty; Jacob Byers was discharged.[28]

Herman Habeck

Discovery of the body of William Habeck, who was murdered by his 19-year-old son, Herman Habeck, early in October 1893 near

Wausau, Wisconsin, did not occur until four weeks after the killing. Herman, with the assistance of a younger brother, 17-year-old Otto, dug a grave and buried the body near the spot where William was butchered with an axe. The crime took place at the family home near the small community of Edgar. While in the woods a short distance from his house, it was said, William began abusing Herman and Otto, who had accompanied him to the woods. Finally, Herman became incensed at the ill treatment and struck him on the head with an axe. The blow knocked the father down, whereupon Herman took a knife and cut William's throat. Otto then assisted Herman in burying the body. The pair felled a tree across the grave and piled brush over it in the hope of covering all traces. When the boys returned home and were asked about the whereabouts of their father by other family members, they said William had sent them home and that he would return later. But days passed, and then weeks, and William did not return. Neighbors became suspicious and a search was begun for the missing man. Herman even accompanied the searchers. At last the body was found and at that point Herman confessed to the crime, giving all the details and telling of the assistance that Otto had rendered. Both sons were arrested and locked up in jail at Wausau. The Habeck family had consisted of the two parents and seven children. According to the boys, their father used up all his money for liquor to the neglect of his family and the family lived in a "very destitute condition."[29]

When an inquest into the death was held the jury returned a verdict that William came to his death from the blow of an axe delivered by Herman and that Herman be held for trial on a charge of murder. That jury declared that Otto should be held as an accessory.[30]

Both boys went to trial for murder and on December 9, 1893, the jury brought in a verdict of guilty of manslaughter against Herman and a verdict of not guilty against Otto. Only seven witnesses were called in the trial; the jury deliberated for 20 hours before reaching a verdict. Judge Bardeen sentenced Herman to seven years' imprisonment at hard labor. Said a journalist; "The crime was a revolting one, the father being chopped to pieces by Herman, and his head severed from his body.... The boys are densely ignorant and the father had always abused them, and on this occasion was about to attack them with a hatchet."[31]

As a result of the tragedy Mrs. Habeck was left a widow caring for the six youngest children. One of those sons, 16-year-old Robert, pled guilty in court in late December 1894 to a charge of attempted assault on a five-year-old girl and was sentenced to six years in the state prison, joining his brother Herman.[32]

William January

On the night of August 8, 1896, near Farber, Missouri, 19-year-old William January hid in the barn on the family property until his father came home from a picnic. Then, when the elder January was putting up his horses, William shot him twice with a shotgun. Seeing that the gunshots had not killed his father, William seized a heavy plank that was nearby and battered his father about the head with it. William confessed the next day and was indicted by the grand jury for murder in the first degree. At his trial William said that his father had been mistreating him and threatening to kill him and his mother and his sisters. From the outset public sympathy in the area was said to be with the young man. After three days the trial of January came to an end, and in early October the jury returned a verdict finding the defendant quilty of murder in the second degree. William was sentenced to a term of 10 years in the penitentiary.[33]

2

Sons, Fathers, and Alcohol

Irwin

In Pennsylvania a man described as an "aged" citizen named Irwin, who resided at Pennsylvania Furnace on the line dividing Huntingdon and Centre counties, was murdered by his own son on March 26, 1846. It was said to have been one of "the horrid results of intemperance" as the son was very much addicted to alcohol "and while laboring under a fit of mania, seized and held his father with one hand and with the other inflicted several deep and mortal wounds with an axe upon his face." Irwin lingered for a few hours before he died. No outcome of the case was reported.[1]

Richard Walkley Jr.

Near Springfield, Massachusetts, on Saturday, October 11, 1851, Richard Walkley Jr. fatally stabbed his father with a knife and then tried to commit suicide. The father was described as an old and respected citizen of the area, while the son "has been a pest of society and a terrible pest in his father's family for years." He had been in jail repeatedly and at the time of the murder was under a bond to keep the peace, a bond that was entered into by the father. "The principal cause of his villainy is drink, which had been indulged in to such an extent as to make him savagely insane under its influence," said a reporter. On that fateful Saturday, both parents and the son sat down together for a meal at around noon. At the end of the meal Richard said to his father, "Are you going to report me?" His father replied, "You did enough yesterday to send you to State Prison." After that remark the son arose from the table, took a long thin bread knife from a drawer, advanced to his father and thrust it into his abdomen just under the ribs. Realizing that neighbors had been summoned, Richard fled from the house. A police officer who soon arrived on the scene set off in pursuit and found Richard in a vacant lot; his throat had been cut with a dull jackknife but he was expected to live. After he was returned to his father's house he was arrested. For years the son had been threatening the father and had used such threats, reportedly, to extort money from his father repeatedly. However, the father was described as too indulgent and affectionate to complain about him officially more than once or twice and so the father had lived with his son from year to year, and from day to day, "in mortal fear." The victim had said that when his son was sober and not drinking he had no trouble with him.[2]

Almost a year after the murder, on September 9, 1852, Richard Walkley Jr. was convicted of murder in the first degree and was sentenced to be executed on a date to be set by the state government. In the middle of November that same year, the Committee on Pardons of the Executive Council of Massachusetts held a session, with one of the cases under consideration being that of Walkley. Reverend Dr. Osgood of Springfield and Reverend Dr. Spear each addressed the panel and strenuously urged that the sentence of death imposed on Walkley be commuted to imprisonment for life. No outcome was reported.[3]

Frank Wilson

Approximately three miles east of Uniontown, Pennsylvania, on February 10, 1884, Alpheus Wilson, 60, was shot and killed by his son Frank. The pair were drinking together and had a quarrel that ended in Alpheus ordering Frank to leave home. Although he complied, Frank returned home in 10 minutes and called his father outside. Frank then drew a revolver and shot him dead. After the shooting Frank fled to the house of a neighbor, Dennis Springer, a short distance away, where he remained all day, threatening to kill anybody who tried to arrest him. Sheriff Sterling and a couple of deputies who had gone to the Springer residence finally were able to arrest him, but not before he tried to shoot the officers. As Frank was being taken away to jail the group passed the Wilson home. His mother came out to see him and he told her that he had intended killing the old man.[4]

Twenty-year-old Frank had shot and killed his father in the presence of his mother and sister. Both Alpheus and the son were employed as miners at the coke works of the Stewart Iron Company, and as February 10 had been a payday they both went into town to buy provisions. While they were in Uniontown both did a fair amount of drinking—the father not as much as the son. Alpheus went home early in the evening, while the boy remained in town until about 9:00 P.M. having, as he described it, a "good time with the boys." Before leaving the town for home Frank had one or two of what he described as "little fights" with his drinking companions. When Frank reached home at about 10:30 P.M. he found his father in the house lying asleep on the floor while his mother and sister were sitting by the fireside. Immediately, Frank began to abuse his father, kicking him violently. While uttering drunken curses he ordered the old man to get up and go to bed. Mrs. Wilson, anticipating trouble, ran to a neighbor's house for assistance but none could be obtained. On her return she found her husband standing up and talking to Frank. For a time the two men continued to quarrel and Alpheus told his son he should leave the house and never return. Frank did so for a short period but quickly returned to the house. Father and son had a drink together, after which the boy stepped outside and told his father he wanted to see him. Going to the door Alpheus said to his son, "If you have anything to say, say it quick," after which Frank shot him through the head. Both women in the house witnessed the murder. Alpheus was described by one reporter as a man who "was an old resident of this county, and was an honest, industrious man. He worked hard and made good wages, but would occasionally drink."[5]

Early in June 1884, Judge Ingram sentenced Frank Wilson to a term of 10 years in the penitentiary.[6]

Peter McDermott

On the evening of June 6, 1888, Peter McDermott, 32, a blacksmith who resided at 484 East 74th Street in New York City, was arrested on suspicion of having killed his father, Patrick McDermott, 65, at the son's residence that afternoon. It was said that "[b]oth men were habitual drunkards." All day on Tuesday, June 5, the pair had been drinking heavily and at one time when they were both intoxicated the son ordered his father to leave his house. Patrick refused to go, saying if his son would not keep him he did not know who would. Subsequently they became reconciled. At midnight on Tuesday the son ordered the father to go out and get beer and not to return if he failed in that mission. Patrick could not obtain any beer, so he remained in the street all night long. At 7:00 A.M. on June 6, Patrick returned to his son's apartment. A quarrel immediately broke out between the two men and Peter's wife ordered both men out of the house. She then left the house to do washing. When she returned home around 2:00 P.M. she discovered her husband had broken open the door. Her father-in-law was also there. They refused to leave and Mrs. McDermott threatened to call a police officer. She went downstairs on her way to get the police when her daughter Mary ran after her to tell her "Grandpa is lying on the floor covered with blood."

Upon returning to the apartment, Mrs. McDermott found the older man as Mary had described. A policeman was summoned and Patrick was taken to a hospital where he was pronounced dead 10 minutes after his arrival. Peter was arrested, in a highly intoxicated state, and claimed he did not know what had happened. He thought Patrick had perhaps hurt himself by falling on the floor or that he, Peter, was so drunk he might have kicked him, though he did not know what he had done. Peter was an ex-convict and had only recently been released after serving 2½ years in jail for assaulting a police officer. Blood was found on the walls of the McDermott home, and the deceased had a crushed nose and multiple skull fractures.[7]

At Peter's trial for murder, Mrs. Ann McDermott, wife of the deceased and the prisoner's mother, said that her husband was very seldom sober, that she had not lived with him for some years before his death and that her son, the defendant, was the only member of the family who could get along with him. There was much testimony to the effect that Patrick had a great habit of falling down for the slightest reason when he was drunk. He was said to have broken many bones that way. It was the claim of the defense that Patrick must have received the injuries that caused his death by falling on the kitchen stove.[8]

On January 24, 1889, Peter McDermott was found guilty of manslaughter for beating his father to death. Late in March, on the 29th, Judge Gildersleeve sentenced him to a term in the state prison of 10 years.[9]

3

Sons, Fathers, and Money

Sadbury

An old man by the name of John Sadbury, living in the eastern part of New Haven County in North Carolina, was shot dead on July 14, 1842, while sitting in his house. Sadbury was upwards of 70 years of age and was blind. Suspicion attached to the son, with the motive reportedly being money. Sadbury was involved in a lawsuit and the son was worried the father stood to lose a lot of money if the lawsuit went against him—money he considered to be his rightful inheritance. When the coroner held an inquest, it was declared by that investigation that the son was the murderer. No other outcome was reported.[1]

Joseph Schnepf

On Wednesday morning, April 3, 1867, in the town of Watertown, Wisconsin, around six miles from Janesville, a savage murder was committed, which, said a journalist, "in heartlessness and brutal atrocity," exceeded any crime ever before known in Jefferson County." Charles Schnepf was a farmer residing in the southwestern part of Watertown with a wife, two sons and two daughters. That morning, Charles and Joseph, the eldest son, left the family home and went into an area less than half a mile away to chop wood. And that was the last ever seen of the old man. Near noon one of the girls called out to them and after the second call Joseph returned to the house alone. When his mother asked where Charles was, Joseph replied his father had been taken with a sudden desire to go to town and had done so, in order to see about some seed and to get some tobacco. When his mother expressed astonishment that Charles would go to town without his coat, Joseph assured her Charles could borrow a coat from someone on the way if the need arose. After the noon meal was finished Joseph harnessed up the horses and with his brother and youngest sister, 14, went to the same area where he and his father had been working that morning. They spent two to three hours collecting scattered brush and then brought the stove wood home. Joseph then returned to the same spot in the woods to burn the scattered brush and decayed wood. It was a much larger fire than was usually the result of such activity and it attracted the attention of several neighbors.[2]

Nothing was seen or heard of Charles, who was well known in the area, for the next four days. With the members of the family not apparently taking any steps to find him the neighbors became curious and alarmed. They made inquiries, visited the Schnepf house, and talked among themselves, but nothing was learned concerning his whereabouts. Neither his wife nor his children seemed to care much about his disappearance. After several discussions among themselves, the neighbors arranged to undertake a general search. Three days were spent on it and it was noted that Joseph tried to keep the searchers away from the area he and his father had last worked and to suggest instead remote, out-of-the-way places to search. When nothing could be found, added to the strange behavior of the Schnepf family, suspicions of foul play were raised. Thus, it was decided to closely inspect the ground where the elder Schnepf had last been, although the son insisted it was of no use. At that area a huge pile of ashes was found and, to one side, a bone that seemed to be human. At that point—April 10—the authorities were called in. When the sheriff and his people searched the mound of ashes they found many human bones, including portions of a skull, a jawbone, scattered teeth, and ribs, as well as buttons and buckles from clothing, and boot nails. Joseph, his mother, and his two sisters were all arrested and on April 12 they were examined by a coroner's jury. In its verdict, the jury declared the remains were those of Charles Schnepf and that he came to his death due to the violence inflicted upon him by his son Joseph Schnepf. Mrs. Schnepf and the other children were released and allowed to go home. Much excitement was created in the community and, according to one report, "It was feared at one time that the indignation would break out in lawless vengeance, but better sentiments prevailed after a little reflection." Charles was of German origin, around 50 years old, and described as a "hard working, industrious farmer," while Joseph, about 22, was said to be "an intelligent and active young man."[3]

Joseph's trial began on December 4, 1867, at Portage City, Wisconsin. Evidence presented was wholly circumstantial. As well, the body had been destroyed beyond the possibility of identification. A reporter who visited Joseph at the jail described him as follows: "He is 22 years of age, of medium height; has black hair, hazel eyes, is tolerably good-looking; clean and respectably dressed. He is a German but speaks English readily." The prosecutor told the court that although the deceased was past the age of liability to military duty, Charles had nevertheless served in the army, in the Civil War. When Charles was about to leave for duty, he had executed a power of attorney in favor of his wife, empowering her to control his property. Upon his return home from the military, the prosecutor continued, Mrs. Schnepf resisted the surrender of the trust and Joseph supported his mother in that struggle. In the eyes of the prosecutor, the motive for the murder was financial. No outcome of the trial was reported.[4]

John C. Ware

The Ware family consisted of Louisa and John Ware and their son, John C. Ware, 24, in 1870 when the family lived on a small farm in the village of Longacoming, in south New Jersey. John C. was a married man and the father of one child but had not been living with his wife for over one year. "The Ware family bore far from a good reputation in the community, old Ware being looked upon as a man of evil and violent temper, and his son a weak-minded passionate, and unremarkable man," wrote a journalist. On August 16, 1870, a sister of John C., along with her husband, called at the family home to borrow some domestic utensils. That request was refused, with the result that angry words were exchanged between Mrs. Williams and her mother, Louisa Ware. John C. entered the house during the row and took his mother's side. After calling his sister several foul names, John C. struck her. Mr. Williams grew angry and grabbed his wife and the pair left the residence, but not before Mr. Williams knocked John C. down. Ware struggled to his feet, seized a Springfield rifle and fired two shots at his sister but missed with both. Mrs. Williams ran into her father along the road and told him what had happened. When the father reached home he and John C. had an argument over a different matter, money. In order to pacify his son John promised to pay him the money as soon as some wood was sold. However, that did not satisfy John C., who picked up his rifle again and shot his father dead on the spot. Horrified, John C. ran a few steps but then stopped and returned to go through the pockets of his victim to take what money his father had on him. As he was about to flee again he was met by Mary Champion, his mother's housekeeper, whom he told to shut her eyes as he escaped to the woods. Just one day later, on August 17, John C. was arrested in Camden, New Jersey, at the ferry terminal as he tried to board a boat for Philadelphia. He confessed to the crime and said it was committed to obtain possession of about $100 that belonged to his father.[5]

When John C. came to trial on a murder charge in January 1871, one of those called to the stand was Louisa Ware. She testified that on the morning of the murder her husband was in "very ill humor" and that he cursed her and threatened to beat her brains out. John C. was present at the time. According to Louisa, her son never went to school and could neither read nor write; he was weak-minded and he had twice attempted to commit suicide, once by hanging and once by taking laudanum. Louisa had seen him take the drug three years earlier, and one year before that he had a fever and attempted to hang himself while out of his mind from the ravages of his fever. Stating she and the deceased had been married for 41 years, Louisa added that John C. had married four years earlier but left his wife after living with her for one year. Benjamin Cheeseman, half brother to Louisa, took the stand to state, with respect to John C., "[H]e was a very ignorant boy, and I think was never inside a schoolhouse or church; I regarded him as weak-minded; his mother is accounted by the family a feeble-minded woman." The defense mounted for John C. was that of insanity. Margaret Simpkins, mother-in-law of the prisoner, testified that he did not support his wife, that she had seen little of him over the previous two years and she did not think he was clear-minded. Simpkins believed John C. had tried to kill her daughter not long after they were married. At the time, he followed his wife into the kitchen carrying a double-barreled gun and fired it at her. However, the weapon failed to discharge. Then he took an axe and chopped up the gun before telling his wife he was going to get a couple of bottles of laudanum and kill himself. Around that time, John C.'s wife gave birth to a child that survived for just seven hours. On the evening of January 31, 1871, the Ware jury returned a verdict of guilty of murder in the first degree against John C. The prisoner exhibited no emotion upon hearing the verdict.[6]

An editor with a Brooklyn newspaper wondered in print if Ware would seek death-bed repentance—knowing the sentence would be death—but admitted that until then he had not done so. Citing a recently executed murderer who became limp with penitence a few days before his execution, the editor said, "Let us see if he of Camden will similarly wilt." Early in February a Philadelphia reporter requested a private interview with Ware, but Judge Woodhull refused to grant one. He was, however, permitted to talk to the prisoner through the intermediary efforts of a guard. The latter questioned Ware at the reporter's prompting. John C. acknowledged that a day earlier he had said to someone else, "I killed my father, and would do it again." The jailor then relayed a query that asked if he had killed his father with the first shot. The convicted man replied, "Yes: the old bastard never gasped."[7]

Ware was first scheduled to be executed on April 10, 1871, but a few days before that date Governor Randolph of New Jersey granted a 30-day stay of execution, before the expiration of which the Court of Pardons of New Jersey would meet and consider the question of the commutation of John C.'s sentence. A few weeks later, an editor with the *New York Times* spoke out about a perceived increase in crime in the area, particularly in the wake of a few recent parricides in New Jersey and New York State, one of which was the Ware case: "In the alarming increase of vice and lawlessness throughout the land, there is none more distressing or disheartening than the recurrence of the awful crime of parricide." More stays of execution followed and finally, in July 1871, Ware was granted a new trial on the ground that the testimony of a witness that had been barred from the trial should have been admitted.[8]

Ware's first trial began on January 25 and lasted six days. It drew large crowds every day and generated much media interest. Principal witness for the prosecution was Mrs. Champion, the housekeeper. The plea of insanity by the defense drew the support of several witnesses, including the mother of the prisoner and several medical people, but it did not prevail. In June 1871, when the scaffold on which Ware was to die stood ready in the Camden jail yard, before a new trial had been ordered, a reporter for the *New York Herald* visited the prisoner and was allowed by Sheriff Morgan to look at the gallows. First a board fence some 30 feet high and 70 feet square was erected and every hole was stopped up to prevent outsiders from looking in; then the scaffold was erected. He wrote: "It consists of two upright posts, twelve feet high, with a cross beam. In one of the posts a pulley is inserted and a rope passed over the wheel. On one end of the rope a solid block of iron weighing three hundred pounds is fastened. This iron block is hoisted from the ground and tied by a small rope to the top of the post. The other end of the rope passes through a pulley in the cross beam and is noosed ready for the reception of the criminal's neck. Everything being in readiness the murderer is led out, the noose adjusted, and at a given signal the small rope that holds the weight is cut. The weight falls rapidly to within three or four inches of the ground and the victim of the law is jerked from life to death in the twinkling of any eye." After his tour of the scaffold—dismantled after the new trial was granted—the reporter visited Ware in the death house. Ware was confined on the top floor of the courthouse where an iron cage 12 feet square and eight feet in height, with floors and ceilings of boilerplate, had been constructed. In that "den" Ware had spent 21 weeks to that date, constantly being watched by two "vigilant keepers." In one corner of the cage was a "dirty mattress covered with two equally dirty quilts, and another corner [was] occupied by a necessary sanitary utensil." And, said the reporter, "Caged like a wild criminal, this uneducated, half-witted young man has spent nearly six months, waiting for death or some final disposition of his case." When the reporter visited the prison again at the end of October, he observed, of the prisoner, "His reason, never very strong, has been badly unsettled by the experiences of the past two years and death will be a relief. He was the pliant tool of a heartless mother who, desirous of getting her husband out of the way for the sake of securing a few hundred dollars selected this half-witted fool to do her bidding and receive the reward of a crime which in all probability properly belongs to herself." At his second trial no new evidence was introduced. It lasted from October 9 to October 14 and after a short period of deliberation the jury returned the same verdict as before—guilty of murder in the first degree. On November 2, John C. Ware was sentenced to be executed on December 15, 1871.[9]

When the *New York Times* summarized the Ware case a day before the execution it noted, among other things, that the Ware hometown of Longacoming had been renamed Berlin by this time. As well, the article gave a different account of the details of the murder. According to this piece, on August 16 the father had one of his not unusual quarrels with his "half insane" wife, whereupon she left the house and went to her married daughter's place. John C. was not present during that row but hearing of it he went home and commenced to "abuse" the old man. Hard words were exchanged and the son became enraged with passion. He then seized an old musket hanging on the wall—it was ordinarily kept loaded—and aimed it at his father, yelling, "You bastard, I'll shoot you" and promptly did so. With the scaffold and its shielding fence once again erected in the jail yard, the only building in the area situated as to furnish an outlook on the yard was a large public school building. It had been ordered closed for the day by the board of education as it was not deemed appropriate that students should witness the execution. That building was kept locked and all curiosity-seeking adults were excluded. Only the sheriff, deputies, officers of the court and official witnesses were to observe the execution.[10]

A few days before the execution Sheriff Henry Fredericks received a final telegram from Governor Randolph stating the execution would go ahead as planned—there would be no last-minute intervention. The sheriff showed that telegram to Ware, said a report, "in the hope that the shocking callousness which he, up to this time, exhibited might be dissipated, but without any effect." On Thursday, the last night of his life, he slept soundly, after having eaten heartily. He last saw his wife and child on Tuesday but showed little emotion. Mrs. Fredericks and some clergymen visited Ware in his iron cage on Friday to try to induce him to join them in prayer. However, he refused and when he did speak it was to use profane language. At 11:20 A.M. on December 15, 1871, John C. Ware was executed by hanging; he died instantly without a struggle.[11]

In the wake of the Ware execution, an editor with the *New York Herald* declared: "The majesty of the law has been once more vindicated and the victim thereof has paid the awful penalty of his most unnatural crime." He added that the unfailing devotion of Ware's counsel led many to believe not a desire for reputation alone was the incentive, but an unshaken belief in the hereditary insanity of his client's family. "There is every indication of hereditary insanity in the Ware family," concluded the editor, "but this was a question not deemed within the province of an uneducated jury, and they convicted the man on the evidence as they heard it."[12]

A different editorial stated Ware "seems to have possessed many brutal attributes. The execution created no small excitement, owing to the celebrity bestowed on the murderer by the local journals.... [H]e died today, fearing nothing, admitting nothing, defying everything, a blasphemous wretch, cursing to the verge of eternity." In summarizing the family, he wrote, "The family was not especially distinguished by advanced intelligence or elevated character. The folks in the vicinity and neighbors used to say that the old man used to beat the old woman and the old woman returned the compliment, both being drunk at such time.... The son John Ware was dogged, ignorant and brutal. The smallest trace of refinement was wanting in him, and he was noted for his despicable animal propensities and passions. His mind was always bent on something low and inhuman." When this article summarized the murder it gave the account of the row John C. had with his brother-in-law, and so forth.[13]

The opening few sentences of his confession, dictated in the death-house, went as follows: "I am twenty-three years of age. I can neither read nor write; and, as I told one of my family a few days ago, if I had received half the attention before I got here that I have since, I would never have seen the inside of this cage." That caused a newspaper editor to remark, "Brought up in ignorance, condemned to the associations of an unhappy home, inheriting the nature, and witnessing the example of a passionate and profligate father, we can scarcely wonder that his life has ended thus early and violently." Clergymen labored with him, members of the YMCA visited him, women called on him or sent messages of kindness: "but he remained obdurate and unrepentant to the last." If only those well-meaning people, thought the journalist, "had shown just a tenth of that interest in him before the crime—to redeem him from a life of ignorance and evil—all those latter efforts would have been unnecessary."[14]

Edwin Hoyt

Late in September 1878, Edwin Hoyt of Sherman, Connecticut, was found guilty of murder in the first degree for killing his 76-year-old father. He went to his father's house on Sunday, June 23, that year, armed with a butcher knife for the express purpose of killing the old man, with whom he had some trouble. Edwin's brother-in-law tried to rescue the old man but could not as Edwin stabbed him repeatedly. After he was arrested, Edwin said, "I did it, and I am glad of it and, if you will fix that rope to my neck and then to that tree, I will climb up myself and jump off, and will bless you all the while you are doing it." He was tried, convicted, and sentenced to be hanged on October 4, 1878.[15]

Appeals led to a new trial for Edwin, which took place in March 1879. Reportedly, he had not been under the influence of alcohol at the time of the killing. Not long before the deed, Edwin had said to a neighbor, with respect to his father, "He has lived long enough, and when I have killed two or three more I shall be ready to die myself." Several neighbors testified to the fact that the son had made threats to his father. Albert Beeman, when working with Edwin a week before the murder, heard him say he did not always expect to be poor. Peter Curry testified he had a conversation with Edwin four or five years earlier in which Hoyt said, regarding his father, "The old cuss used to lift my wages until I ran away and I would like to put a ball through his heart if I thought it would penetrate."[16]

Edwin, 36, had a wife and five children. He testified in his own behalf at the trial. He said he had served for three years in the United States Army and when he attempted to reenlist was rejected, although he claimed he did not know the reason for the rejection. His health had never been good since the Civil War, he explained, relating several instances of falling in a kind of fit, before and since the war and during his time in the service. On the stand, he said he was always on friendly terms with his father and denied ever making any threats against the elder Hoyt. According to this story he had not contacted his father for some time and the first he knew of the murder was when he read about it in a Hartford newspaper. The prosecution introduced several letters (to his wife) not in evidence at the first trial. One was written shortly before the first trial and in it Edwin said he was writing without the knowledge of the jailer. He requested his wife to swear he had been a kind husband and to deny he had ever abused her, to swear that he thought a good deal about his father and that she had never heard him say anything against the old man and that he, Edwin, acted strangely from time to time and was sometimes not in his right mind. The estate of the deceased totaled less than $3,000 and that was divided between six heirs, one of whom was Edwin. He had assigned his entire share over to his lawyer to cover his legal bill.[17]

More legal appeals were made; but when the Supreme Court refused a final appeal on March 19, 1880, Edwin was sentenced to be executed by hanging for the second time. This time the date set was May 13, 1880. On the morning of May 11, Edwin was informed that the state governor had refused to interfere and the execution would go ahead as scheduled. Reportedly, Edwin refused to believe the governor had refused to grant a reprieve, that it was all newspaper talk. His wife visited him for the last time on May 10 and when leaving she asked the jailer to show her the preparations for the execution. She was taken to the area where the hanging was to take place and remarked, "I am glad he is to be hanged, and would like to see him hang now." Four hundred tickets of admission to the execution enclosure were to be issued.[18]

On May 13, 1880, Edwin Hoyt died almost instantly on the scaffold. A reporter commented that he had shown a "very ugly disposition" during his life and that his wife had experienced his bad temper many times. Her life had been placed in danger, as Edwin had once discharged a shotgun at her, seriously wounding her. On the Sunday of the murder, though, he had nothing in particular to exasperate him except the refusal of his brother-in-law to accompany him on a fishing trip. Having been refused, he went home and, taking a butcher knife from his house, told his wife he was going to kill his father. During his case the prosecution said the motive for the killing was animosity toward the father, "who had always exercised great severity toward him and who, he believed, had decided to wholly disinherit him." The defense, in both trials, was that of insanity.[19]

Henry Gunn

Justin L. Gunn, a well known businessman of New York City, was found murdered in his summer residence near Bridgewater, Massachusetts, on the morning of September 24, 1879. His horribly disfigured body was found on the floor of his bedroom and there was evidence a struggle had taken place in the room. Blood was splattered all over the room, while in an adjacent room was found a trunk that had been broken open and rifled. It was known that Gunn kept money and other valuables in the trunk but it had nothing of value in it on the day of the murder. Among the missing valuable articles were a gold watch and a chain, worth $500, that Justin always wore. Also notably absent was Justin's son Henry Gunn, who had been with his father the day before the murder but had since disappeared. Justin was a 52-year-old New Englander by birth who was engaged in the printing business in New York City. It was a business he had prospered in and at the time of his death he was worth upwards of $75,000. Six years earlier his first wife had died, leaving him with two sons, Henry, now 23, and Melvin, 21. Melvin was married and lived with his wife in Brooklyn, while Henry continued to live at home. Henry was said to have always been "a shiftless and dependent youth, relying altogether on his father for support, and by his extravagant and wild habits always causing his father much annoyance." Justin had always catered to Henry, paid his bills, and so forth, but kept on chiding him and hoped for his reformation.[20]

Not long after his first wife died, Justin Gunn married a Miss Towle, of Pittsfield, Massachusetts, who was then about 24. She bore him a daughter, five years old at the time of Justin's murder. According to one reporter's account, "Soon after his second marriage his son Henry's vagaries became very marked and persistent, and a constant menace to the domestic peace of the family." Justin grew disconsolate, and by degrees became careless in his personal habits. Additionally, he turned more and more to drinking. To curb the habit he decided to retire to the country and spend the rest of his life on a truck farm, away from the vices and temptations of the big city. He also thought it might reform Henry. Therefore, in the previous May he had purchased a 20 acre farm about four miles from Bridgewater. Soon after the purchase he went to live on it with Henry. His wife continued to live in Brooklyn. Justin's intention was to dispose of his city property that fall and to unite the family at Bridgewater by the end of 1879 at the latest. For a time everything seemed to go well and in due course Henry was placed in charge of the farming business in the country. Justin's wife and young daughter spent much of the summer on the farm, having returned to the city just two weeks before the murder. It was also reported that Henry was continually importuning his father for money. Justin's refusal of what he viewed as unreasonable demands for money often led to bitter quarrels between father and son.[21]

Henry was finally captured by the police in Boston around the middle of October. One Massachusetts newspaper declared, "The crime was one of the foulest and most atrocious in the criminal annals of this State, and public indignation ran so high that an untiring search had been made for the dastardly assassin, by night and day." When captured, Henry freely admitted to the murder but alleged his father scolded him and struck him. After a fight, in which Henry got the worst of it, the son got a hatchet and struck his father from behind, instantly killing him. After taking all the money and valuables he could find around the house, Henry fled and traveled from Boston to New York and back, twice, since the time he had killed his father. As well, he had spent some time in Lowell, Massachusetts. While he was on the run he was arrested once for drunkenness but the police did not realize who had fallen into their hands and Henry was discharged. No disposition of the case was reported.[22]

William Dwenger

In 1879 an old man named Dwenger, who owned a large ranch some 30 miles outside of Silver City, New Mexico, came back home from a prospecting trip into the neighboring states. He brought with him a German woman about 35 years of age, well-educated, who was said to be able to speak three or four languages. They settled into life on the old man's ranch as a couple and lived together for about one year before they were married. The remaining people who lived on the ranch were the old man's two sons, William, aged about 20, and a boy of six or seven. Also in residence was an old man referred to as Parson Young, who was permitted to hang about the place. About one month after the marriage took place the elder Dwenger disappeared with the other members of the group giving out the story that he had gone to Mexico, a not unusual thing to do, as he had made such trips in the past. The nearest neighbor to the ranch lived 15 miles away. About two months later the man with whom Dwenger was said to have departed with for Mexico returned to the area and, on being questioned, said the old man had not gone with him. Rumors soon spread in the area that something was wrong and that Dwenger had been murdered. His wife and son were the prime suspects. Sheriff Whitehall immediately arrested all at the ranch. Finally the son confessed to having murdered his father and told the authorities where the deed had been committed and where the body was buried. It was found at that spot.[23]

As it was learned, both William and Young had fallen in love with the woman and for some time prior to the murder had both "been unduly intimate with her." But the presence of old Dwenger was a hindrance to all and after discussing the best means to get rid of him, the three finally decided the woman should marry him so as to become his widow and thus fall heir to his property—amounting to several thousands of dollars, with $800 in the bank and the rest in the value of the property. Thus the pair married and, in carrying out the second part of the plan, old Dwenger was murdered about one month after his wedding day. On the day of the murder, the group took a trip to Dwenger's mine, where Young engaged the old man in conversation while William shot his father in the back. They buried his body near the mine. When the three came to trial they were all found guilty. Parson Young was executed, Mrs. Dwenger was sentenced to 10 years imprisonment, and William Dwenger was sentenced to a term of 99 years in jail.[24]

A different account identified Parson Young as an itinerant preacher who was stopping with the family. One morning while at the breakfast table, according to William's testimony, the three conceived the plot to get rid of the old man in order to get his property and divide it between them. A prospective burial hole was prepared in advance far out in the mountains and the victim was readily enticed to that area. Mrs. Dwenger had prepared a bag, which they took along to bring his clothes back in. After they killed him they stripped the body of its clothing and later cut those items up to make part of a bed quilt that was later produced in court as evidence. After his arrest the "inhuman son" confessed and the trio were convicted. Despite the life sentence New Mexico Governor Ross released William Dwenger in 1887, after only six years' incarceration. That prompted a reporter to comment that Ross "with his pardoning power has turned this brute in human form at liberty." In addition, "There was a general feeling of surprise and disgust when the news reached here that Dwenger, self-accused of murdering in cold blood his own father, was by executive clemency again a free man."[25]

James McMenemon

Early reports that surfaced from an area 12 miles west of Muscatine, Iowa, indicated that John McMenemon, a 65-year-old farmer, had been shot and killed by his 15-year-old daughter, Mary, on May 19, 1882. According to the first reports the father and daughter were quarreling when the girl's brother James, 18, handed her a revolver with which she shot her father dead through the chest. The wife and mother of the family was in an insane asylum. While in jail, though, Mary confessed to a different story. In fact, the murder was committed by James, in order that the children might inherit John's estate and live as they pleased on the farm. It was arranged between James and Mary, though, that Mary should confess to the killing with the idea being that a plea of self defense and her extreme youth would save her from punishment, allowing the siblings to get away with the deed.[26]

Early in February 1883, James McMenemon was sentenced by Judge Hayes to the state penitentiary for a term of life imprisonment. "He received his sentence with hardened nonchalance," said an observer. Apparently no charges were ever brought against Mary.[27]

Wash Boyer

In November 1891, David Boyer, a wealthy citizen of Cooke County, Tennessee, disappeared. Then his son Wash Boyer exhibited a deed to the family property telling the neighbors his father had sold the farm to him and gone off to Texas for good. But in March 1892 the body of the elder Boyer was found in a cave. Wash was arrested, tried, and convicted of murdering his father and sentenced to 20 years in the penitentiary. Rufus Holt, who had served as a witness to the forged deed, was sentenced to eight years in jail. A confession from Holt was made public in September 1893. In that confession Holt said that he and Wash met the older Boyer in the woods and that Wash beat his father to death with a club. Then the two of them carried the body to a nearby cave, where they hid it. For his part in the affair, Holt received an old mule in payment from Wash. After they deposited the body of David Boyer in the cave, Wash threw in several dead sheep as well, to ward off suspicion.[28]

Archibald Kelso

On September 17, 1896, the body of Henry Kelso was found at his home near Pittsburgh. His head was severed from the body and burned and the body was thrown into a river. It was soon learned that the murder had been committed by his son, Archibald Kelso, for the purpose of robbery. Archibald escaped and for 10 months detectives searched for the fugitive. After following his trail literally from coast to coast, detectives finally arrested him in Ponca, Oklahoma Territory, in the middle of July 1897. On his way back east, under the control of detectives, the prisoner managed to jump through a rail car window at Emington, Illinois, making his escape once again. On September 14, 1897, detectives caught up with him again, chasing him into the water near Port Washington, Wisconsin. The authorities believed he died in that lake but no body was immediately recovered. Detective Arthur Black of Pittsburgh was thrown into the lake by Archibald before the latter took his own fatal plunge. Black was rescued by Morris Goldfun, another Pittsburgh detective who, as he brought his nearly drowned comrade ashore, had to fight off Archibald's friends with his pistol.[29]

John Henry Collins

Much interest was shown in Lawrence, Kansas, and the surrounding area, over the arrest of John Henry Collins, a student at Kansas State University, on a charge of murdering his father. Prior to being taken into custody, he had what was described as "an unblemished record." Early on the morning of May 13, 1898, John Collins, a wealthy farmer who lived near

Lawrence, was shot dead in his bed with his own gun, which had been taken from his closet in the same room. At first it was thought the killer was a burglar, but no evidence of forced entry was discovered. The only people at home at the time of the shooting were Mrs. Collins, second wife of the deceased, and his children by his first wife, John Henry and Grace. When questioned by the authorities, the wife said she slept soundly on the night of May 12–13, until she was awakened by something at 5:00 A.M. She went back to sleep only to be awakened again at 5:15 A.M., this time by the sound of two gunshots. The bedroom the couple shared was full of smoke and her husband groaned, "Oh, Helen, I am shot." She ran to other rooms in the house to arouse John Henry and Grace. Mr. Collins died a few moments later, saying no more. John Henry had just returned home from college even though the term was still underway. When he was chastised by his father for leaving college during the term, the son pleaded illness. Investigation revealed that the father's life had been heavily insured in favor of his two children and suspicion began to center on the son. Grace insisted that as she came out of her room in response to the noise of gunshots, John Henry came out of his room at the same time for the same reason. With his mother and sister firmly standing behind John Henry in his claim of innocence, and with other extended family members all taking the same position, some observers felt a conspiracy must have been involved. However, the police could not make John Henry confess.[30]

A further motive was revealed when it was learned that John Henry was madly in love with Frances Babcock, a "belle" of Lawrence, with the Babcocks being "a proud and aristocratic family." John Henry was at the Babcock home nearly every day. However, he had no money to take her out properly and his father was known to be "close in money matters." He allowed his son only $25 a month for all of his college expenses, including board, and scolded him when he exceeded his allowance and ran into debt. As John Henry was madly in love with Frances but had no money and was insanely jealous of her, detectives theorized the only way he saw of getting money in order to spend the summer at the seashore with her was by murdering his father. The Babcock family had already arranged to spend the full summer at the seashore, near Atlantic City, and John Henry was determined to join the Babcocks. If he murdered his father he would come into a large sum of money from his father's insurance policy. As the authorities continued to investigate the case, John Henry remained defiant and spoke sneeringly to close friends of the "addle pated" detectives from

Topeka. Once he commented, "Talk about them catching the murderer of my father. They couldn't catch a freight car on a side track." Stymied in the case, the authorities called in a private detective by the name of Dell Harbaugh. When he spoke to the Babcock family, the daughter John Henry was pursuing told Harbaugh that several times John Henry told her that blacks were tailing his father, and that blacks planned to kill his father, and so forth. Harbaugh also learned that John Henry had supposedly lost his watch and diamond stud a week or so before the murder. Therefore, the detective surmised the son had hired a black man to kill his father and that he had paid the black man with the watch and stud. Then he found two black men who corroborated the story; the men were Johnson Jordan and Jesse Harper. They admitted to having the watch and stud but claimed they had only been stringing John Henry along to get what they could out of him and never had any intention of killing the older Collins. Harbaugh concluded the son must have committed the murder himself, probably on the spur of the moment with little advance preparation. For example, if he had wanted to protect himself from suspicion by making the killing look like the work of burglars then he should have left a window open, ransacked a trunk, and so on. John Henry Collins was finally arrested on June 17.[31]

The climax of the Collins trial came on December 8, 1898, when Frances Babcock, "the pretty young society leader of Lawrence," took the witness stand to testify against John Henry. "So firmly convinced is Miss Babcock that John killed his father that she and her mother refused to have anything further to do with him," said a reporter. She told of receiving telegrams from him after the murder admonishing her to "tell nothing," that is, how John Henry had predicted the murder of his father by some secret enemy. Once, while the couple was out riding he accidentally dropped a loaded revolver from his pocket. Frances reproached him for carrying weapons but he impressed upon her that the weapon would be needed for an important occasion. Reportedly, her testimony caused John Henry to break down completely and, "It caused general weeping among the women in court."[32]

At 9:00 P.M. on December 24, 1898, the jury in the Collins murder trial returned a verdict of guilty of murder in the first degree against John Henry. Besides being a student, he was described as a licensed lay reader of the leading Protestant Episcopal Church of Topeka. Mr. Collins carried a total of $26,000 worth of life insurance and $6,500 of that sum was to go to John Henry. The son had lived beyond his allowance while at college at Lawrence and he had contracted numerous debts at the university town that he could not pay. In this account Jesse Harper of Lawrence and Johnson Jordan of Topeka were called two of the "most notorious negroes in Kansas." They were important state witnesses and swore that, working through Harper, John Henry had hired Jordan to kill his father but after securing what money and valuables they could from the son the pair had refused to do the job, at which point, according to their testimony, John Henry boasted that he would "do the job" himself.[33]

With respect to the conviction of Collins, an editorial in a Colorado newspaper declared the crime was "the most heinous of all crimes in the code. The evidence, familiar now to all our readers, was of a most convincing character and it is difficult to see how an intelligent jury could have found a different verdict." The piece argued that if the father had been something like a cruel tyrant "there would have been some slight palliation for the crime. But he was a fond and indulgent parent on terms of most intimate affection with his unnatural son…. The motive for the crime was so cheap and trivial and the method adopted so deliberate in design that the malignity and wickedness of the murder place it among the darkest deeds ever perpetrated. Self-indulgence, vanity, and misguided passion have had a terrible ending in the case of young Collins."[34]

At Topeka, Kansas, on March 27, 1899, John Henry Collins received the death penalty from Judge Hazen. When asked if he had anything to say, he once again pleaded his innocence, declaring, "I know I am innocent. I did not kill my father."[35]

However, that account of receiving the death penalty was either in error or the sentence was changed suddenly, because Collins actually received a life imprisonment sentence. At 9:20 A.M. on April 5, 1899, John Henry Collins arrived at the state penitentiary at Lansing, Kansas. Crowds gathered at the train depots to catch sight of him as he made his way to the notorious Leavenworth Prison. Upon his arrival his escorts turned him over to the prison clerk and he became convict number 8882. He signed in on the convict ledger that required the prisoner to give the names of his best friend and closest relative. In his case he listed his sister, Grace Collins, as both. Collins stated he had spent 14 of his 22 years in school. Convict 8882 was then given a bath, a shave, a close haircut, and a "good behavior" suit of prison clothes, that is, a set of clothing without stripes. Finally, he was taken before Warden Landis for a talk. Landis decided — his prisoner had no occupation — to assign him to the penitentiary tailor shop. Emmett Dalton, the noted train robber of the infamous Dalton gang, was a cutter and foreman in that shop and it would be his duty to instruct Collins. On the morning of April 6 John Henry Collins went to work in the tailor shop.[36]

George Schan

George J. Schan, an employee of the State of New York, was shot and killed at his home in New York City on November 13, 1899, by his son George Schan, a student. The father was in bed when he was shot and died instantly from two gunshots to the head. The wife of the victim and mother of the killer had died 18 months earlier, leaving, it was said, considerable property to be divided among her husband and her two sons. However, the father remarried and refused to probate the will of his first wife, leading to much friction in the family. Both sons moved out of the family home when their father remarried. The other son was a member of the United States military and was then stationed in Manila. Both sons repeatedly asked the father to divide the property and, in lieu of that, they called upon him for money, requests that were always denied. George went to his father's house early on the morning of the thirteenth. Finding his father in bed—his stepmother was in an adjoining room—he demanded, once again, some money. The father refused again and became enraged, making as if to get out of bed, whereupon the son drew a gun and fired. After the shooting George calmly placed the weapon on a dresser and sat down quietly to await the police.[37]

When his stepmother rushed into the room in response to the shots, she said she found George trying to pull a diamond ring off of his father's finger. When the police arrived they found George sitting in another room smoking a cigarette and reading a newspaper. In this account the young man was described as a "cigarette fiend" and dental student. His friends said that the excessive use of cigarettes "unbalanced his mind." No other outcome of this case was reported.[38]

4

Sons, Fathers, and Other Causes

Joseph Bebon

A young man named Joseph Bebon was arrested on the night of August 19, 1860, for stabbing his father with a knife. Earlier that evening the son had called upon the father at the latter's Brooklyn, New York, home in relation to some business about which they disagreed; words ensued between the pair and Joseph pulled out a large knife and stabbed his father several times. On August 31 Coroner Murphy commenced an investigation into the death of Peter Bebon. In the view of one observer, "[T]he house is one of a row of small, ill-looking frame structures, and the neighborhood is not attractive." It was reported that Peter left considerable property, to which Joseph was the sole heir. Peter did not die immediately after being stabbed but lingered for some time. At one point it seemed as if he would recover but on the night of August 30 Peter got out of bed, dislodged his bandages and subsequently bled to death. The deceased's widow described the affray on August 19 by stating that the prisoner and his wife, Margaret, came to Peter's home, that Margaret Bebon indulged in front of the house (on the sidewalk) in violent and abusive language directed at her mother-in-law. As a result Peter went outside to remonstrate with her while at the same time seizing hold of her. Thereupon Joseph rushed at his father and stabbed Peter, while the latter struck Joseph in the face. Widow Bebon also testified to previous disputes between the parties. Her testimony did not differ materially from that of the deceased that had been given during an antemortem examination.[1]

On November 21, 1860, Joseph Bebon was found guilty of manslaughter in the third degree. Joseph said he was 23 years old, a native of France, and had been in the United States for 18 years. A tailor by trade, he had a wife and one child, and had never been in prison. When Judge Garrison passed sentence, he commented, "You were indicted for a lesser offense than the testimony adduced on your trial would seem to warrant. You might have been indicted for a more serious offense, and might probably have been convicted under such indictment. The court is disposed to look on your case more leniently, perhaps, than it deserves, the recollection of your unnatural offense will always haunt you; this will be of itself a sufficient punishment, but the law is not satisfied with it." With the maximum punishment for that category of crime being four years imprisonment, and the minimum being two years, Garrison sentenced Joseph Bebon to the state prison for a term of two years and six months, with hard labor. According to a reporter, "Bebon seems to be much more intelligent than his appearance warrants. He thanked the Court after the sentence with a suavity that seems never to desert a Frenchman."[2]

Charles Brooks

On March 13, 1863, a farmer from Vincentown, New Jersey, by the name of Job Brooks was found dead in a ditch on the roadside in his village. His throat had been cut and he had been battered about the head. The prime suspect in the case was his son Charles H. Brooks. But before Charles could be arrested he disappeared and fled to the West. Subsequently he was captured and brought back to New Jersey, where he was convicted of murder in the first degree in April; he was sentenced to death in September of that year. Before and after his trial he made several confessions in which he implicated his mother and brother-in-law, Timothy Ridgway, in the murder as instigators and accessories before the fact. Sometimes in his confessions he blamed only himself, declaring he had acted alone. As a result of his confessions the other two people named were arrested and tried for murder. However, at their trial Brooks swore he had done the deed alone. As a result the pair were accordingly acquitted and Brooks was finally sentenced by Judge Vandyke to receive capital punishment. "He evinced, from the beginning, the utmost indifference in the whole affair," remarked a journalist. During Charles' confinement he was visited by a variety of clergymen but none made the slightest impression on him. Just before his execution, noted an account, "Profanity was a marked feature of his conversation on the last day and his levity was repulsive to all his visitors." Upon being told he might have had his sentence commuted to life if only he had told the truth consistently in his various confessions, he replied, "I'd rather be hung any day than go to State Prison for life. The Sheriff feels worse about this than I do. I'll sleep first-rate tonight but he won't." When asked how he could be so happy-go-lucky in the face of death, Brooks said, "What's the use of worrying? I feel all right. A man might as well be gay and happy if he is going to be hung. You can't but die once." On the day of his execution, in December 1863, thousands of people showed up for the event although only about 600 were admitted to the enclosure. Brooks slept well on his last night, ate a hearty breakfast and refused to meet with any of the many clergymen seeking an audience with him. He expressed no sorrow for his crime and displayed no guilt. On the scaffold he declared, "I want the people of Burlington county to know that I am not the guiltiest man of the three. I was led into this crime. Timothy Ridgway is the guilty man. I struck the first blow and Ridgway finished him." He continued: "I was intoxicated when I did it. I was urged ever since last November [1862] by my mother and Ridgway to kill my father. My mother coaxed me to do it, and offered me seventy-five dollars if I would kill my father. If justice was done Timothy Ridgway ought to stand here today and be executed in my place. He coaxed me to kill my father." According to Brooks, when his mother and brother-in-law were in prison awaiting their trial they told Charles he would get a new trial if he testified they had nothing to do with the murder. "That's the reason I swore as I did when they were tried. Timothy Ridgway and my mother ought to be executed here today. I always tried to get along well, but two rogues brought me to this. Mother tormented father for six years, cutting off his hair and selling his clothes. She believed in fortune telling."[3]

Warren Rice

William Rice was a 60-year-old farmer who lived in retirement with his wife near Concord, Massachusetts. They had living with them a 26-year-old son, Warren Rice, who, it was said, had been insane for a number of years, but only periodically. His mania always induced him to do deeds of violence and he had twice been confined in the Worcester Insane Hospital. At about 6:00 P.M. on Friday, February 24, 1865, he came home to find his parents sitting at the table. Warren had an iron farm tool in his hand with which he suddenly and inexplicably attacked his father and beat him until the old man was senseless. Then he threw him down the cellar stairs. When his terrified mother screamed out, Warren grabbed her and threatened to kill her if she did not keep quiet and if she ever told anybody what he had done. Playing along with her son, Mrs. Rice assumed a calm demeanor and talked to him for some hours, pretending to devise a plan with Warren whereby the two of them could hide the crime and go on to run the farm themselves. During that conversation the old man was heard groaning in the cellar and Warren went downstairs and beat him again, this time until he was dead. Warren then went to inform the neighbors that his father had accidentally died from falling down the cellar steps—part of the plan devised by the mother. When the neighbors arrived at the Rice residence it was obvious the father had been murdered and Warren was immediately arrested. A son older than Warren was then confined at the State Lunatic Hospital at Worcester; a sister of the deceased committed suicide while in a state of insanity; and a brother of the deceased killed another brother while laboring under insanity. No other outcome of the case was reported.[4]

Isaac Carpenter

On Friday morning, November 2, 1866, the Carpenter family sat down to breakfast in their home near Mayfield, Ohio, at about 8:00. Isaac finished his meal before the rest and went out, remarking to his father, Ezra, that he would harness the team and the two of them would haul in cornstalks from the field. Ezra followed his son outside a few minutes later and almost directly Ezra's wife and daughter heard angry words exchanged between the two men. The two women went outside to try and prevent any trouble that might arise. On the way to the field the men had to pass through a gate. Isaac went to open it and one of the horses snapped at him, tearing his sleeve. An enraged Isaac seized a stick and began to beat the animal. Soon the father ordered his son to stop hitting the horse, whereupon Isaac turned on his father and tried to hit him with the stick; Ezra warded off the blows with a pitchfork. That was the situation when the two women arrived on the scene. Mrs. Carpenter prevailed upon her son to put down the stick and go away. He did so, returning to the house to change his shirt. Coming back to the wagon he seemed to have calmed down but suddenly became irate again. Isaac seized a stone from the ground and hurled it at his father. It caught the older man just below the ear and knocked him off the wagon. Carrying his badly injured father back to the house, Isaac laid him on the couch and then went for a doctor, although he had to be prodded somewhat by the two women before he consented to go for a physician. Determined to keep the real facts hidden the two women made up a story. When a neighbor arrived—Isaac was still absent—the women told the neighbor the horse had been startled, causing Ezra to be thrown from the wagon, and when he fell to the ground he received his injury from one of the wagon stakes. Mrs. Carpenter told Isaac that if he left that part of the country she would keep the secret; he agreed to do so. The false story was told to all who inquired but many did not believe it as the Carpenters were known as a family that engaged in frequent rows. After keeping her secret for two weeks, Mrs. Carpenter disclosed the truth to her younger son, James, who had not known the real facts up to that point. Despite his promise to leave the area, Isaac had remained at home. Worried the morose and moody Isaac might strike out again at a family member, James went to the authorities. One day later Isaac was arrested and committed to jail to await his trial for manslaughter.[5]

Ezra was described as a longtime resident of Mayfield, a mild and inoffensive man who was respected and esteemed by his neighbors. His domestic relations, though, were not entirely happy. His wife was said to have a violent temper, as did some of the couple's children. Isaac, the third son, was described as particularly wayward and one who engaged in constant fights with his father. So great was the animosity between Ezra and Isaac that the son had left home and been gone for some years. However, after a three-year stint in the U.S. Army that ended in 1865, Isaac returned to the family home to work the farm with his family. No other outcome was reported for this case.[6]

James Davis

The murder of Silas Davis of Stetson, Maine, in May 1874, by his insane son, James P. Davis, was called one of the "most revolting crimes" ever committed in the state. The wife of the murdered man witnessed the deed from the house and immediately had her son arrested. He appeared calm and unconcerned when taken into custody. James said he and his father were in the woods when Silas said to him, "James, I am getting old and want you to cut my head off; do it quick." Silas laid his head on the chopping black and James struck; "the first blow glanced, the second cut him badly, and the third time I hit him his head came off and rolled away. I had to do it as it was my duty and I am glad I performed it. Mother and father had laid a plan to kill me, but I was too sharp for them. The matter don't trouble me. I did right, but I feel bad to think the old man couldn't have lived to do better." The truth was that James knocked his father down and then dragged him to the block where he beheaded him. No disposition of the case was reported.[7]

J. T. Clarke

A brief report from a small Ontario newspaper at the beginning of December 1875 told of a homicide that occurred a short time earlier near Arden, Ontario. For the two months prior to the murder, J.T. Clarke, of Arden, formerly a Methodist Episcopalian minister had been "afflicted with insanity." He had gotten his friends—apparently aware of his condition—to promise that they would not send him to an asylum but keep him at home. At the time of the deed, the wife of the "maniac" was lying ill upstairs in her bedroom and Clarke wanted to go upstairs and see her. However, his father attempted to prevent him from doing so and in the struggle that followed the "infuriated Bedlamite" kicked his father and inflicted various other injuries that led to the old man's death after about 10 days. After having beaten his father, J.T. Clarke went upstairs, seized his two-year-old son and threw the child down the stairs, breaking the boy's collar bone. After those "little eccentricities he was secured and placed in confinement." Presumably he was committed to an asylum, but no other report on this case was published.[8]

Joseph Charest

From Ste. Anne de la Perade, Quebec, came a report that outlined a "most brutal" murder that had occurred in the community on January 18, 1878. Aubert Charest, 78, had a 24-year-old son named Joseph Charest, a "hunchback" whom he held in great favor in spite of the young man's "hideous deformity and bad temper." Old Charest's niece, aged 16, lived some 10 miles from the Charest home and Joseph often visited her, hoping to persuade her to marry him. She grew tired of his attentions and some weeks before had asked Aubert to speak to Joseph and convince him to drop his amorous suit. Joseph heard of that and threatened to kill both of them. On the 18th Aubert was sitting quietly after dinner smoking his pipe when Joseph came up behind him and beat him with a club. There was a servant girl and a man servant in the house "but the French peasants have a horror of hunchbacks," declared a reporter, "and instead of attempting to save the old man they fled upstairs and took to praying." After he had finished beating his father, Joseph dragged the still alive but unconscious man into the yard and left him to freeze to death. By then Joseph had become "maniacal" and he danced around the yard and called to the servants to come down and see how he punished those who crossed his path. A party of neighbors arrived and Joseph fled. Aubert died before a priest arrived. As it was thought Joseph had gone to kill his cousin, a posse was formed and went to the girl's home. After dark that evening Joseph did, in fact, show up at that house. He knocked on the door and was admitted, but was quickly overpowered by the waiting posse and taken off to jail at Trois Rivieres. No disposition of the case was reported.[9]

Martin Coleman Jr.

Martin Coleman, a Newark, New Jersey, brass refiner, died at his residence on Tuesday, January 21, 1879, from wounds inflicted by his son Martin Jr., aged 20. The young man had charge of several horses and in the previous week his father thought he had been neglecting them and spoke to him in a tone the youth resented, replying that he would look after the horses when he was ready. That angered the father, who picked up a boot and struck his son with it, whereupon the son drew a knife and stabbed his father in the arm. Due to unexplained reasons there was a considerable delay in getting a physician to attend the injured man. By that time the father had lost a great deal of blood. He continued to sink until Tuesday night, when he died. The police were not notified at all and the first they heard of the situation was when word was passed to them from the county physician, who had learned of the situation from the undertaker. By then the son had fled the city. Late at night on January 23 he was arrested by the police in New York City. When taken into custody he admitted he had stabbed his father on January 16, but denied having any intention of killing him. The Essex grand jury returned a true bill on February 1 against Martin for manslaughter in the death of his father. In the middle of February, in court in Newark, New Jersey, Martin Coleman Jr. pled guilty to manslaughter and was sentenced to the state prison for a term of five years.[10]

Felix Rooney

New York City coroner Brady was put in possession of some facts on January 13, 1881, regarding the death of Thomas Rooney, who was said to have committed suicide on December 25, 1880. Those facts made it appear probable that he had been murdered by his own son, Felix Rooney. Thomas had been a street sweeper employed by the New York City street cleaning department and lived in rooms on the second floor of a tenement house at 407 West 39th Street. On the afternoon of Christmas Day it was reported at a police station that Thomas was lying dead in his rooms, having cut his throat. An investigating police officer found the dead man with his throat slashed and much blood, but no disorder about the rooms. Mrs. Bridget Rooney (wife of the deceased) was also found in the rooms, wailing loudly about her husband's death, with a number of neighbors gathered around her trying to comfort the widow.

She told the police her husband had been of very intemperate habits and when drunk he had often abused her. On Christmas Eve he had gone on a spree and came home drunk the next morning, whereupon he quarreled with his wife, beat her, and drove her from the dwelling. Bridget took refuge with a neighbor and returned home at about 3:00 P.M. Christmas Day. She was horrified to find her husband lying dead on the floor with his throat cut. Bridget also said that on two previous occasions Thomas had tried to commit suicide by taking poison. A search for the weapon—it looked like a razor cut—was made but it was not found. Notwithstanding the suspicious circumstances, police accepted the theory of suicide. An inquest was held and a verdict of suicide was returned. Thomas Rooney was buried.[11]

The new information was provided when Joseph Rooney (son of Thomas), Mrs. Margaret Rooney (wife of Joseph) and Matthew Rooney (cousin of Joseph and Felix) went to see the authorities on January 13. They did not believe the death had been a suicide but that Thomas had been murdered by his son Felix Rooney. Joseph said his father was sober on Christmas morning and went to Mass at a Catholic church in the neighborhood. After church he had a few drinks—but was not drunk—and went home. Joseph then went out himself for a few drinks and returned home slightly under the influence. He met his mother, who told him his father was drunk upstairs and in a very angry mood. Therefore Joseph did not stay at the house but went to his brother Patrick's place and lay down for a while until he became sober. When he awoke Mary

Ann Rooney (wife of Patrick) told him Thomas was dead and that he had cut his own throat. Joseph said he did not believe it and started to leave. On looking for his hat he found it gone and in its place the hat of Felix. He asked Mary Ann about the hat and she said while he was asleep Felix had been there, washed his hands and left, taking the wrong hat, Joseph's, by mistake. Joseph thought that was strange as he knew Felix did not get along with Patrick and had not spoken to him or visited his house for two years. Margaret Rooney said that some days after the death Felix came to see her, saying he was in trouble, and begging her for money with which to leave the city. She refused to give him any. After leaving her he went to the home of Michael Halloran (husband to one of the daughters of Thomas, and brother-in-law to Felix). Michael took him to a railroad station and put him on a train. Matthew, while washing and preparing the corpse said he was asked by the wife or daughter of the deceased (he could not remember which) to hide a blood-stained knife in the shroud he was placing on the body. Felix was an ex-convict. Since the death of Thomas, Felix had robbed a man on the street of his gold watch, presumably to get money to leave the city. A warrant was then out for the arrest of Felix Rooney but there was no clue as to his whereabouts.[12]

On the following day the coroner directed the police to bring before him Bridget Rooney, her daughter Julia, her son Patrick and his wife, Mary Ann, Michael Halloran and his wife, Kate, Maria Murphy (she boarded with Patrick), Maggie Rooney (Bridget's daughter-in-law), Matthew Rooney, and Joseph Rooney (Bridget's son) in order that he might question them. "All were forlorn-looking persons," said an account. Julia testified that she witnessed a quarrel between Thomas and Felix and she tried to separate them when the stabbing took place. She saw Felix slash his father with a razor. When it was over Felix said nothing and fled the scene, taking the razor with him. She afterward told other family members what had happened. Matthew suggested the family take a knife and throw it into the blood near the body so as to make it appear to be a suicide. Julia and Bridget refused to go along with that idea. The other family members all took advantage of not being in the room when the murder took place and all pretended to know nothing, even though all had been told the story. And all of them knew of Felix's strange behavior, or of the efforts made to keep him out of the way. The Hallorans admitted they harbored Felix at their place until January 30, when they gave him $12 and sent him to Trenton. Taken as a unit, Captain Washburn of the New York Police Department described the Rooney clan as having "bad character." One of the murdered man's sons had been killed in a brawl in a stable some 10 years earlier. The murdered man once kept a liquor saloon on Seventh Avenue, noted a reporter, "that was resorted to by thieves, and Felix was a desperate thief and ruffian." By the end of that day's examination the coroner and the police were convinced the guilt of Felix as the murderer of Thomas Rooney had been established.[13]

Felix remained on the run and nothing more was reported on the fugitive until July 1887, some 6½ years after the murder. Reportedly, he had eluded the grasp of the police all that time, although there were some near captures. Police followed Felix through several states but were always a little too late to capture him. He was said to have been in New York City on several occasions since the killing. In the previous November he came to Manhattan on a schooner and spent a night under his mother's roof. He sailed away the next morning as the police prepared to close in on him. In July 1887 the police received a tip that Felix had been seen walking along Sixth Avenue in New York. Police went and checked out the area but found nothing. Some of the numerous tips received over the years, police officials acknowledged, could have been erroneous. Over the years he had been heard from, supposedly, from time to time in different states.[14]

Another six years passed before Rooney was mentioned again. By that time it was almost 13 years since the murder had been committed and the police were no closer to catching him. He had, as before, been traced to various places but the authorities always seemed to arrive on the scene just after Rooney had once again vanished. Reportedly, he had made several trips to New York City over those years to visit relatives. Two or three weeks earlier the police were informed he was at a rooming house on the Bowery. That house was thoroughly searched but Felix had already fled the place, if he had been there at all. Police reserves were called out and they searched every lodging house in the neighborhood but Rooney was not found. Apparently, he was never found. At any rate there were no more mentions of Felix Rooney in the press.[15]

James G. Allison

In the summer of 1879 a family named Allison lived about 13 miles north of Indiana, Pennsylvania. For the previous several years they had great trouble among themselves. The Allison family possessed a large and valuable 300 acre farm that belonged to the two brothers and two sisters in the family. Three of them resided on the land, which remained undivided. Robert, having purchased the share of one sister, was owner of half the land; Alexander owned a 25 percent share of the property, as did Mrs. Young, the married sister. Some years earlier, because of the ill treatment of some of the members of his family toward him, Robert finally was compelled to leave his own residence and live with his brother Alexander— the houses being about a quarter of a mile apart. During his absence Robert's wife and sons attended to Robert's part of the farm. In April 1880, acting on legal advice, he tried to take possession of his own residence and in the attempt was seriously beaten by his eldest son, James G. Allison, and then ejected from the premises. A criminal prosecution followed and an indictment was presented to the grand jury in June for assault, and a true bill found. On Thursday, June 17, the parties reached what was described as an "amicable settlement" and agreed that any matters still in disagreement between them would be submitted to arbitration for a final settlement.[16]

One day later, on Friday, June 18, Robert and Alexander loaded a wagon with bark, intending to haul it to Indiana on Saturday to sell; the bark formed a part of the dispute between Robert and his son James. At dusk that evening a little son of Alexander Young had been on an errand to the house of Robert Allison, occupied by Mrs. Allison and her two sons, James and Alonzo. As the little boy left Robert's house James called him over and told him to tell Robert (at Alexander's place) that Alonzo wanted to see him out at the road at dark. After the child delivered the message he went home. Robert went down to the road at dark and, hearing a person whistling, called out to see if it was Alonzo. He was answered by James, who said, "No, it is not Alonzo, you damned old son of a bitch, I will show you who it is," and he immediately made for the father, who retreated toward the house. Catching up with his father, James fired four shots in all, three hitting Robert, one in the back of the head. Those statements came from the wounded man before he died. James was arrested at his house on Saturday. "He is a man aged 28 years, tall and rough looking, with a dark threatening countenance. He appeared to be a little excited, but made no resistance. He did not seem to realize his perilous situation and denied the shooting," said an account. Mary Allison (wife of the deceased) declared at the coroner's inquest that she did not go near Robert and did not see him, as the couple had been separated for four or five years and she was not on good terms with him. John Allison (son of Alexander) heard the shots and the voices of his uncle and cousin as the latter shot the former. The jury at the coroner's inquest returned a verdict that the cause of death was by a shooting at the hands of James Allison and that it was an act of "deliberate murder."[17]

Legal appeals delayed the execution, which was finally fixed for February 17, 1882. On death row Allison remained indifferent, as he had since he was taken into custody, and refused to answer any questions with respect to the crime. The only relative who visited him was a female cousin. His mother, his brother, a sister, and the families of his uncle and aunt never visited him in prison.[18]

At 10:00 A.M. on the day of his execution his mother, sister and brother called at the jail but James refused to see them. As well, he refused to shave and refused to allow the sheriff to dress him in a new suit (a customary practice at executions throughout America). The only words he spoke from the gallows were "I have been fetched here wrong." James Allison was executed by hanging on February 17, 1882, at 11:00 A.M. At the trial, evidence showed that a bad feeling had existed among the members of the Allison family for a long time due to, it was said, Robert's "dissolute habits."[19]

As required by law an official notice was published in the newspaper to the effect that James G. Allison had indeed been duly hanged. The notice was sworn by the clerk of the court and bore the names and signatures of the 12 official witnesses, also required by law—"respectable citizens of the Commonwealth of Pennsylvania, residing in the County of Indiana...."[20]

James Weir

General James Weir of St. Clairsville, Ohio, was murdered by his son James Weir, 35, on Saturday, October 22, 1881. It was said to be a crime committed in the heat of passion and evidently without premeditation. General Weir's daughter Ada, 12, had been in the employ of Miss Cady, a dressmaker, over the previous summer. Cady wanted to adopt the child. It was a plan favored by James but the general would not consent to it. On Saturday, James asked his father to sign an instrument binding the girl to Cady but the old man refused. That act so enraged James that he struck his 78-year-old father with his fist. It was a blow that broke the older man's nose, and in the ensuing fall the general's skull was fractured.

Doctors were immediately called but declared the old man could not survive. General Weir died on Monday morning. In between the attack and the death, James Weir slipped away and was not heard from again. Years earlier General Weir, born in 1803, was one of the most prominent citizens of Belmont County. For more than 40 years he practiced law successfully. As well, he represented his county in the Ohio legislature for several years. Of later years, though, it was reported he had lost prestige, retired from his law practice, and was leading a lonely and unhappy life. In December 1880, his son George shot a man named Sterling Riggs and was then in jail under indictment for murder in the first degree. James was considered "the best" of the family but had a "most violent temper."[21]

General Weir was married twice but tried to get a divorce from his second wife. However, the courts refused his petition for a divorce and the couple resumed living together. Mrs. Weir died in 1876. She had given birth to eight children, five of whom died of consumption. The remaining three were James, George, and Ada. "It would have been better for all concerned if consumption could have taken these two boys also, as subsequent events have proved," noted a sardonic reporter. James grew to be a man of fine personal appearance but of a violent nature. When he was a youth he knocked a young man's eye out in St. Clairsville with a hammer, which came about as a result of a dispute over a game of cards. On another occasion James struck a man on the head, causing permanent injury. James found employment as a letter carrier in Cincinnati but got into a fight in which he almost broke someone's arm. He was tried on a charge for that assault but was acquitted. Another time, he fired a shot at an employee of the Cincinnati post office but was never arrested. In 1877 he returned to live with his father, ostensibly to run the general's estate. Family rows were reported to be frequent events and former friends had almost given up going to the Weir residence because of the constant fighting. James was known to have often struck his aged father to try to get his own way. James and George also fought regularly and James threatened to kill George one time after the latter had blocked the former's efforts to get the old man to sign over his property to James. All three of the men went around the house armed with guns. Events reached a head on that Saturday over Ada. James and his father had fought all summer over the future course of Ada's life. James would send her to Cady and then the general would demand that she return. Finally, Cady insisted that she was willing to keep Ada but she needed a legal agreement to prevent the constant coming and going imposed on the child. When the general balked on that Saturday at signing an agreement allowing Cady to adopt Ada, James threatened to kill him if he did not sign. After James had attacked his father and after he was satisfied the general would die, he rifled a bureau of all the money it contained and escaped. No attempt was made to stop him although many knew he planned to disappear. No other outcome of this case was reported.[22]

James Lambert

On a Saturday evening in the middle of May 1883, a murder that was described as being of an "unusually brutal character" was committed in the Canadian province of Ontario, 1 1/2 miles east of the village of Williamsford Station, in the township of Holland. At around 4:00 P.M. a farmer named George Lambert, about 50, went into his house for supper and while he was in the process of washing his hands was shot through the back by his son James, about 20, a man said to be "of eccentric habits but not heretofore looked on as dangerous." Hearing the shot, the victim's wife rushed to the room only to find James reloading in preparation for a second shot; his mother implored him to stop. Nevertheless, he fired a second shot into his father—a head shot that killed him instantly. James then dragged the body out of the house some 40 yards to the foot of the garden, where he began to dig a grave. As well, he got some lumber that he commenced to measure and to saw up for a coffin. By that time 15 to 20 neighbors had assembled but were unable or unwilling to do anything as James threatened to shoot anybody who came near him. Finally, the neighbors were able to overpower him and took him off to the village jail. James explained that in committing the murder he was carrying out his father's instructions. It was reported that James wished to get the farm and the fact of his being kept from doing so generated the feelings that prompted him to commit the murderous act. At the coroner's inquest the jury returned a verdict of willful murder. James was taken to Owen Sound where he was to be held until his trial took place. No disposition of the case was reported.[23]

Samuel McCauley

A dispatch from Westmoreland County in Pennsylvania in August 1883 told of a "brutal parricide" that had occurred one mile from Salina.

Samuel McCauley shot and killed his father in the presence of his mother, brother, and two sisters. The cause of the quarrel was said to have been a lawsuit between father and son. Reportedly, the elder McCauley was a well-to-do farmer but tightfisted when it came to money. His "unnatural son" lived the life of a hermit in a cabin on the family farm property, a small portion of which he tilled for his living. The lawsuit in question was brought by the father to oust his son from the property. When the pair met on August 6, they quarreled bitterly over the issue. During that argument Samuel calmly drew a weapon and shot his father dead. He then fled the scene through the fields and was just making the cover of the woods when he was overtaken by his brother and some neighbors who had pursued the son. After his capture Samuel was taken off to jail. One account described him as follows: "The murderer is middle aged, of a savage disposition and never mixed with public affairs in the least."[24]

After a trial that lasted 14 days, in February 1884, the jury returned a verdict against Samuel McCauley of guilty of murder in the first degree. "The patricide had saved considerable money from school teaching and was abundantly able to support himself, yet had repeatedly asked to live at home and had been repeatedly driven away by his father," said a reporter. "He was looked upon as a crank and insanity was his defense." No report on sentencing was published.[25]

Stanley Griffith

On January 1, 1884, a quarrel took place on the farm of Mr. Griffith near Salem, Ohio. He argued about the farm work with his son Stanley Griffith. The father wanted the assistance of the son but Stanley refused and stormed out of the house in an angry mood, taking a revolver with him. Later in the day the father went out to look for Stanley. Soon thereafter when a neighbor heard a shot he thought it was a gun fired by a hunter. A little later Stanley went to a neighbor to say his father had committed suicide; he borrowed a horse from the neighbor so he could go and fetch a doctor. Mr. Griffith's body was found in the woods with a bullet hole in the chest. Numerous tracks indicated a struggle had taken place there and the blood-stained snow that was nearby, but away from the body, led authorities to believe the killer had tried to clean his hands in the snow after the killing of the old man and the handling of the corpse. After Stanley had called on the doctor and told the physician the suicide story, he escaped in the confusion before it became apparent Stanley was the killer. When the elder Griffith left the house he had $20, which was not found on the body.[26]

Almost a year later, in December 1884, Stanley stood trial on a charge of murder in the second degree. However, at the trial both sides agreed to a plea of guilty of manslaughter. Stanley was sentenced to a term of 12 years imprisonment at hard labor in the Ohio penitentiary. Later, Stanley was transferred to the Lancaster Industrial School in Ohio and was released from custody in December 1886, just two years after being incarcerated. Upon his release he went back home to live at Salem.[27]

Cicero Jefferson

On April 29, 1884, Cicero Jefferson confessed to the murder of his father, Hiram Jefferson, committed by himself and his two brothers-in-law. As evidence that his confession was given freely and not made under duress, it was reported that Cicero's admission was sworn and freely testified in the presence of a "large audience." Cicero was 25, lived in Carroll City, Iowa, and said that he last saw his father on the night of Friday, April 25. That evening Cicero and his brothers-in-law, Joel J. Wilson and John A. Smyth (often Smythe), left the Carroll City residence of Wilson at about 8:00 on that Friday. They rode close to Hiram's house where they stopped and made plans on how to proceed. Next they burst into Hiram's house and dragged the father out of bed and into the next room where they proceeded to choke and smother him. One of the two in-laws, according to Cicero's account, took a rope and noosed it about Hiram's neck. Then they dragged him outside by the rope. Throughout all of this Hiram remained alive and conscious and was begging for mercy. When the group reached a tree the three killers strung Hiram up and left him there lynched to death, although Cicero thought he might have been dead before the actual lynching. As a finishing touch Wilson tore the father's shirt open and tied it over the older man's head; the shirt was the only clothing Hiram had on. When the lynching had been completed, around midnight, the three men rode back to Wilson's place. Cicero's confession agreed with the story that Hiram's wife had told as she watched her husband dragged out of their home and lynched. According to an early article the three men—then all in jail—were in no danger then from the citizens of the area.[28]

With respect to the motive for killing Hiram, one account said it had appeared that Wilson had been told that his wife (Hiram's daughter) had not always been virtuous. When Wilson confronted his wife with the allegation, she admitted to having been intimate with her father through compulsion and that she had once been "in trouble" by him. That angered Wilson to the point where he said he would either leave his wife or kill the old man. She wanted him to do neither and she consulted with Smyth. The result of the consultation was the lynching on Friday night. Many believed a different story. Under that tale Smyth was the one who had been intimate with Wilson's wife and those two worked out the plan whereby they would charge it all off to the father.[29]

Further details of the murderous night revealed the three men showed up at the Jefferson home on the Friday night on horseback and wearing masks. They were noisy and boisterous and it was dark so Mrs. Jefferson did not recognize them but Hiram apparently did, at least he recognized Cicero. Regarding the family, a reporter remarked, "Neither Jefferson, his wife, nor their children were considered very strong mentally, and Cicero is far below the average young man in intelligence, and is just such a fellow as might be expected to be led into anything by such a man as Smyth."[30]

Hiram Jefferson, 65, had come to Iowa from Pittsfield, Illinois, 18 years earlier and settled on the farm near where he met his death. He raised a family of one boy and five girls. Three years earlier John Smyth, "a rough, drinking character, married a daughter and soon succeeded in causing a disturbance in the family, arraying mother and children against the father. Threats were made against the latter's life," asserted one account. "The family is not a bright one, and the son is said to be almost an idiot."[31]

Reportedly, when Smyth married one of Hiram's daughters he accused the elder Jefferson of committing incest with one of his daughters and threats were made by Smyth and others against the father. Smyth had moved to a new place a year earlier and induced both Hiram and Lucy (the daughter who was the victim of the alleged abuse) to leave the family home and live with him and his family. Frequent threats against the life of the old man were said to have been made by several relatives during the preceding two years. Herein, Hiram was described as "crippled and not very strong mentally, and was scrupulously honest and upright in all his dealings and a kind husband and father. His son Cicero and son-in-law Smyth have so harassed him that for the past year he has been partially insane at times." During that last year or so of his life, none of Hiram's children lived in the family home anymore. The article then mentioned the story about the old man being accused of incest with Wilson's wife, and then commented, "The general impression here is that the incest business is a hoax. That such a report was out about two years ago, there is no question, but it is generally believed that Smyth is responsible for these stories and that the old man is innocent. Wilson married his wife, Jefferson's daughter [Lucy] last February."[32]

All three of the accused were lodged in jail in Audubon, Iowa, awaiting their trial. Then, at about 4:00 A.M. on February 4, 1885, a mob battered down the walls of the jail in Audubon, Iowa, and lynched John A. Smyth, Joel J. Wilson, and Cicero Jefferson. Smyth and Wilson fought "like tigers" and were shot dead by the mob in their cells. Cicero was taken to the bandstand in the park and hung dead there. Catalyst for the lynching at that time was said to have been a ruling made a few days earlier by a judge that the venue for the trial would be changed to another county. That angered the people of Audubon, who vowed the prisoners would never be allowed to leave Audubon County, at least not alive.[33]

The prison compound in Audubon had a jail and a residence area— the latter for the sheriff and his family, alone. Early that morning Sheriff Hebert and family (asleep in the residence area) and deputy sheriffs Workman and J.H. Jenkins (both asleep in the jail itself) were awakened by a pounding on the front door. Hebert looked outside to see a crowd he estimated at from 500 to 750 men gathered around the jail, who demanded the Jefferson murderers. After some arguing back and forth, the sheriff took his revolver and fired several shots over the heads of the mob. Nevertheless, the mob moved to quickly overpower the authorities. After Wilson and Smyth were shot dead, their bodies were taken out of the jail and hung to the stringers of the high fence that surrounded the jail.[34]

The work of the mob lasted from about 2:30 A.M. to 4:00 A.M., according to one report, and, "Public opinion approve[d] the lynching." A coroner's jury held an inquest into the three deaths on the afternoon of February 4 and returned a verdict that Smyth and Wilson came to their deaths by shooting and Cicero Jefferson came to his death by hanging "at the hands of unknown parties."[35]

Regarding the mob, a reporter declared, "The crowd that filled the corridor was not a mob at all in the usual sense of the term, but a well organized body of deliberate men who went quietly to work in a separate way and accomplished their purposes without any unnecessary noise...."

They were all masked. The parties that did the most shooting were apparently young men but acted under orders of a leader."[36]

John Neave

John Neave deliberately murdered his father, Joseph Neave, on the afternoon of July 27, 1887, at Falmouth, Kentucky, in a dispute over the division of the crops. "A mob is organizing to lynch the son who has barricaded himself in a barn," observed a journalist. Joseph had gone to the farm that he owned but did not live on to see John, who lived on the farm and worked it, to get his share of the crop of wheat. After the killing the son briefly barricaded himself on the property but was soon taken into custody by the authorities. At the end of March 1888, after being convicted on a murder charge, John Neave was sentenced to a term of life imprisonment.[37]

Robert Elder

Hammonton, New Jersey, not far from Atlantic City, was the site of a murder on Saturday night, August 4, 1888, when Robert Elder shot and fatally wounded his father, John E. Elder. The latter had been separated from his wife for some time and Robert, 18, was said to have shot his father to avenge the wrongs John had done to his mother. It was reported that Mrs. Elder had been compelled to leave her husband because of his association with other women. John was reputed to have countered such allegations by claiming his wife had been unfaithful to him. It was a charge that was "indignantly resented" by his son Robert.[38]

A week later another account presented a different version as to the cause of the shooting when it declared, "The two men wanted to marry the same woman and quarreled about her."[39]

At his trial later in 1888 Robert was convicted of murder in the first degree and on November 10 Judge Reed at May's Landing, New Jersey, sentenced him to be executed by hanging on January 3, 1889.[40]

On that day at noon Robert was executed, with death being almost instantaneous. In this news story the killing was said to have resulted from the ill treatment of Robert's mother and brother by John. It was a killing that had been witnessed by Robert's grandfather, aged 90. John was 60, while Robert Elder was said herein to have been 27.[41]

The causes that led up to the murder were reported to have involved a long story of domestic unhappiness in which were arrayed the father on one side and the mother and six children (including Robert) on the other. The condemned man spent much of his last night listening to hymns that were sung to him by friends. His family all visited him for the last time on January 2. "To all of them young Elder presented a buoyant appearance, declaring himself not only ready, but anxious to die, since he believed, as he said, that his crime was committed in self defense," said a reporter, "and that for either the real or fanciful wrongs which he had suffered at his father's hands, he felt that he had inflicted a just punishment on his parent."[42]

Elder was executed by an "upward jerk" gallows—a method that had given way almost everywhere to the more familiar trapdoor gallows. When the weight fell, "Elder's body was jerked almost to the top beam of the scaffold, and then it fell back with a quiver and there was a convulsive movement of the arms and legs. County physician Riley, after the body had hung for five minutes, said there was no pulsation of the heart, and ten minutes afterward he was pronounced dead." Reportedly, Robert had frequent quarrels with his father because of the father's cruel treatment of his 14-year-old brother, Thomas. Robert went to his father's house on the day of the murder to get his younger brother's clothes. He quarreled with John and when the pair came out of the house John made a threatening advance to his son. Robert drew a revolver and shot his father four times in the chest. Following the shooting, Robert fled the scene and escaped to the home of his uncle at Medford, but he gave himself up to the police the next day. At the trial it was shown that Robert had frequently threatened to kill his father and the son admitted he traveled to Philadelphia a few days before the shooting, where he purchased the revolver he used to kill his father. His defense at the trial was that he had been in mortal dread of his father and had shot him in self defense.[43]

A.F. Hoffeditz

In Anaconda, Montana, on the night of Saturday, November 23, 1889, A.F. Hoffeditz shot and killed his father and then shot himself through the head. A.F. kept a secondhand furniture store in Anaconda. Three months earlier his father, J.F. Hoffeditz, almost 70 years of age, came out from Nazareth, Pennsylvania, and since that time had been helping his son by working in the store. On that Saturday evening, A.F.

informed his wife he would not be home that night but would sleep in the store, with his father, after the close of business. The store was open until 9:00 that evening and customers saw both father and son attending to business in the usual fashion, nothing seemed amiss. At 9:00 P.M. the store was closed and nothing unusual was heard therein during the night by occupants of the neighboring buildings. Mrs. Hoffeditz prepared breakfast for both her husband and her father-in-law at around 8:00 on Sunday, but neither of them appeared for the meal. She waited for an hour and then went down to the store to check on the two men. She was able to get in through a window and went to the sleeping room, which was located in the center of the building. On the floor she found the old man dead from a bullet to the head and also on the floor was the body of her husband, also shot through the head. A.F. was still clutching the revolver in his hand. He was about 32, and died around 7:00 P.M. on Sunday. "There was no difficulty of any nature whatever between himself and his father, and his terrible deed was undoubtedly nothing but a manifestation of insanity," declared an observer.[44]

Paul Holtz

A murder took place in a tenement in West Chicago, on the night of December 15, 1890, wherein lived Carl Holtz, an "aged widower," in an upper flat with his 16-year-old son, Paul Holtz. Father and son slept in the same bed. On the night of the fifteenth, when the boy went to bed he took with him an old table knife. After his father had retired for the night and gone to sleep, Paul got up and cut his throat from ear to ear, severing the jugular vein and windpipe. Then Paul rushed to a nearby police station where he told the authorities that his father had attempted to commit suicide. When the police reached the flat the old man was still alive but could not speak. Carl had crawled from the bed and on a piece of yellow wrapping paper, bespattered with his blood he wrote in German, "Paul Holtz did it." A doctor bandaged up the throat and Carl was able to utter a few hoarse words. With a finger pointing to his son he rasped, "You have killed me, Paul, but you can never enjoy the money. God will punish you for this." A few moments later he died. The money referred to was a $2,000 life insurance policy.[45]

Paul was taken to the police station where, on being questioned, he admitting to having killed his father. "I did it because he starved me," said the boy. "I work in a picture-frame factory and earn $6 a week, but my father takes it from me and does not give me enough to eat. He was a cabinetmaker. He did not earn much more than I do, and spent most of his money foolishly."[46]

As to the idea he had killed his father for the insurance money, it was a charge that Paul strenuously denied. Neighbors said the boy had always been quiet, "but peculiar in his ways. Some think his mind is abnormal." In May 1891, Paul Holtz was found guilty of murder and sentenced to 14 years imprisonment.[47]

James B. Carpenter

At Mifflintown, Pennsylvania, an inquest was held on December 14, 1893, into the death of James C. Carpenter, a blind huckster, whose mutilated body was found in a creek. Testimony was that on a Sunday the dead man had a bitter quarrel with his son James B. Carpenter in which the wife/mother joined in and sided with the son. A few hours after that the older man disappeared and was never heard of again until his body was found by searchers. Both James B. and Mrs. Hettie Carpenter were on the witness stand and told contradictory stories about what had happened. At the conclusion of the inquest the jury found the older man had been murdered. As a result James B. was arrested, as was Hettie, the latter after her husband's funeral, also on the fourteenth.[48]

The father had been murdered on December 10 and was about 56 years old. After being tried and convicted of the murder, James B. Carpenter was executed on the morning of June 14, 1894.[49]

Elijah Moore

The Reverend Jesse Moore was found murdered in his bed at home on November 16, 1899, near Dexter, Missouri. One day later his son Elijah Moore was arrested for the crime, although he protested his innocence. Jesse was a Methodist minister and as far as was known he had no enemies. Although three sons slept in the same room with their father (one was Elijah), all of them swore they heard no shot on the day in question. A shotgun was found on a rack on the rear porch with one barrel empty; it had been recently discharged. At the coroner's inquest, Elijah, the eldest son, testified that in the week before his death his father loaned the shotgun to a neighbor whom he, Elijah, did not know. Elijah said he believed the unknown neighbor returned with the gun, killed his father and placed the weapon in the rack. The coroner's inquest returned a verdict of murder at the hands of person or persons unknown.[50]

A day or so later, on November 20, Elijah, 19, made a full confession. He had planned the murder two weeks before its commission, claiming his father was cruel to his family and allowed his children no pleasure. Elijah got up at 3:00 A.M., got the shotgun, and shot his father by moonlight, hung the gun back up on the rack and then went back to bed. According to the boy, his father was a hard, cruel man, rigid in his discipline. At Dexter, Elijah Moore was sentenced on March 29, 1900, to be executed by hanging, on May 16, 1900. No report of the hanging was published.[51]

5

Sons, Mothers, and Alcohol

John Shea Jr.

In a tenement on Wednesday night, December 11, 1867, "a fearful tragedy such as never before was equaled in this vicinity for brutality and heartlessness was enacted," declared a journalist. An Irish family lived there in Springfield, Massachusetts, John and Mary Shea with their five children. John Jr., 19, Denis, 16, and Maggie, 10, were John's children from a previous marriage. The other two were younger, Kate and Patsy Connors, children of Mary from a previous marriage. John and Mary had been married about two years. About 8:30 A.M. on December 12, John and his eldest son called at the home of Dr. McLean and asked him to come with them and attend a woman to see if she was alive or dead. When the physician arrived at the Shea residence he found Mary lying dead on the bed. She was covered in blood and her body was badly bruised all over and she had every appearance of having been beaten to death. Police were informed and they immediately arrested John and his eldest son, although the crime appeared, from the evidence before the coroner's jury and from the accusation of the father, to have been committed solely by John Jr. The father was held in custody as a witness. It appeared that Mary had been beaten and kicked the night before by John Jr. and then she was placed on the bed where the two youngest children slept. The father was out until 2:00 or 3:00 A.M. before he came home drunk and threw himself on the same bed with the dying woman and lay there for the rest of the night. After the arrest of young Shea and his father a jury was summoned by Coroner Trask, who viewed the premises and examined several witnesses. Shea Jr., it was reported, "has long been known to the police officers as a desperate character, and one that would not hesitate at committing any crime." He had once been to reform school, frequently appeared before the police court for drunkenness and in the previous summer had served a sentence of three months in the house of correction for beating the woman he had finally killed. For many months he had no regular employment and lived at his father's house when he was not in jail. Said a reporter, "His father is a drunken, dissolute man, who gets his living from hand to mouth, but who is not particularly vicious, while his step-mother was comparatively peaceful and inoffensive."[1]

John Shea Jr. was convicted on May 26, 1868, of manslaughter in the death of Mary Shea and sentenced to eight years in the state prison.[2]

Michael Mead

New York City coroner Flynn held an inquest on December 29, 1869, over the remains of Mrs. Margaret Mead, 80, who had been brutally kicked to death at her residence, 14 Baxter Street, New York, by her son Michael Mead. The wife and son of the accused were called to testify against him. Catharine Mead, the wife, said that on the night of December 18 she was awakened by her children screaming and saw Michael in the other room kicking his mother, who was on the floor. Afraid to say anything or to get up to interfere to try to save her mother-in-law, Catharine did nothing. On the previous evening Michael had given his wife a pair of black eyes. He had frequently beaten his mother. Michael had reportedly been drinking to excess for the previous four months. When Catharine arose on the morning of the nineteenth, Mrs. Mead still lay on the floor with a bruised and bloodied face and body. Still alive then, Mrs. Mead was unable to get up; she died that evening. Doctor Harron was called in to attend the elderly woman on the 19th and was told she had injured herself when she fell down the stairs. Harron could do nothing and advised that a priest should be summoned. On the next morning, the twentieth, Michael called upon Harron to issue a death certificate but he refused to do so and called in the coroner. Thomas Mead, grandson of the deceased and son of Michael, testified that on the night of the eighteenth his father came home and kicked Margaret Mead. Thomas had seen his father kick her several times in the past. The coroner's jury returned a verdict that the old lady came to her death at the hands of Michael. He was 41, born in Ireland, and was by trade a shoemaker. Mead denied his guilt and was committed to the city prison, the Tombs, to await trial.[3]

When he was brought to trial in February 1870 on a murder charge, Mead declared he was willing to plead guilty to manslaughter in the second degree. It was an option the prosecution accepted. Before he was sentenced Michael told the court he was not yet 20 years old when he came to America, residing for 21 years in New York City. He had been in the United States only 18 months when he sent to Ireland for his mother and made a home for her living with him in New York. He said, "[S]ince then I never did her any injury; my mother was a hard drinking woman; she was several times sent to the [Blackwell's] Island [prison] by Justice Dowling, and I often got her off; I am sorry for what occurred; I am ashamed." Judge Vandervoort then sentenced him, saying, "Mead, you are charged with one of the most heinous crimes known to the law. You have killed your mother on account of rum. You first knocked her down and then brutally kicked her in that helpless condition. You have had some time to reflect on the enormity of your crime, and you must already be aware that it is one for which you can never make amends here." He continued, "I see nothing in these papers why I should not give you the full sentence allowed by the law. The sentence of the Court is that you be confined in the State Prison at Sing Sing, at hard labor, for seven years." At the conclusion of sentencing Michael Mead was manacled together with a prisoner sentenced immediately before him—Jack Reynolds, sentenced to death for murder. The pair were then led out of the courtroom through a side door, attended by a large force of deputies. According to a news account, "They were then led down the broad stairs on the outside of the new Court House into Chambers Street. Thence they were carried through Chambers Street to Centre Street [to the Tombs] and followed by an immense crowd of roughs and curiosity seekers."[4]

Joseph Dykes

Some quarrel broke out on the night of August 14, 1872, between Mrs. Margaret Dykes of West 28th Street, New York City, and her son Joseph Dykes. During that quarrel Joseph seized a club and beat his mother violently to death with repeated blows to the head. Margaret lingered near death for close to two weeks before she finally succumbed. At the coroner's inquest later in August evidence showed the deceased had been systematically beaten and kicked by her "brutal son, who was of very intemperate habits." Several of the tenants in the rooming house testified that they had often seen Joseph beat his mother in "the most inhuman manner." That jury returned a verdict that Margaret Dykes came to her death at the hands of her son Joseph. He was 30 years old, born in Ireland and a stone cutter by occupation.[5]

Joseph Dykes was tried for the murder of his mother on October 25, 1872, in the court of general sessions. When the case was called it was found that almost none of the witnesses for the prosecution were present. Thereupon Joseph pled guilty to manslaughter in the fourth degree. By consent, District Attorney Sullivan read into the record the testimony taken at the coroner's inquest. From that it was learned that Dykes had been in the habit of beating and kicking his mother and that on the night of August 14-15, he, being drunk at the time, "assaulted her with great violence and kicked her in the most brutal manner." Joseph Dykes was sentenced to two years' imprisonment with hard labor.[6]

Patrick Morrissey

On Sunday afternoon, June 23, 1872, Ann Morrissey was murdered by her 28-year-old son, Patrick Morrissey, in Buffalo, New York. A shocked reporter observed that in the late 19th century in the midst "of a people noted for their enlightenment and Christianity, we find a fiend in human shape guilty of driving a large carving knife into the heart of the mother who bore him." Patrick was born in 1843 in Nenagh, in the county of Tipperary, Ireland, and came to America with his mother when he was just seven months old. In his early life and until he reached the age of 11, when he became a sailor, Patrick's occupation was that of a ferry boy on a craft called the *Buffalo Creek*, carrying passengers from the central wharf to the island, earning during the summer months from $1 to $5 per day, which he gave to his mother. Police records revealed he began his criminal career when he was 12, his first offense being the stealing of a watch and $42 in gold from a drunken sailor, for which he was sentenced to the Rochester House of Refuge. In 1869 he was convicted of larceny and sentenced to the Auburn State Prison in New York for a term of three years and six months. But after serving just seven months he was released on a pardon from the state's governor, mainly through the intervention of his mother who lobbied tirelessly to obtain her son's release.[7]

Patrick was implicated in the robbery of some people from the East in August 1871. To escape the pursuing police he fled Buffalo and went to New York City. Once there he was said to have been shanghaied by the keeper of a sailor's boardinghouse and shipped out onboard a South

American ship heading to Liverpool. He returned to Buffalo just one week before the murder. From the time of his return he stayed at the boardinghouse operated by his mother. Ann had been a widow for several years, was about 55, and had four children, three daughters and Patrick. She kept a boardinghouse and saloon. At 1:30 P.M. on the fateful day, Patrick left home intent on finding a vessel upon which to sail. However, he had no luck and soon returned home quarrelsome and intoxicated. Patrick came upon his mother in the dining room preparing to serve her lodgers a meal; she had a large carving knife with her. He began to verbally abuse his mother. At first she paid no attention, thinking he was joking, but when she realized he was not she told him to be quiet and to leave the house until he sobered up and settled down or she would call the police. In response, Patrick then called her a "damned bitch," seized the carving knife from her hand and plunged it up to the hilt into her chest. Nobody saw the stabbing; but the cook, Mrs. Springston, entered the room in time to see Patrick throw the bloodied knife onto the table. Ann staggered several feet before collapsing into the arms of lodger Blackledge, who had come in response to the commotion. As Blackledge supported Ann, Patrick exclaimed, "My God, I've killed my mother, I've done it, I've done it." He was quickly taken into custody, declared he had murdered his mother and demanded a lawyer before answering any questions. Morrissey was placed on trial for the murder on July 9, with the defense being the crime was committed in the heat of passion while the accused was under the influence of liquor and thus unaccountable for his acts. The jury was out for just 18 minutes before returning with a verdict of guilty of murder in the first degree. He was sentenced to be executed on September 6, 1872.[8]

Some seven or eight years earlier Patrick was married to a girl named Ellen Connolly of Buffalo but reportedly left her immediately after the conclusion of the ceremony, never having lived with her as man and wife. She subsequently obtained a divorce and married again. During his stay in Liverpool on his last ocean voyage he was married to a young woman named Julia Drought. Ten days after that marriage he sailed for America with the understanding being that he would send for her as soon as he was able to provide a home for her and support her. She never heard from him again. Just before his execution he gave an interview to a *New York Herald* reporter, during which he said, "There are a large number of sailors in New York who will remember me very well when they see this in the *Herald* and will feel sorry for my sad fate. If my death can save one of them from the evils of intemperance I am satisfied." When he was with that reporter Patrick did not deny the killing of his mother but protested he was innocent of having killed her with premeditation and that he had no conscious recollection of the crime. Attempts to obtain a new trial or a reprieve were all unsuccessful. Patrick Morrissey was executed by hanging on September 6, 1872, and died instantly of a broken neck.[9]

Another account cast a different light on the murder. With respect to Ann Morrissey it stated, "It was understood that she sometimes got inebriated, and had at all times a savage and unbearable temper. This latter fact was sworn to by two of her daughters at the trial. It is also alleged that there is not one of the children who does not bear the marks of wounds inflicted by their mother."[10]

Thomas Callaghan

Shortly after noon on August 29, 1875, a police officer was stopped on the street by a woman who was greatly agitated and who informed him there was a woman lying dead in a room on the top floor of a house on Fifth Avenue and that she had been murdered by her son. Neighbors said she had died a violent death; she had been carousing with her son during the night and it was thought he killed her during a drunken brawl. Thomas Callaghan had last been seen on the premises at about 10:00 A.M. on August 29. He was arrested that afternoon. A reporter with the *New York Times* went to the premises and learned the details: "The house in which the murder was committed is a two-story brick dwelling, very dilapidated, and filthy in the extreme. It is inhabited by white and colored people who do not bear a very enviable reputation." A small front room on the top floor was occupied by Mrs. Mary Callaghan, a 49-year-old Irishwoman, her 28-year-old son, Thomas, and daughter Katie, 15. Mary had been a widow for 12 or 13 years, her husband having drowned in the Erie Canal near Rochester, New York. The rest of the family consisted of another daughter, a widow named Ellen Duncan, then a live-in servant in Lancaster, New Hampshire, and a son James, who was serving with the Sixth United States Cavalry in the West. From the facts he ascertained, the reporter said the "family record is not a very creditable one." Ellen, the oldest daughter, had married a black man, and Katie, employed in a feather-making factory, was rumored to be intimately involved with a black man. Thomas had lived an "irregular" life. He enlisted in the 77th Regiment, New York State Volunteers, during the Civil War and at its end he entered the regular army, enlisting in the Fifteenth United States Infantry, and served with that unit until November 1874, when he returned to New York City as a civilian. Two years earlier, at the age of 18, James had enlisted in the cavalry. Since Thomas had returned home it was said that "he has been doing nothing for a living and has been leading a very dissipated life." Thomas heard that his mother was on "too intimate" terms with the black men living in the rooming house, and that gave rise to frequent quarrels between mother and son. Mrs. Callaghan drank to excess and was known to have been drunk for a week at a time. "The room occupied by the Callaghans was very poorly furnished and everything in the apartment had the air of squalid poverty," noted the reporter.[11]

From a statement made by Katie, some three weeks earlier Thomas, in a drunken rage, beat both her and her mother. Mrs. Callaghan had him arrested and he was locked up. However, when he was taken to court the next day she refused to prosecute and Thomas was discharged. He then went away for a bit to Albany or Troy, New York, returning home about one week before the murder. During that final week Mary and Thomas had been constantly drunk and quarreling and fighting all the time. Katie said she came home at 10:00 Saturday night and found them both drunk and fighting. As she was afraid she would be beaten, Katie left the house and stayed away until midnight, thinking her mother and brother would be asleep by then. But when she got home at midnight they were still up and fighting. Katie remained in the room until around 2:00 A.M. during which time her mother and brother abused her, and Thomas threatened to kill her. Therefore, Katie left the room again and slept on the rear stoop of the house until between 5:00 and 6:00 A.M. on August 29, when she took refuge at a neighbor's place. At 9:00 A.M. Thomas banged on the neighbor's door and demanded to know if Katie was there. The neighbor said she was not. He went away muttering that his mother was dying and he would kill his sister if he got hold of her. Katie did not return to the room until after the discovery of the body, by a different neighbor who stopped in to see Mary, not long after Thomas had left the flat that Sunday morning.[12]

New York coroner Croker held an inquest into the death of Mary Callaghan on September 2. Among other injuries, the deceased had sustained broken ribs and had bruises and contusions all over her body, arms, legs, and face. She had literally been beaten to death. Katie had been the last to see Mary alive, around 2:00 on the Sunday morning. She was then lying on the floor, where she would later be found dead by the neighbor.

Katie told the inquest how on previous occasions she and her mother had been beaten by Thomas. After being arrested Thomas denied knowing anything about his mother's death but did admit he had beaten her on the Saturday night, because she had called him a thief and a loafer. There were, however, no direct witnesses to the murder and when the jury returned with a verdict it said nothing more than that Thomas "had a hand in it." Croker asked them what they meant by that and as they could not explain it to the satisfaction of Croker, he refused to accept what he termed such a "stupid" verdict and directed them to retire for further deliberations to see if they could reach an "intelligent" verdict. In a short time the jury returned and rendered a verdict "that the deceased came to her death by shock from injuries at the hands of her son Thomas Callaghan." Croker accepted that verdict. Thomas was committed to the City Prison (the Tombs) to await the action of the grand jury while the hapless Katie was committed to the house of detention—to be held in custody as a witness.[13]

Thomas Callaghan went on trial for murder on October 21, 1875. In this account the Callaghan flat was described as a "miserable chamber" divided into a room and a bedroom by a sheet hung in the middle of the single room. It was learned at the trial that when Thomas left the apartment on Sunday morning, August 29, he had with him a Bible he had taken from the family home and that he tried unsuccessfully that morning to pawn it. Later on that same morning he pawned, for a few dollars, all the clothing and bedding that had been in the flat. Thomas testified that on the Saturday evening his mother, while drunk, threw a pitcher at his head and that in retaliation he slapped her face but used no other violence toward her. On the following morning, he explained, he set off to pawn the items in order to raise money so he could bury his mother. It was while he was coming back home from the pawn shops downtown that he was arrested.[14]

It was a very short-lived trial because the jury retired to deliberate at 1:00 P.M., October 21, the day the trial started. While the jury was out it was reported that Thomas, who did "nothing particular" for a living, sat conversing with one of his sisters and smiling. The defense was that Thomas did not cause his mother's death by beating and kicking her but that she was frequently drunk and on this occasion she had fallen over the stove and down off the stoop and in that fashion sustained the injuries that proved fatal. At the trial, said a reporter, "The evidence disclosed a painful state of degradation and drunkenness." At 2:00 P.M. the jury returned with a verdict of guilty of manslaughter in the second degree.

Judge Barrett said there was no doubt that the prisoner had killed his mother "in a cruel, brutal and unusual manner"; but the jury had given him the benefit of the doubt as to whether it was done intentionally. Barrett added there was no reason why he should not receive the full penalty of the law and he therefore sentenced Thomas Callaghan to a term of seven years imprisonment at Sing Sing.[15]

A different account reported on how Thomas spent the one hour while the jury was out reaching its verdict by stating, "Callaghan and a married sister sat in a corner of the court-room weeping and anxiously awaiting the results of the jurors' deliberations."[16]

William Burke

In dramatic fashion, William Burke, a well known "young vagabond" burst into the circuit court during a session in the morning of April 29, 1893, in Rockford, Illinois, to announce he had murdered his mother. Police officers found the blackened and decomposing corpse of the woman lying in bed where the son had shot her, presumably on Monday night, April 24, 1893. Since that time he had been drunk and had gone in and out of the house in which the corpse lay. It was thought that Burke was drunk when he committed the crime and that he did it for money. Burke had been employed sometime earlier by G. Maffoli, a contractor and saloonkeeper, to do some work; he earned $4. That was paid him but shortly thereafter his mother called on Maffoli for the money, saying William told her he had not been paid. That led to a court case that was postponed until Tuesday, April 25. William showed up but not his mother, she having been killed the previous night, and the case was dismissed. One theory was that the mother had heard something about the case during earlier court sessions, something that led her to believe William lied to her about the $4 and that a quarrel was initiated over the matter that led to Mrs. Burke's murder.[17]

When Burke appeared in court on May 6 he told Judge Shaw that he wished to plead guilty. When the court explained to him that he might plead not guilty and counsel would be assigned to defend him, he replied, "I do not want anyone to defend me. I am guilty of murdering my mother, the only friend I had on earth, and I deserve to hang." According to his story to police he came home on the Monday night crazed with drink. Mrs. Burke was then asleep in bed and he shot her through the heart while she slept.[18]

However, Burke was defended by counsel, using the argument the defendant was insane. After deliberating for several hours the jury returned on May 20, 1894, with a verdict of guilty of murder. The first ballot taken by the jury stood at 11 votes for acquittal on the ground of insanity and one vote to hang him. William Burke was sentenced to a term of life imprisonment in the penitentiary.[19]

Benjamin Parrott

In Hamilton, Ontario, Benjamin Parrott came home on February 8, 1899, partly under the influence of liquor. After quarreling with his mother he killed her with an axe, first striking her on the arm with the sharp edge and then beating her on the head with the blunt side. It was described as a murder committed "in a cold-blooded, cruel manner." After being tried and convicted of murder in the first degree, Benjamin Parrot was hung in the Hamilton jail yard at 7:43 A.M. on June 23, 1899. He died without fear, said a reporter, "and the young man of low instincts and foul and careless tongue passed into the beyond with but little apparent fear. If there was a repentance for his crime it was not manifest to those who were with him at the last, and the matricide gave little hope of having undergone a change spiritually. He died as he had lived, a coarse, unrepentant sinner." Parrott's execution was witnessed by about 30 people, including four reporters; one from each of the three Hamilton papers and one from the Associated Press agency. Parrott died instantly from a broken neck. His two sisters lived in Buffalo and one—Mrs. Parks—visited him in jail the day before he was executed. She said, "My brother should never have been hanged. He has suffered from convulsions ever since he was a child and never was responsible for his actions." Before his body was placed into a jail yard grave three doctors examined the brain and found it had been strong and healthy; it weighed 50 ounces, about two ounces over normal. And that, said the article, "proved that he was not insane." He was thought to be about 30 years old. On the day of the murder he had been drinking and quarreling with his mother all day, off and on, from the morning onward, as he had often done in the past. At about 5:15 P.M. he took an axe to her because she had tired to lock him out of the house. She ran out into the street but he followed her, overtook her, and attacked and killed her with the axe. She did not die until the following morning when she expired in the hospital. He was arrested on the evening of February 8 and on April 19 was tried and convicted before Chief Justice Armorer. On the afternoon of his last day, June 22, Parrott delivered a signed document to two clergymen. It said, in part, "I am very sorry for what I have done to my mother and hope God has forgiven me.... I hope that any of my companions who have not given their hearts to God will do so, and that young people will be warned by my example not to lead a life of drink and bad companions." Just before leaving his jail cell for the gallows, Parrott cursed the police officer who arrested him and asked for a brandy, which was given to him. At the gallows he cursed the hangman. His last words were "Give me a chew of tobacco."[20]

6

Sons, Mothers, and Money

Joseph W. Freeman

A report came on the night of January 14, 1874, that an old lady, connected with one of the most respectable families of Bergen City, New Jersey, had been murdered in "cold blood" by her son. Mary E. Freeman, widow of Joseph H. Freeman, was the victim. Her son Joseph W. Freeman had, it was said, "much difficulty with different members of the family. Bergen had recently been amalgamated into Jersey City. Some months earlier Joseph W. charged his brother-in-law Alexander Annin with being a worthless fellow and, after quarreling with him, threw him out of the family house. During the three or four weeks prior to the killing, Joseph W. had been trying to induce his mother to give him $2,000. She consistently refused. On the night of the 14th at around 9:00 he went to his mother's bedroom on the second floor of the house. Once more he asked her for money and once more she refused him. Becoming agitated by the refusal he drew a revolver from his pocket. Fearing for her safety, Mary tried to flee from the room, according to the story of one of his sisters, who was in the room at the time, but her son deliberately aimed at his mother and fired. The ball struck her in the back and she fell over the threshold of the door leading from the room. Joseph W. threw down the weapon and escaped from the house. He was in such an agitated state as he fled that a policeman walking a beat noticed him and asked him what was wrong. On being pressed by the officer he admitted he had shot his mother. When he was taken to a police station Joseph W. said he was 27, a native of New Jersey, and currently unemployed. Upon being questioned as to the motive for his act, he said the shooting was accidental, that he had intended to shoot himself but missed, the ball striking his mother by mistake. Mary's late husband Joseph H. had been a person well known throughout Hudson County. The family owned a large amount of property in the area and held "high social position." According to one account, the son Joseph W. "has the reputation of being a sober man but of extremely violent disposition. He is also a man of eccentric habits, and his sanity has frequently been questioned."[1]

Much excitement and curiosity was generated in the neighborhood as a result of the shooting, and all day on the 15th crowds of curiosity seekers gathered around the residence. Many endeavored to gain admittance but the family "had no desire to gratify a morbid curiosity, hence none but relatives and immediate friends of the family were admitted." Besides Mary and Joseph W. the family consisted of two daughters and another son, Alman Freeman, described as a well known physician in Jersey City. Some three years earlier the eldest daughter had looked with favor upon the attentions of a young man named Turner Frank but the girl's family was strenuously opposed to the match because of Frank's poverty. However, the pair secretly married, whereupon the Freeman family became enraged and barred them from the house. Frank had no occupation and no means of support; the couple was soon reduced to extreme destitution. They decided to separate. The bride was allowed to return to her family home on the condition she never see or communicate with her husband again. About one year earlier Joseph H. had died, leaving all his property to his widow in order to prevent the possibility of his son-in-law deriving any benefit from it. Later, Mary gradually became reconciled with her daughter. The result was that the rest of the family feared that the growing influence of the latter would have the effect of ingratiating Turner Frank into her mother's good graces. However, it was also said there were no reasonable grounds for such fears. And that was how matters stood on the day of the killing. After drawing his pistol upon being refused the $2,000 again, Joseph W. did threaten to shoot himself before he turned the weapon on his mother. At the coroner's inquest, Mrs. Frank—the daughter in the room at the time of the shooting—testified to the above facts. She added that her brother was not of an affectionate nature and she also believed his mind was unsettled. According to Mrs. Frank, her brother shot their mother from a distance of around three feet. Another sister, Myra, testified her brother had never lived happily with the family. Still another sister, Harriet, said she thought Joseph W. showed symptoms of insanity at times. The coroner's jury committed Joseph W. for trial.[2]

An editorial in the *New York Times* a day after the murder said that it was "charitable" to suppose that Joseph W. was insane: "It is not less just, however, to demand that he shall be punished in such a way as to make insanity of this sort less prone to bloodshed.... The atrocity of the crime is so great and so exceptional that few will believe a sane man capable of it. It is well to remember, nevertheless, that insanity has degrees, and that mental aberration to a very extreme stage is usually accompanied by a sense of right and wrong." The writer went on to warn that "we must beware of the maudlin sympathy which finds in that aberration a reason for remitting the punishment which the law imposes.... [S]o long as the law makes hanging the penalty of murder, it is better that one absolutely insane murderer should be hanged than that ninety-nine partly insane persons should be stimulated to murder by his escape. The general good ought to be paramount to any individual interest." Claiming that he had no desire to prejudice the case of Joseph W., the editor concluded: "But there seems to be no doubt of his guilt, and little doubt that insanity will be set up as his defense. It is a defense which, even though duly made, has too long been accepted without question."[3]

Joseph W. had spent some time away from home, traveling out west before the murder. And when he returned home, said sister Harriet, he was even more melancholic than before he went way. He used to take all of the medicines he found about the house, regardless of for whom they were intended. He often became agitated in talking with his family, regularly becoming excited over trivial matters. After returning from the west he had a head wound that he often complained about. He wanted the $2,000 in order to start a business.[4]

Joseph W. went to trial in March 1874, and the courtroom was packed every day. The trial concluded on March 14. When Judge Bedle charged the jurors he differentiated between the degrees of murder. If the killing had been committed with purposeful intent it was murder in the first degree; if Joseph W. in trying to kill himself accidentally killed his mother, he was guilty of murder in the second degree. If the prisoner drew his pistol for the purpose of threatening his mother and it accidentally went off, killing her, then his crime was manslaughter. Bedle then explained the law of insanity, as it applied to criminal acts, to the jury and, remarked a reporter, "after he had concluded left no doubt in the minds of the jurors of the prisoner's sanity." After six hours of deliberations the jury returned with a verdict of guilty of manslaughter. When he addressed the prisoner for sentencing, Bedle declared the jurors had done right in disregarding the insanity plea and in not returning a verdict of guilty of murder in the first degree. Joseph W. Freeman was sentenced to a term of 10 years' imprisonment in the state prison—the maximum penalty. An observer in the courtroom said the prisoner received the verdict and sentence "with the most stoical indifference."[5]

John Kodisch

At the beginning of 1883, it was reported that John Kodisch and his wife, Annie Kodisch, of Watertown, Wisconsin, were in custody and charged with the murder of John's elderly mother. It was a death that occurred on December 13, 1882, and was not regarded as suspicious at the time. However, the body was exhumed later, the authorities declaring the old woman had been murdered. Motive for the deed was thought to have been a desire on the part of John and his wife to obtain possession of the mother's money.[6]

When the trial took place in Jefferson in February it was revealed that John and Annie had compelled the old woman, 95 years old, to sleep outside in the barn during the coldest nights of the previous December, where she was found dead one morning. The later discovery of cuts and bruises on the body showed that violence had been added to exposure in the efforts to shorten the woman's life. Near the end of February the pair were both found guilty of murder in the first degree. "They are stolid and ignorant Bohemians and though they have resided in this country for nearly thirty years are unable to speak a word of English," said an account. The trial lasted one week and aroused much interest, "the courtroom being daily crowded with spectators, many of whom were ladies." No other disposition of the case was reported.[7]

John Davison

John Davison, 35, was a man described as a drunkard and someone whose sanity was the subject of some doubt. He was the father of two children and picked up a meager living for a time from a newsstand. He lived with his mother in an apartment on the third floor of a tenement in Philadelphia. Both were said to be addicted to liquor and engaged in frequent and noisy quarrels with each other. As well, they were known to have disputes over the inheritance from the late father and husband. On May 4, 1882, Davison returned home drunk and within a few minutes was engaged in an argument with his mother over the disputed money. John stormed out of the apartment but returned a few hours later to pick up the argument again. Neighbors heard yelling and the noise of dishes and furniture breaking. The racket ended with the heavy thud of what the neighbors took to be a body falling. When they investigated they found Mrs. Davison dead on the floor, covered with blood and with a hatchet wound that had opened her skull. Davison escaped from the building but was soon captured, jailed and indicted for murder in the first degree. He was awaiting his day in court when, on the afternoon of July 11, guards found him in his cell in Philadelphia's county prison, dead from suicide. Davison had hung himself to a bar of his cell door. He had stripped himself naked and had torn his shirt into strips with which to make a hanging rope. Then he evidently stood on a stool that he kicked away. He slowly strangled to death. Davison's wife was sent for the next morning but she refused to claim the body, saying she had already had trouble enough with the deceased.[8]

Philip Held

Philip Held was a young farmer who lived four miles west of Le Mars, Iowa. On April 22, 1888, he shot and killed his mother and shortly afterward committed suicide. Trouble that had existed in the family for some time culminated on the 22nd over the matter of the selling of a horse, according to an early report. Mattie Thomas was the only witness to the murder and stated the son fired two shots at his mother and then went upstairs. Shortly thereafter the neighbors heard another shot and when they went upstairs they found Philip dead from a self-inflicted gunshot to the head. Reportedly, the son "had always borne a good reputation" in the area. A year earlier his father had died suddenly after having been kicked by a horse. Mrs. Held was 57. Because she had a brother then serving a term in prison for manslaughter it was said, "The sanity of the family is doubted." Said a reporter, "There is no doubt that Held would have been lynched had not he taken his own life." The Held property was worth about $10,000 and Mrs. Held was survived by three unmarried daughters.[9]

A later story reported the murder scene was around 25 miles from Sioux City, Iowa, and the murder took place on a Saturday between 5:00 and 6:00 P.M. Philip, 28, had some words with his mother about the division of the property left by his father; and after quarreling with her for some time, during which he used "vile language," Philip drew a revolver and shot her twice. Said an account, "Realizing his awful deed young Held went at once to his room upstairs and sat down on his bed. He then placed the muzzle of the revolver in his mouth and pulled the trigger, scattering his brains over the ceiling." Since nobody witnessed the suicide the foregoing was perhaps best viewed as fanciful exaggeration to titillate the reader. Reportedly, in this story, two of Philip's sisters arrived home after a trip to town in time to see their mother fall dead through the open doorway.[10]

Elmer Sharkey

At an early hour on January 11, 1889, near the town of Eaton, Ohio, the murder of Mrs. Sharkey took place. She was found badly beaten and dead. Her son, Elmer Sharkey, authorized his cousin, prosecuting attorney John Klesinger, to offer a reward of $1,000 for the arrest of the murderer of his mother. Nevertheless, said a reporter, "[T]he chain of circumstantial evidence is coiling itself around the son in such a convincing manner that the public mind seems to have settled down upon him as being the guilty party." Within a day or two of the murder Elmer was not in custody, but he was being watched.[11]

Around 2:00 A.M. on the eleventh, Elmer went running to the house of a Mr. Clark, a tenant on his mother's farm, and aroused the household, saying burglars were in the house attacking his mother. He said he had also been attacked but had managed to escape and fled to give the alarm. By his account he had jumped out of a second story window to make his escape. Clark and a neighbor ran to the Sharkey residence, where they found the front door had been opened after the glass was broken. Mrs. Sharkey slept in a ground floor room and she was found on the carpet with one arm broken "and her brains beaten out." Reportedly, the instrument used to kill the woman was an ordinary maul. It was still in the room with blood and hairs sticking to it. Not a thing in the house was disturbed and there was no evidence to suggest that burglars had been there. Everything pointed to Elmer as the killer. Mrs. Sharkey had objected to her son's plans to marry a neighborhood girl with the surname Straw, and that had frequently been a bone of contention between mother and son. Elmer was an only child and Mrs. Sharkey had threatened to disown him if he ever married the girl.[12]

The coroner held an inquest on Saturday afternoon, the day of the murder, that went on into Sunday. No sooner had Elmer authorized the $1,000 reward for the arrest and conviction of his mother's killer than a neighbor, Herman Hughes, had himself sworn in as a deputy sheriff and promptly arrested Elmer, who wildly protested his innocence. After the funeral on Sunday afternoon, Elmer was escorted back home by the authorities and locked up there. Soon thereafter he made a confession in which he said that on the Friday evening, he and his mother had a bitter quarrel, which she concluded by saying that the next day she intended to go to town and have a new will made, from which she would omit him. As he was crazed with anger at the time, he said he struck her as she sat in a chair, knocking her out of it and onto the floor. In falling, her head struck the sharp edge of a table and she seemed to Elmer to be dead. Realizing the desperate situation he was in, he continued, he determined to make it look like someone else had done the killing. He went to the woodshed, came back with a maul, and beat her with it. That was at about midnight. Then he panicked and sat around for a while wondering what to do. At length he devised a plan of action to make it look like a robbery before running to the neighbor's place with the concocted story. When news of his confession spread in town threats of revenge became frequent. "At this hour it looks as though Sharkey will be dangling at the end of a rope before many hours. He has been removed to the jail for safe keeping, and crowds of excited and angry men are around that building," said a news story. "The crowd is constantly increasing, and the air is full of ominous shouts and threats."[13]

A day or two later the sheriff still had the jail guarded by an armed force of men but the fear of a lynching had subsided. People appeared to be willing to let the law take its course. Upon the death of his mother, Caroline, Elmer fell heir to 130 acres of what was described as very fine land.[14]

Sharkey went on trial for the murder of his mother on April 22 and more than 100 witnesses were called to testify. It was reported, "Intense interest was manifested in the case, there being a large number of ladies in attendance." That trial ended on May 3 when the jury found Sharkey guilty of murder in the first degree. During the trail a strenuous effort was made by the defense to establish the idea of hereditary insanity and to that end a number of experts were examined. However, it was a tactic that failed with the jury. Elmer was 22 years old.[15]

When a motion for a new trial was denied Sharkey was sentenced to be executed in Columbus, Ohio, with the date fixed at August 1, 1890.

Legal motions led to a reprieve until September 26, then again to November 14 and finally to December 19, 1890. During those stays Sharkey's lawyers continued to bring forward supposed "strong medical testimony" showing Elmer to have been insane at the time of the murder. But none of it was successful.[16]

On December 19, Elmer Sharkey and Henry Popp (a condemned man having nothing to do with Elmer and his crime) were executed in the annex of the state penitentiary at Columbus, shortly after midnight. Elmer was the first to be executed and Popp ascended the scaffold some 30 minutes later. In total, Sharkey had two trials and was convicted of murder in the first degree at both. Toward the end of his time he claimed that his confession was forced out of him through the threat of leaving him to the lynch mob if he did not admit to the crime. At that stage he was regularly claiming that he had no remembrance of committing the crime. To the end, his lawyers tried to get a commutation of sentence on the ground of having insanity in the family. Elmer stepped on the scaffold at 12:05 on the morning of December 19, and 15 minutes later he was pronounced dead. His neck was not broken from the hanging and death resulted from strangulation. He made a statement from the gallows: "I will answer to God for what I have done and He will forgive all." Eight minutes after being pronounced dead his body had been removed and the scaffold prepared for Popp, who stepped out from his cell at 12:29 A.M.[17]

Despite his employment of the most eminent counsel, Elmer had been convicted by juries in two different counties at two separate trials and the supreme court of Ohio, the state board of pardons, and the governor of Ohio all passed adversely on his case, with the defense arguments relying on various insanity pleas, from "ordinary" insanity to hereditary insanity to epileptic insanity. Sharkey was able to afford such counsel because he had heavily mortgaged the property he fell heir to after he murdered his mother. After both mother and son were dead, the administrators of the mother's estate tried to block the payment of the legal fees. Elmer's lawyers recovered their fees in the lower courts but heirs took it to a higher court, bringing up the legal question of whether the son could dispose of the property after he had removed by murder the source from which it came. Several cases profiled in this book feature people who were able to hire lawyers only because they used the property they had inherited from the person they had murdered to pay those lawyers. Cases such as that of Sharkey were among the early ones that led to reforms wherein, generally, people would not profit financially from their crimes.[18]

R. Irving Latimer

A murder was committed on the night of Thursday, January 24, 1899, at Jackson, Michigan. Mrs. Mary H. Latimer, a widow living with her son R. Irving Latimer, a druggist, was shot twice in the head after retiring. She was found on the morning of January 25 lying in a pool of blood. Irving had gone to Detroit on the evening of the 24th, telling the clerk he employed in his store that he was going there to act as a pallbearer at a funeral for a deceased friend. As of noon on the 25th no message had reached Irving about the death of his mother as his friends did not know how to contact him in Detroit. There was then reported to be no clues as to the identity of the murderer.[19]

Yet, on January 30, Irving was arrested for the murder of his mother. His examination by the authorities began in Jackson on January 31 at 10:00 A.M. "Although he retains an air of stolid indifference, he does not look as fresh as he did a few days ago," commented an observer. Mary's body had been found on the Friday morning by Harry Nicholls, who was wall-papering the house. William Henry Johnson, a Detroit barber, testified he shaved Irving on the morning of the twenty-fifth. When taking the chair, Latimer said to the barber, "Give me a shave once over in a hurry." Johnson revealed that his customer seemed very nervous and was trembling. Also, Latimer asked the barber for permission to wash himself. He went to the sink and when he took off his cuffs, the barber noticed blood, which came off on the towel. One of the cuffs was also bloody. Asked by Johnson about that, Latimer said his nose had been bleeding. After he had finished washing, Latimer stepped to the door of the barber shop, looked up and down the street, and then fainted. At the conclusion of the examination Latimer was bound over to the circuit court for trial.[20]

A few days later, as Latimer waited in jail, a reporter disdainfully remarked that Irving "has become the pet of a lot of foolish women in Jackson, who send him bouquets and wreaths of flowers, delicacies and valuable presents. His cell looks like a bower of roses. Many of his admirers try to see him in jail." At his examination the courtroom had been crowded and half the audience was composed of "handsomely dressed and respectable women. When Latimer entered he greeted his friends in a nonchalant way and was effusively welcomed, though in a subdued manner by his society friends."[21]

In Jackson, on April 8, 1889, the trial of Irving Latimer began. From an early hour, long before the courtroom opened, there was a large crowd outside hoping to get in. "The murder, which was characterized by a cold blooded atrocity, created a great sensation at the time and the trial is likely to renew it to fever heat," speculated a reporter. Latimer was described as a young druggist "rather given to a fast life." His father had died suddenly some years earlier under circumstances that, it was said, "pointed strongly to murder by poison." He had been an old and respected citizen of Jackson; but as the coroner's jury that investigated the old man's death returned an open verdict nothing more was done with the case. Since that time Latimer and his mother had lived alone in the family house. Reportedly, in pursuit of the fast life, Irving had neglected his pharmacy business and as a result was heavily in debt. Although Latimer supposedly had an alibi of being out of town when the murder took place, suspicion soon fell on him. Railroad employees were then found who swore Latimer had returned to Jackson from Detroit after dark on the 24th and then had gone back again to Detroit later in the night of January 24-25. From the testimony of the chambermaid of the Detroit hotel at which he had registered on the afternoon of the 24th, it was revealed that he had not occupied the bed in his hotel room on the night of January 24-25. When he appeared in court, it was reported, "The alleged murderer was attired like a society leader, with embroidered bosom shirt, wide trousers with a silk stripe and patent leather shoes. He was smiling and confident." Perhaps he should not have been so confident, since the prosecution declared it had enough evidence "to hang Latimer ten times over." Rumor had it that the defense would come forward with an alibi: a woman that Irving had supposedly spent the night with in Detroit. However, in the event, no such person materialized.[22]

On May 6 Irving Latimer was found guilty of murder in the first degree in the death of his mother, Mary Latimer, after the jury had been out for just 17 minutes of deliberations. The first ballot stood at 10 for conviction and two blanks; on the second ballot 12 votes were cast for guilty of murder in the first degree. A few days later he was sentenced to a term of life imprisonment at the state prison in Michigan.[23]

A few months later, in July, a journalist who observed Latimer in jail remarked that he "is either insane or is playing the insane dodge with remarkable shrewdness. When alone in his cell he weeps and wails, sings and prays for forgiveness, these outbursts being succeeded by spells of melancholy, when he will speak to nobody. When at work he keeps muttering to himself constantly, and when eating will fix his eyes on an object and frequently has to be aroused by his keeper before he will finish his meal. The man is pale and emaciated, and nearly everybody about the prison except Warden Hatch looks upon him as insane." His appeal was due to come before the Supreme Court of Michigan in the September term.[24]

Apparently the insanity dodge did not succeed, because it was reported at the end of August that Latimer had been detected in a plot to blow up the prison and a quantity of explosives had been found within the prison walls. Upon the discovery of the plot, Latimer was immediately placed in the solitary dungeon. For the preceding six weeks, it was reported, the warden had felt Irving was at the head of a scheme to blow up the prison and therefore he was watched closely. A couple of days earlier a man was discovered retrieving a package, near the north wall of the prison compound, which had been thrown over the wall by outsiders during the night. A guard confiscated the package, having traced it to Latimer's possession. It contained a quantity of Hercules powder explosive. Warden Hatch refused to release any more details of the plot, wanting to keep the matter quiet so he might catch Latimer's accomplices from the outside. Hatch would not say what his prisoner had said with respect to the plot. From other sources, supposedly reliable, it was learned by newsmen that certain other prisoners had made use of Latimer's money to secure outside assistance to implement the scheme to blow up the prison and in so doing let some 300 convicts loose. The scheme had been contemplated for the previous year and did not originate with Latimer.[25]

When a reporter went to see Latimer in jail eight months after the well-publicized plot, the newsman remarked that the prisoner was beginning to realize what life imprisonment meant: "His face is pinched, his eyes leaden and lusterless and he moves like a machine." Latimer said to a visitor, "It's a slow, lingering death, it's hell upon earth."[26]

A news report in February 1891 stated that Warden Davis, having replaced Warden Hatch, had moved Latimer from the cell in which Hatch had placed him. A guard then sat in front of the prisoner's new cell all night, whereas before the prisoner had been isolated. Davis said he wanted his "celebrated" convict where the guard could have an eye on him all the time.[27]

For one reason or another that close supervision ultimately failed. Irving Latimer reclaimed the headlines in March 1893 when it was reported he was at liberty and armed with a rifle. According to one early report he escaped at around 1:00 on the morning of March 27 after drugging George W. Haight, who had charge of the upstairs prison gate. As a result of the poison, Haight died some two hours later. Prison Captain Gill, night keeper, was under arrest and charged with being an accomplice of the prisoner in the escape. As he was escaping, Latimer tried to release the prisoners near his own cell but failed in that effort before he made his own escape by way of the front gates. Before going he secured a rifle and a quantity of ammunition. This article gave a brief recap of the murder of Mary Latimer and the earlier death of the prisoner's father under suspicious circumstance. Then, it demonized Irving further by declaring, "[T]here is but little doubt that Irving poisoned his father," even though it had nothing new to say about the old case.[28]

Latimer got out of jail by getting the keys and walking out the front door of the prison compound, declared another early report. This piece also summarized the death of the father, pointing out the deceased man had been heavily insured in favor of his wife and son and leaving an indirect inference rather than a direct one that Irving must have been the killer. Said the article, "Those who know him say there is not one chance in a thousand of ever taking him alive. There is the most intense excitement and hundreds of men are searching the city and surrounding county. Telegrams have been sent all over the state and it seems impossible he can escape." For some time Irving had occupied the cell nearest the door to the guardroom and it was said that for a while he had been allowed certain privileges by Night Captain M.F. Gill not accorded to other convicts "and on several occasions lately he has been permitted to take luncheon with Captain Gill in the lower corridor" outside of his cell. At about 9:00 P.M. on March 26, Latimer and Gill had their lunch together and it was not shown that the prisoner was ever in his cell after that time, but allowed to wander about. At midnight, after having drunk several glasses of hot chocolate prepared by Latimer, Gill was taken sick. Keeper C.E. Rice and Latimer took care of him. Soon afterward the noise of a heavy fall and the rattling of dishes were heard in the guardroom upstairs and Latimer, it was thought, took the captain's keys and rushed upstairs to see what was the matter. Rice said he went to the guardroom with the prisoner, but that was not believed, under the circumstances. George Haight was the keeper of the guardroom, and he had just sat down and started his midnight meal when he suddenly fell to the floor in a fit and died soon thereafter.[29]

In a different account it was said that Latimer had been in the habit of taking a cup of chocolate to Gill and on the evening of the escape he stirred poison into it. According to this account one of the reasons Gill allowed Irving out to have a meal with him in the evening, even though it was against the rules to allow a convict out of his cell after lockdown was imposed in the late afternoon, was because Latimer was stringing Gill along with a phony story. Latimer told his keeper about $2,800 buried on an island in Rhode Island. Gill let his prisoner out each evening to learn more details, as Latimer doled out those details slowly over time. Irving had also been in the habit of taking a cup of chocolate nearly every night upstairs to Haight, passing it through a slide in the grating. During the meal on the night of the twenty-sixth, Latimer took a glass of chocolate to Haight as usual. When Haight collapsed upstairs, Gill was too ill to attend; Irving said he would go for the doctor. Latimer took the keys but instead of going to the doctor's quarters he used the keys to open the front door and was gone. Guard E.C. Rice was also arrested for complicity in the escape. It was felt that either Rice knew what was going on and what would happen, or, if he did not know, he was criminally careless. Under questioning, Gill acknowledged that Latimer had been in the habit of making chocolate for Haight and Gill and that Irving had taken Haight's cup up to him that night. Also, he acknowledged his prisoner had been telling him a tale of buried treasure.[30]

The well-publicized escape of Latimer had generated what was reported as a state of "outrage" in Michigan, with political fallout, and many members of the Michigan Legislature demanded a full investigation and so forth. More and more the whole affair was looked upon as a conspiracy, especially as Gill recovered very quickly from his sickness and just 15 minutes after Latimer had fled was up and about and outside, ostensibly looking for Latimer. As well, the prisoner knew where all the keys were kept, all the various levers that had to be disengaged, and so on. Also, it was considered strange, noted a reporter, that "a prisoner of Latimer's vicious disposition and well-known desperation should be given the freedom that he had enjoyed for a long time, which is denied a great many prisoners serving short time for crimes trivial in character as compared to his." Not only had it been customary to give him the run of the corridor and the captain's quarters but he was also allowed to procure patent medicines for sale to other inmates. The poison administered by him on the 26th to Gill and to Haight was procured for him, at his request, by G. Taber, chief clerk of the prison, at Webb's drugstore. Irving had made a request for the drug, prussic acid, two or three days earlier; but the druggist then refused to let him have it, whereupon Latimer wrote the druggist a "sharp letter." Taber said Latimer told him he wanted prussic acid to use in the preparation of dry photographic plates.[31]

Between 8:30 and 9:00 P.M. on March 28, Latimer was captured at Jerome, a little town about 20 miles from Jackson and the state prison. He went into a store in Jerome to purchase a pair of shoes and the shopkeeper recognized him. Alerted to that, Latimer fled the store and ran along the railroad tracks pursued by several people from the store and surrounding area. That group of people caught him and held him for the authorities; the escapee was back in the state penitentiary at Jackson by 3:45 A.M. on March 29. During the ride from Jerome to the prison he told the authorities of the escape. He had been at work on the plan for over a year. As a druggist he had, of course, a strong knowledge of poisons and their effects. Latimer said he had no intention of killing Haight and gave Gill the same amount of poison he had given Haight. He administered to them a dose of opium and prussic acid. The intended effect was for the opium to cause sleep, the prussic acid making it take effect at once. Latimer said a mistake must have been made, as he reiterated that he had not intended to kill anyone and that he would rather have rotted in prison than to have killed Haight. Also, he added that Gill was not to blame for the escape in any way except through his carelessness. What Latimer did not know was that Haight suffered from a bad heart and it was thought that fact might have explained why Haight had died while Gill had not expired.[32]

On the afternoon of March 29 Latimer was placed in a solitary cell, where he was expected to remain for some time. As the prisoner entered solitary, said a journalist, "[T]he wonderful nerve which has stood by him ever since the murder, completely deserted him and he broke down and cried like a child."[33]

An editorial about the Latimer case appeared in the *Washington Post* on March 31 and began by saying, "[T]he Michigan man who seems to have a mania for reducing the population of that State, has, very naturally, revived the discussion of capital punishment," then not in effect in Michigan. According to the piece, Irving had killed his mother in order to come into possession of her property: "His deed was so heartless and committed through such mercenary motives that at the time there was a general regret that Michigan laws prevented punishment stronger than imprisonment for life." Pointing out that Latimer could not be punished for his second murder—the guard—the editorial warned, "Nor is this all. Latimer is a most desperate criminal and there is nothing to restrain him from future murderous efforts to escape." Noted was the fact the *Detroit Tribune* newspaper was then advocating capital punishment for Michigan because, said the *Washington Post* editor, "[I]t does seem that the laws of a State are rather lax when the performances of Irving Latimer can be kept up with no greater punishment than a deprivation of his liberty. In his present position, with not the least hope of clemency, Latimer is but encouraged to do murder in the hope that he may escape from prison. It is an instance where the law places a premium on crime."[34]

On March 31, 1893, an inquest was held into the death of Haight. Gill said it was a common thing to see convicts out of their cells after lockdown. He also said that on at least one occasion he had seen Deputy Warden Cellum lunching with the convicts after lockdown. Going even further, Gill admitted he had left the prison once when he had supposedly been on duty and had gone to Pat Casey's saloon for a couple of drinks. In reply to another query from the coroner, Gill testified that a convict, Dr. Mason, serving a term for the murder of a young girl by criminal malpractice, had been permitted to leave the prison three nights a week to be "in the society of his wife." Mason would return to the prison early in the morning after each such visit. According to Gill, he let Latimer out of his cell on the night of the 26th because he was hoping that night to "get a sure-thing diagram of the place where the $2,800 was buried" from his prisoner. However, he admitted he had never asked the warden if he might let Latimer out after lockdown time and he did not know if the warden was aware the practice occurred; but he insisted Warden Davis had seen other convicts out of their cells long after the lockdown hour. After giving his testimony, Gill was taken back to the jail—as a prisoner— as he could not get bail on the charge of aiding Irving's escape.[35]

Warden Davis testified he had no idea that prisoners were let out of their cells after lockdown time and that he had no idea drugs were taken into the prison for convicts, that he had always forbidden the practice and that he had no idea Latimer did anything of the kind. He added that Taber had never spoken to him about Latimer's ordering prussic acid and had no idea what the convicts received from the outside. Davis acknowledged Taber bought stuff for inmates and the chaplain bought articles for the convicts occasionally. Also, packages were not opened. Packages might be sent to the prison by messengers and the contents of those packages were determined not by inspection but only from the bills accompanying the packages. Taber testified he did not know the meaning of prussic acid in medical jurisprudence and took it for granted that everything Latimer ordered was all right. He considered himself only as a "common carrier" and had no idea that prussic acid was a deadly poison. At the conclusion of the inquest the jury ruled that Haight died from the toxic prussic acid administered to him by Latimer and that Irving had been able to secure the poison through the carelessness of Taber and to administer it through the carelessness and neglect of Night Captain Morris P. Gill.[36]

On October 27, 1893, the state prison board ordered Latimer to be released from solitary confinement and set to work in the prison. He had been in solitary since March 29 and, said a reporter, "after seven months of the most rigid solitary confinement in the history of Jackson prison, has emerged from it with as much flesh and apparently as good spirits as when he began." Some time earlier he had been interviewed by a member of the board but made no request except to be furnished with some good reading material. He said he had only the Bible to read and had gone through it several times; he wanted a little change. Just days earlier the prison physician had told the board that Irving's health was failing, despite appearances to the contrary, and advised he be given some exercise or he might collapse. So the board ordered his release from solitary and a return to prison work.[37]

7

Sons, Mothers, and Other Causes

Newkirk

On the Friday or Saturday, May 18 or 19, 1849, a man named New-kirk, who lived some 12 or 15 miles from the city of Liberty, Missouri, shot and killed his mother, who was reported to be nearly 100 years old. After the killing he reloaded his gun and, using fierce threats, ordered a nearby 12-year-old black child to take the weapon and shoot him. The boy did as he was told but deliberately fired the gun wide of the mark. An enraged Newkirk whipped the boy before sending him off to fetch a neighbor. When the neighbor arrived Newkirk said to him, "I have shot my mother—do you think they will hang me?" Soon thereafter he disappeared and remained at large during the few days immediately after the murder. One newspaper account observed, "We believe his neighbors generally think he is insane." No outcome of the case was reported.[1]

Ezra Brainerd

Ezra Brainerd was executed by hanging at Trois Rivieres, Quebec, on October 25, 1860, for murdering his mother some months earlier. After his conviction strong efforts were made to have his sentence commuted on the ground of insanity, but to no avail. A crowd estimated at 2,000 had assembled to watch the execution. As the condemned man stood on the scaffold with the noose around his neck the Reverend Caron said to him, "Brainerd, humble yourself, repent, in ten minutes you will be no more, and facing your Creator." Caron repeated those words twice but to no effect. A reporter remarked, "He was deaf to all the entreaties of his spiritual advisors, and refused to be baptized before stepping on the scaffold. When the drop fell he seemed to suffer horribly," as his neck was not broken by the drop. "Whirling rapidly around with the rope, his body was visibly agitated by his convulsive efforts to loosen his hands, every nerve seemed to writhe in agony, and after a short struggle a horrid choked sound issued beneath his clenched teeth," continued the account. "Gradually it ceased, and with it the upheavings of the chest and the agitation of the limbs. A few gasps and in a few moments Ezra Brainerd had expiated his crime."[2]

Edward Cromie

Coroner Jackman was called upon on June 12, 1860, to investigate the death of a 42-year-old Irishwoman by the name of Margaret Cromie, who died at Bellevue Hospital in New York City on Monday night, June 11, from the effects of a beating administered to her on June 5. From the evidence, Edward Cromie returned to live at his mother's house around the end of May, after an absence from home of five years. At the time of his return to the family home the place was occupied by Margaret and her daughter, the father having recently left his wife because of her "violent temper and drunken habits." For a few days Edward lived peaceably with his mother but finally took offense at her treatment of his sister Mary and a violent altercation occurred between the pair. Margaret told Edward to stop abusing her in her own home when, as daughter Mary testified, her brother struck her mother three or four times with his fist and knocked her down to the floor. After she went down Edward stomped on her face and chest. Then he threw her on the bed and choked her, saying he would kill her, as she had lived long enough. Mary went for the authorities and Edward fled the scene. Both mother and son were sober when the trouble started although the mother often became intoxicated and remained in that condition for days at a time. Coroner Jackman's jury declared that Edward Cromie inflicted the beating that caused Margaret Cromie's death. An arrest warrant was issued for the 27-year-old Edward and police commenced a search. A later report indicated Edward had been indicted for murder, with the case to be heard at the October term of the Court of Oyer and Terminer. However, no other disposition was reported.[3]

Thomas Alexander McGill

Around 5:00 P.M. on December 8, 1861, Thomas Alexander McGill, residing at 292 First Avenue, New York City, went home grossly intoxicated and found, said a reporter, some "unreasonable cause" for a quarrel between himself and his mother, Mrs. McGill, who lived in the same house but resided on the 5th floor in rooms separate from those of her son. What passed between them was then unknown but Thomas grabbed his mother, took her to the window of her 5th floor room and threw her out onto the sidewalk beneath. She was horribly mangled and died instantly. A police officer went to the room and arrested the "cruel and treacherous" son.[4]

One day later an inquest was held into the death of Mrs. McGill. Francis Conlon, 14, was playing in the back yard of 290 First Avenue and testified that all at once he saw something black coming out of the window of the top floor of the adjoining house. He soon realized that it was a woman. After Thomas threw her out Conlon heard him say as she descended, "Now, you are going to hell" as he leaned out of the window watching her fall. Charles H. Whitford resided in the room next to the deceased and told the inquest Thomas had been delirious most of the time for the previous week and Whitford judged him to be crazy. On the day of the murder he heard them talking in Mrs. McGill's room. Thomas wanted to know who sold her rum. Mrs. McGill made no reply, whereupon Thomas said he would give her five minutes to tell him and if she did not comply with his request he would throw her out of the window. Then Whitford heard the sounds of a struggle before Thomas did indeed throw his mother out of the window. While dragging her to the window Thomas frequently exclaimed, "I am the brother to the Almighty" and similar expressions. William J. Miller, the prisoner's employer, testified he was a merchant, that Thomas had worked for him for one year and Miller regarded him as a sober, industrious and inoffensive man who was good tempered, tractable, and entirely honest. However, Miller added the prisoner had shown symptoms of insanity for two or three days prior to the murder and on the night before the killing "appeared quite beside himself, and I had no doubt of his insanity, but as he had been in a similar way before—(about eight months ago)—I did not think it very serious." The police officer who took Thomas into custody said when he was arrested Thomas was very wild and "even furious." A brother of Thomas testified that some 10 years earlier the prisoner had a sunstroke that affected his head and rendered him partially insane for several months. Subsequently, he recovered and had remained in good health up to about eight months earlier. He soon recovered from the attack of eight months earlier and was fine until the end of November, at which time he began to display "insanity behavior" again, just after a girl refused to marry him. After the testimony had been taken the coroner's jury came to a verdict that the deceased was thrown to her death by Thomas McGill, who was "laboring under a paroxysm of insanity at the time." He was held over for a jury to determine his sanity. Thomas was 54 years old.[5]

At the request of the district attorney, a medical report on the prisoner was prepared and delivered on December 13, 1861. Thomas has been born in Ireland and had lived in the United States for 13 years. For some three years he was a cashier for a dry goods merchant; then for a time he was employed in canvassing for listings for the city directory. As well, he had peddled books on his own account. For the year before the murder he had worked for Miller. Two doctors had examined him and, according to their report "Many of his delusions are of the most profane and obscene character, and all of them absurd to the last degree." He was still confined in the city prison but plans were then being implemented to remove him immediately to a "lunatic asylum." That medical report stated McGill was then insane—in fact, "a maniac of the most dangerous description." From McGill's statements and appearance the medical examiners concluded his insanity was either "mania recurrens"—recurring—or an attack of acute mania or the result of a "debauch." They further stated that public safety seemed to require some form of legal action to prevent his immediate discharge from an asylum. If placed in an asylum under an ordinary commitment for insanity he could, at any time, be discharged at the request of his friends. If the form of insanity was found to be "paroxysmal," whenever a lucid interval for the patient occurred it was the duty of the superintendent to discharge him, even if no application was made for the patient's release. Also pointed out by the doctors was the fact that the reception of a homicidal maniac produced an injurious effect on the ordinary patients of an insane asylum and that the rooms of such an institution were not properly constructed for the safekeeping of homicidal patients. Acting on those facts, the doctors urged the state to make special provisions for the detention of "criminal lunatics." And because of cases such as that of Thomas McGill, and others, such special provisions eventually were made.[6]

Moses Terwilliger

Moses Snyder Terwilliger was placed in the county jail early in April 1871 on a charge of murder. "The prisoner is a tall, slim man, gray headed" and somewhere between 50 and 60 years of age, said a report. The prisoner, with his mother, had resided near the town of Shawangunk, New York. His mother was 87 years old. It was also said the accused man was "subject to fits of temporary insanity." Two nights before he was jailed, Moses was in bed while his mother was still up and about. Suddenly Moses got up, went to the other room, grabbed his mother and strangled her to death with his bare hands. After the killing he dragged her body down to the cellar and then set fire to the house and to the barn, both of which were destroyed. Neighbors going to church on that Sunday morning saw the smoke from the fire and went to the Terwilliger farm to try to help. Attempting to open the door to the burning house they found it locked. Moses, inside the house, yelled at them that they could not come in. After forcing the door open, they entered the house and Moses assaulted one of the would-be rescuers. He was also asked repeatedly where his mother was before he took them to the cellar. When those neighbors tried to go downstairs to the cellar, Moses attacked them again. Finally he was subdued. In a confession he later made he admitted choking his mother. When she said to him, "Don't choke me," Moses replied, "I have tried to choke you twice before, and now is as good a time as any; she didn't say anything more, and I choked her until she was dead." Moses said he was 57. Said a journalist, "He has been crazy for some time past, and many think it very imprudent to have left him at large, as he was considered dangerous." No disposition of the case was reported.[7]

Charles Merrill

Charles Merrill killed his mother at China, a small town near Augusta, Maine, in February 1881. He chopped her body into pieces and burned them after killing her in a barn near the house. She had been missing for several days and Charles was arrested on suspicion. While in custody he quickly confessed to the crime, on February 27, and told the authorities what he had done with a portion of the remains he had not burned. "A crowd quickly gathered to lynch him, but the officers evaded it and took him to Augusta" for safety, stated a news account.[8]

After Merrill had been in jail for a couple of weeks and more facts and background on the man emerged, a journalist was moved to cite him as an example of "total depravity." Since his incarceration, evidence had accumulated that went to show his "moral rottenness." On the night of

June 17, 1880, two large barns belonging to Oliver Hammon of China, a neighbor of the Merrills, were burned to the ground. Reportedly, Charles had confessed to that. Speculation was that his reason for committing arson was that Charles wanted to purchase a calf from Hammon but the latter refused to sell: "So this young monster took this method to get even, probably hoping that in the confusion he could steal the calf without being detected." When Charles had been thrown out of the family home by his mother the previous September—after an altercation with Mrs. Merrill—he went to live for a time with a relative by the name of Sumner Merrill. With the son in jail, Sumner was saying that Charles had tried to recruit him as an accomplice in crime, suggesting they should set fire to the barn of neighbor Nat Jones and thus steal some of the neighbor's sheep in the resultant confusion.[9]

On the afternoon of Sunday, February 27, rumors filled the air of the small town that an atrocious murder had taken place and that the police had the confessed murderer in custody. Observers saw a young man being hustled into jail. It was learned that on Saturday, February 19, 1881, Charles had slain his mother by striking her head with a hammer. He tried to conceal the evidence of his guilt by chopping the body into pieces and burning the bits in the fireplace in the house. The torso had been concealed by him in the woods. Frank Percival, deputy sheriff of Kennebec County, went to the Merrill residence on Friday, February 25, where he found Mrs. Lilly, a daughter of Mrs. Merrill. Charles was not at home then but arrived later. When Percival asked him where his mother was, Charles said she had gone away on the previous Monday but had not told him where she was going. Charles added that he had been looking for her for a day or two but could not find her, although he had looked all over. A quick search by Percival revealed that all of Mrs. Merrills' clothes were gone. At 8:00 A.M. the next day Percival returned to the house and began a systematic search, with a lot of helpers. The first suspicious thing to be discovered was blood on the manure pile in the corner of the barn. Going through the pile, the searchers found pieces of burnt and semi-burnt meat, which they put in a basket and took to the local medical man, Doctor Nelson. Merrill was arrested at 5:00 P.M. on Saturday. On Sunday afternoon, after Merrill had confessed, Percival took Charles to Augusta for safety. On the way the prisoner pointed to the spot where the torso was buried. Also found in the manure pile were ashes, bones, fragments of cotton cloth, and so forth.[10]

As Charles sat in jail, more details of the murder were revealed. In the afternoon of the fateful day, Charles and his mother had been out in the horse and sleigh together. He asked her if he could have the horse and sleigh for the evening. Mrs. Merrill made no reply but then went to get the sleigh robes to hide them, as she had done before, to keep Charles from taking them, and making it more difficult if not impossible for him to use the rig. When he saw what she was doing he tried to prevent her from hiding the robes. Getting furious, he worked himself into a frenzy, picked up a hammer that was nearby, and attacked his mother with it, killing her. When his mother had ejected him from the family home the previous fall Charles had boarded with Sumner for around 13 weeks, returning to the family home at the end of January 1881. Merrill was described by most people who knew him as "peaceable and quiet."[11]

Charles Merrill was 23 years old and had spent his boyhood on a farm in Windsor. A few years earlier the family had moved to the farm they occupied at the time of the murder. Taking the stand at his trial he said he had left home in the fall of 1880 and voted the Greenback ticket in the fall election. Coming home he had an altercation with his mother, who removed his bed from the house. She told him he could no longer have a home there as he had voted wrong. That night he slept on the sofa and then went and stayed at his sister's house for a few days. Next he went to a friend's place, where he did some farming work and stayed a brief time. Then he went to stay with Sumner before finally returning to the family home in January 1881 where he did the chores in exchange for his board. Charles had been home abut four weeks when the murder took place. According to Merrill, he had no difficulties with his mother except that she would not let him use the horse when he wanted the animal and would hide the harness so he could not use the horse; then came the afternoon of Saturday, February 19. At the close of his trial, on May 13, 1881, the jury was out deliberating for just six minutes before returning with a verdict of guilty of murder in the first degree. On May 14 Charles Merrill was sentenced to life imprisonment in the state prison, with hard labor.[12]

The sentence caused the editor of a Maine newspaper to comment: "What a doom is imprisonment for life to a robust man only twenty-three years old. Hanging is merciful compared to such a fate. Will men never be warned of the dread consequences of taking human life?... Forty, fifty, sixty years in a rock-ribbed prison, shut out from association with his fellow men, from human sympathy, from the sight of friends, kept in restraint like a wild beast, that is what awaits the man who slew his mother, and there are none to say he does not deserve the punishment he is to receive."[13]

George Schneider

George Schneider (sometimes Snyder), 40, a farmer who lived near Darrtown, 15 miles from Hamilton, Ohio, was arrested and lodged in jail in Hamilton on the night of December 5, 1884, charged with the murder of his mother, Catharine Schneider, 75, who had been missing from her home in Hamilton since the end of October. His story was that she had visited his place in October for a day or two. On the day of her departure he started out with her, driving her to the train station so she could take the next train home to Hamilton. On the way, George explained, they were attacked by two robbers who demanded Catharine's money and, upon her refusal to hand it over, shot her dead. As well, they made George promise, under a threat of death, to say nothing to anyone about the murder. Then they made George bury the body. However, when Catharine's body was exhumed it was found that she had been buried in her night clothes. Not surprisingly that raised suspicions and it soon became apparent the son had killed the mother in his own home. However, that report of being buried in her night clothing proved to be false.[14]

One news account referred to the murder as "[a] most inhuman and unnatural matricide." What had tipped the authorities off is that a couple of days before George was arrested the victim's 12-year-old grandson (George's son) stated that his father had killed his grandmother with a shovel and then buried her body behind a haystack. That story also turned out to be false.[15]

While in jail, George confessed to having killed his mother, but not until just before his execution. In due course he was convicted in court of murder in the first degree and on March 10, 1885, he was sentenced to be executed on June 1. After a brief stay, George Schneider was executed on the morning of June 19, 1885, at Hamilton, Ohio. Catharine Schneider was the mother of five living children. She lived alone in a small house in Hamilton and was described as "very parsimonious." It was known that she had saved up about $125 and that she carried that money around with her wherever she went. Occasionally she visited her children, the three married daughters more often than the two sons. On Friday afternoon, October 31, 1884, she went with her son Henry's wife from Hamilton to Darrtown, carrying her little basket of money with her. At Darrtown the two women parted, Mrs. Henry Schneider going to her home 1 1/2 miles east of Darrtown and Catharine going on to her son George's home, 2 1/2 miles southwest of Darrtown. That was the last time she was ever seen alive, "except by her unnatural son, who murdered her," declared a reporter. Nothing more was said about her until Thursday, December 4, when George and his wife visited Henry, at which time George was asked "where was mother?" That question was asked because the other three children had been writing to Henry with the same query. George hesitated a moment and then without showing any emotion answered, "I will tell you, Henry—mother is dead. Two tramps killed her by the old oak tree close to my house the same night that she came there." Embellishing his tale, George added, of his mother, "She told me when they were murdering her that she knew them and that they had followed her all day. They let me off on account of my family, and they swore me to never say anything about it. One of the men was a German and one was an American." George went on to say that he did not know either one of them and after the murder they made him go back to his house, get a shovel, and bury his mother. One of them robbed her of the $125. The next morning he went back to the spot and found one leg and one hand sticking up out of the ground so he got some brush to cover them up.[16]

George's story raised suspicions and Henry and a brother-in-law went out at once to find the body. At Schneider's preliminary examination "it required a cordon of officers to protect him from lynching." Throughout his time in jail, over the course of his trial, and up until June 10, just nine days before his execution, George stuck to his story about the two tramps while protesting his innocence. Then he made his confession. In it he said his mother had frequently threatened to poison his wife and that on the night of the murder Catharine abused his wife dreadfully and quarreled at the supper table. After supper his mother asked her son to take her to the station so she could take the train home to Hamilton. He took her in an open wagon and about one-quarter of a mile from the house she got off the wagon to open a gate for the rig and as she got out she said, "George, if your wife was dead I would have a home." Then he got out and picked up a club and beat her to death with it. After hurriedly burying her he went back home to his wife and children. As well, he robbed her of her money, herein said to be about $90. His family knew nothing of the murder, he insisted. After his first confession he repeated the story "with several variations." George Schneider was 33 when he was executed.[17]

Asbury Hawkins

When the body of Mrs. Cynthia Hawkins was found on October 2, 1887, on the road a little more than a mile from the village of Islip, Long Island, New York, great excitement was generated in the small community. Within a short time of the discovery of the body it was said there seemed to be little doubt that Francis Asbury Hawkins, 28, induced his mother to leave the house on that fateful night shortly after 9:00 on the pretense that his uncle Seth Clock was very sick and that while driving towards Seth's place he killed her. Mrs. Hawkins had induced a young girl to whom Asbury was engaged to break off the match and that was thought to have led to the crime. One day after the body was found the coroner's jury returned a verdict that Mrs. Hawkins met her death at the hands of Asbury "who feloniously killed and murdered her." She was about 50 years old and the widow of Captain Franklin Hawkins who, a few years earlier, had been one of the best known residents of the south shore of Long Island. He left an estate valued at $30,000. Supposedly, Asbury had made a full confession to another uncle, Nathaniel Oakley Clock. His confession stated that while the pair were on the road in the buggy, she criticized his girlfriend and forbade him to marry her. After some heated words he drew a revolver and shot her through the head. Then he beat her over the head with the butt of the revolver. Asbury then dragged the body out of the wagon and laid it on the road. He then threw the pistol into a pond and washed the blood out of the wagon the next day.[18]

According to one account, "So strong was the web of circumstances that the matricide broke down completely and made a full confession yesterday [3rd] morning." Franklin Hawkins was for years engaged in the lumber and coal business at Islip and he was connected by birth and marriage to most of the old families in the area. When he died some seven years earlier he left that $30,000 estate and three children—Asbury, 22, Grace, 15, and Franklin Jr., eight. Asbury had been the source of a great deal of anxiety to his parents for several years because of a disposition to associate "with the servants in preference to girls in his own sphere of life. They tried in every way to make him give up these associations, but without avail." Three years earlier Asbury had left Islip to live with his uncle at Bay Shore, Long Island, being employed in the latter's grocery store as a clerk at $10 a week. While he was there he became acquainted with Hattie Schreck, who was a clerk in a nearby ice cream parlor. She got a "strong hold" on his affections and when she left the ice cream store to become a servant in the family of Dr. Mowbray he continued his attentions to her and promised marriage. His mother, Cynthia, learned of the relationship and tried to break up the connection. That led to frequent quarrels between mother and son.[19]

A few weeks before the murder, Schreck left Bay Shore and went to Northport, about 15 miles away, on the north shore of Long Island. Every Sunday thereafter Asbury hired a horse and buggy at a livery stable in Bay Shore and, after stopping at his mother's home in Islip, drove over to Northport and spent the rest of the day with Hattie. About two weeks before the murder he began to drink heavily and, speculated a reporter, "This was probably caused by the knowledge that the marriage with Miss Schreck could not longer be delayed consistently with the preservation of Hattie's good name." Still, Asbury could not receive consent to marry from his mother. When he showed up at his mother's house on the night of the murder he told Cynthia her sister was ill and not expected to live and wanted to see her at once. Cynthia set out with Asbury and as they drove along they argued once again about the Hattie situation. Ashbury drew his revolver. After the killing he returned the rig to the livery and told the stableman he wanted the same rig the next morning. On the next day, Sunday, he got the rig, drove it to Northport and scrubbed it clean. However, the stableman had noticed the blood in it when Asbury returned it on the Saturday night. As Asbury spent his Sunday in Northport the body of his mother was discovered about 9:00 A.M. on Sunday. A distinctive hoof print allowed the police to follow tracks and trace them back to the livery, where the stableman also told them about the blood he had seen in the rig. When Asbury returned the rig to the livery at 4:30 P.M. on Sunday the police were waiting there to arrest him. As well, the hapless Asbury had been seen throwing the pistol into the pond and the authorities soon recovered the weapon. When the story spread that Asbury had been arrested and charged with the murder it was reported that a mob soon formed and a lynching of the prisoner was threatened, but cooler heads prevailed. When he was first questioned by the police Asbury had tried to explain the blood in the buggy by saying he had a serious nose bleed.[20]

As the initial excitement over the case waned, it was speculated the defense would be a plea of insanity. "It is believed that the well-to-do and widely extended families of the Clocks and Hawkinses will use every effort to avert the stigma which would attach to their names by the hanging of one of their number," said an account. One of those relatives, Philander

J. Hawkins, declared Asbury was very excitable and of a quarrelsome disposition, falling into an uncontrollable rage whenever his will was crossed. He attributed that to a disorganization of the young man's physical system, due to a severe illness he had as a child and for which, as a cure, he had to be dosed with large quantities of morphine.[21]

Contrary to the intention of Asbury, his girlfriend Hattie Schreck would not inherit his property in the event of his death. Three months after his arrest he assigned and conveyed to his uncle, Seth Clock, all of his property, worth about $10,000. Clock was instructed to pay Asbury's legal bills out of his estate and to divide any money that remained equally between his two siblings. As a reporter noted, "Miss Schreck has not visited her condemned lover of late."[22]

By April 1888, Asbury had been tried and convicted and was under a sentence of death awaiting a decision by the Court of Appeals. At that time, said a journalist, he "threw off his stolid indifference to his fate long enough to concoct a plan to secure his liberty and cheat the hangman." Reportedly, the keeper of the Suffolk County Jail allowed him privileges that were denied to most inmates. But Asbury did not keep his plot secret. Another prisoner by the name of Rev. Mr. Wilson was set by the sheriff to watch Asbury, thinking the latter might attempt suicide if his last legal appeal failed. However, Asbury did not know the man was a plant and took Wilson into his confidence and told him of his plan to escape. Wilson, though, kept faith with him and did not reveal the plan; it was discovered by accident. In some fashion Asbury got possession of a number of saws and files. Officials suspected that Hattie may have smuggled the tools in when she visited the prisoner. But it was also thought it could have been almost any one of his relatives as they were all said to be anxious that he escape the gallows. Asbury hid the tools by tying them around his leg. He gave some of the tools to Wilson, who hid them on his person in a similar fashion. One day Wilson was called to see the keeper and when he sat down in the presence of the prison official the string around his leg broke and out tumbled the tools. Wilson quickly confessed everything. Under the escape plan, Asbury and Wilson thought they could saw through the bars of their cell. No work in that direction had yet been started as they had no lubricant and Asbury was waiting for a delivery of oil. More tools were found in Asbury's cell when it was thoroughly searched. After that plot was exposed, Asbury was kept shackled and Hattie had to visit him in jail from a distance, under the eye of a guard.[23]

When Asbury's appeal to the court of appeals was dismissed he was taken before Justice Willard Bartlett on October 22, 1888, for re-sentencing. He was sentenced to be executed by hanging on Tuesday, December 11, 1888.[24]

When Asbury was tried in December 1887 the defense was insanity and an absence of premeditation. His father, it was reported, had been insane for some months before his death in 1880. The jury was out for only three hours before it returned with a verdict of guilty of murder in the first degree. At his trial and when his sentence was pronounced "he was perfectly unmoved and seemed indifferent. He is a well built young fellow, weighing about 170 pounds and not ill looking," remarked a reporter.[25]

At 8:30 A.M. at Riverhead, Long Island, on December 11, 1888, Francis Asbury Hawkins was executed or, as one newspaper account put it in its subhead, "Francis Hawkins is swung off and started on his downward trip to his future abode." A slightly different account was given herein about his meeting Hattie. When Asbury was 18 he went to work at his uncle Seth Clock's store at Bay Shore. In Seth's house was a domestic named Hattie Schreck, who had been taken from an orphan asylum in New York City. All Asbury's relatives were greatly dissatisfied when he announced he was engaged to Hattie. The girl was dismissed by Seth and went to Northport. But Asbury kept visiting her and they planned to marry in October. His execution was witnessed by 22 people.[26]

On December 13 Asbury was buried at a cemetery near Islip. Hattie was there and, said a report; "His sweetheart wept bitterly at his grave."[27]

Herman Probst

A tragedy that occurred in a three-story frame tenement house in Jersey City, New Jersey, on July 3, 1889, involved Herman Probst and his widowed mother, Elizabeth Probst. Herman, 31, was employed as a driver with the American Express Company and on the day in question he shot his mother dead and then fired a bullet into his own brain. Mrs. Charles Meisel ran a butcher shop on the ground floor of the tenement and said she heard what she thought was a pistol shot at 7:00 A.M. but paid no attention to it. Later she noticed that a bullet had pierced the ceiling of her apartment and ended up in the crib where her baby was sleeping. It was not until the afternoon of that day that Meisel noticed the unusual quiet in the room overhead that was occupied by the widow Probst and her son. A little before 2:00 P.M. she went upstairs and knocked at the widow's door. There was no response and she became alarmed. When she summoned a policeman he also got no response to his knocks on the door and so he forced it open. As the door crashed open there was the sound of a pistol shot from within and as the police officer entered the room he saw Herman fall backward onto a bed with blood spurting out of his head. In the next room lay the lifeless body of Mrs. Probst, shot through the head. Motive for the shooting was called a "mystery, but it is believed Probst suddenly became deranged. The neighbors say he was temperate, steady and devoted to his mother's interest. He was a regular attendant at church and was looked upon as a model son." Mrs. Probst was thought to be about 50 years old.[28]

Herman left the following letter addressed to his brother August Probst, a baker: "I hope you and all your folks are getting along well. Have us buried in Greenwood in father's grave. Be sure and have as cheap a funeral as possible. Tell the doctors to examine my kidneys and forehead. That will tell all the tale why we would be better off dead. I did not want mother to live after I am dead. She would worry to death in this wicked world. Also have mother's left side and kidneys examined. That will tell all about her sufferings. Me and mother would have been better off dead years before" (Signed). August reckoned his brother was insane.[29]

Herman survived his suicide attempt, for a time. It was learned that as a boy he had injured his head in a fall and it was speculated that Herman had never fully recovered from the effects of that fall. A few days after the shooting he was able to ask for a glass of water but he refused to talk about the shooting. A sister-in-law stated that he had acted oddly for the previous month and that he was devoted to his mother, who was described as a "confirmed invalid." So devoted was he that he frequently grieved over his mother's misfortune. As a result of his self-inflicted injuries, Herman Probst died in Jersey City on July 14, 1889.[30]

Ralph Ray

Ralph Ray, 20, wanted for the murder of his mother, was captured near the end of September 1891, in New Mexico by Sheriff Longneck and then was returned to the scene of the crime, Durango, Colorado, on September 27. He made a confession to the sheriff in which he gave the details of the crime. Ray said that after he and his mother had eaten breakfast on Wednesday morning, September 23, he went to the barn and took two drinks of whiskey from a bottle he had hidden in the hay. Returning to the house he told his mother he was going to Farmington, New Mexico, to attend the fair. Mrs. Ray remonstrated with him as she did not want to be left alone. That angered him and as his mother walked past him in the kitchen Ralph struck her a blow on the back of the head with a nearby hatchet he had picked up, sinking it into her head to the handle. Mrs. Ray dropped to the floor and her son then plunged his hunting knife into her chest three times. Then he wrapped the body up in a quilt, mounted his horse, and set off to flee to Mexico. Ralph's father, Mr. Ray, returned home from his mine that night unexpectedly early, and the crime was discovered sooner than Ralph had anticipated or he would have successfully made his escape across the border. He was arraigned in court on September 28 and pled guilty to a murder charge. "Mr. Ray, the gray-headed father of the young murderer, has gone insane over the terrible affair and his life is despaired of," said an account.[31]

After killing and wrapping up the body, Ralph had left a note that his mother had been killed and that he had gone in pursuit of the murderers, giving a general direction away from which he was really headed. When he finished the note he went to the pasture, selected the fastest horse, and fled the area, having no idea the murder would be discovered until the expected return of his father on Saturday night. That was 3 1/2 days after the killing, and Ralph expected to be beyond the reach of the law by then. However, Mr. Ray, who had been out at his mine for a week before the murder came home unexpectedly. Edwin Ray, the father, reportedly was then prostrate at the Strater Hotel under the watchful eye of a physician and a nurse. His mind was said to be unbalanced and he did not know his son was the murderer of his wife. When Ralph was informed of his father's "pitiable condition" his response was: "Oh, he'll get over that all right." As to the likely outcome of the situation, a news article declared, "[T]he young man will undoubtedly hang."[32]

Two months after the murder, near the end of November, Ralph Ray of Durango, Colorado, was sentenced to life imprisonment for the murder of his mother.[33]

Charles Samsmuller

Charles Samsmuller, a shoemaker who lived with his mother, Lena Samsmuller, on East 12th Street in New York City, killed her in May 1894.

Then he killed himself. Lena was over 90 years of age; Charles was 50. They had lived at the same place for about nine years and as far as the neighbors could tell, Charles was devoted to his mother, as she was to him. He had been out of work for some time but he had money in the bank and there was money in the house. Authorities could find no motive for the murder and one reporter speculated, "He probably was despondent because he was out of work, and was not content to die alone." Lena was described as weak and frail and she had not been out of her house for over a year. They lived in the second floor rear of a frame tenement building. So feeble was Lena that often she could not do her own housework and a neighbor regularly came to do it for her for free. "Mrs. Samsmuller was a kind-hearted old woman and everybody in the neighborhood liked her," said an account.[34]

8

Daughters and Parents

Anna Cajay

Described as a most "shocking and unnatural crime," a news account went on to declare that a young woman who gave her name as Anna Cajay had attacked her mother with an axe, which she buried in the older woman's skull for the purpose of obtaining the $35 her mother possessed. Officer Wade of the New York City police was patrolling along Elizabeth Street about 5:30 A.M. on February 8, 1859, when he heard the cry of murder, followed by stifled groans. When he rushed to the site of the noise he found an aged black woman lying on the floor with an axe buried in her skull. Standing over her was a young black woman who had been stifling her groans with the bedclothes. Cajay was said to have been living in the apartment in "criminal intimacy" with a man. Her mother lived there also. Anna and her paramour were both arrested and jailed. Cajay said her paramour had urged her to "the dreadful crime." No other outcome of the case was reported.[1]

Leila Burgess

Little was reported on the case of Leila Burgess. A brief account noted that her trial concluded in Gainesville, Georgia, on October 18, 1884. She had been on trial for the murder of her father. Two months earlier Leila and her sister had been preparing to go to church. Being hurried up by their father, Leila ran back into the house to adjust her bangs and when her father started to chastise her again for delaying the family's departure, she took up an axe that was lying nearby and split his skull open. Convicted of manslaughter, Leila Burgess was sentenced to a term of life imprisonment.[2]

Four years after that brief report another account was published that gave a little more detail on Leila and the murder. She was then reported to be serving out her life term in the Dade County, Georgia, coal mines. Her father, James Burgess, had lived near Martin in the western part of Georgia and had two daughters, Leila being the youngest. Some three years before his death James joined the church and became a regular attendee at the services. He was pained to see that his two daughters, then grown to young womanhood, did not care to attend the religious services with the regularity that he did and, said the account, "the bitterest kind of discord grew up." Later James told the girls that a revival meeting was about to open in the town and that he expected them to attend every service and if they did not there would be somebody to whip. For three mornings in a row the girls failed to appear at the sunrise revival meetings. On the fourth morning James pulled the girls out of bed and began to chastise one of them severely. When he had beaten her into submission he began to do the same to the other. Leila, the first one beaten, slipped out of the room, grabbed an axe and killed him instantly with a single blow to his head.[3]

Mary Marean

Mrs. Mary B. Marean, a widow living in one of the most respectable localities in Cambridge, Massachusetts, on the morning of October 31, 1892, killed her mother, Mrs. Ann L. Brownlee, 70, by striking her on the head with a wrench. Marean told the police about the murder in a calm and unconcerned way. She said she and her mother were chatting pleasantly on the morning of the 31st at their home. The old lady kissed Marean and told her she was a very dutiful and faithful daughter. As the mother started to go upstairs, the daughter walked up behind her and struck her on the head with the wrench, killing her instantly. It was said that Marean had suffered a severe attack of grippe two years earlier and never fully recovered form its effects. "Of late she has shown signs of insanity, but did not seem violent, and her mother had no trouble in controlling her," said a reporter. Marean was about 50 years old.[4]

Marean told the police she did not know why she killed her mother. A neighbor said that Marean came to her house on the morning in question to calmly inform her that she had killed her mother. At first the neighbor thought it was a joke but when Marean insisted it was true the neighbor went to the house, whereupon she discovered the body and then notified the police.[5]

Later details revealed that for a long time Marean had been in very low spirits. She seemed to have a fear that she would die first and leave behind her poor old mother without anyone to care for her. "This thought so preyed upon her mind that she frequently spoke of it to others. The couple had just enough money to get along moderately, but nothing to spare.... There is no doubt about her insanity and she will probably be committed to any asylum." And, in fact, Mary Marean was committed to the insane asylum at Worcester, Massachusetts, in November 1892.[6]

Caroline Valois

A warrant was issued on November 20, 1895, for the arrest of Mrs. Caroline Valois of Saundersville, Rhode Island, charging her with the murder of her father, John W. Roessler, on the night of October 31. Her whereabouts were then unknown. On November 1, Mrs. Roessler (wife of the deceased) and her daughter Caroline informed the authorities that Roessler had been found dead by them in bed with a bullet hole in the head and they thought he had committed suicide due to a recent bout of despondency. Although coroner Woods accepted the story of suicide, the people of Saundersville did not, as stories spread that John had been murdered. Many stories of trouble in the family, of fights and arguments, were freely circulated in the community and when medical examiner Smith heard those stories he conducted an autopsy. Smith found suspicious evidence and an inquest was held on November 20. At the inquest it was shown that by the nature of the wound Roessler could not have committed suicide.[7]

At the inquest on November 20 the mother and daughter told conflicting stories about what had happened on the night of John's death and it was also brought out that the relations between the father and daughter had been strained. Also, it was learned that a deed of sale of all of Roessler's property, which had been made out to Valois, was not in the father's handwriting. Valois had sworn the deed was in her father's handwriting. Other evidence was revealed about two revolvers in the house. One was borrowed before John's death by Valois in Providence. Valois claimed the other one had been purchased by her father in Providence the day before his death, but the police were unable to learn of any sale being made in Providence to a man of Roessler's description on the day in question. According to coroner Woods, Valois explained to him, before anyone suggested that her behavior was suspicious, that she was not responsible for the death of her father. Mr. Page, who was her counsel in a divorce case, said that he thought Valois was insane. No other reports on this case were published.[8]

Cordelia Hill

Cordelia Hill, who resided at Rippon, West Virginia, shot her father, Robert Hill, on February 19, 1895. Robert had been "unmercifully chastising" his 10-year-old son when the boy broke away and ran to his mother for protection. Robert Hill then began to beat his wife, throwing her to the floor and choking her. Cordelia ran into the room with a revolver, placed it near the back of her father's head and fired. Death was instantaneous. An indictment for murder was found against "the child" a few hours after the shooting. Cordelia was just 11 years old. It was a case settled with amazing speed, as the trail was held on February 25, just six days after the shooting. The mother and Cordelia were the chief witnesses. Cordelia said it was the first time in her life she had ever handled a gun. That trial lasted about three hours and a verdict of not guilty was reached by the jury in half an hour, also on February 25. She had uttered not a word or showed the slightest excitement before or after the shooting. All Cordelia would say was that she shot her father because she thought he was going to kill her mother.[9]

Alice Fleming

Mrs. Mary Alice Almont Fleming buried her mother on September 3, 1895, and was then promptly arrested for murdering her, at the close of the funeral service. She followed the body to the grave under the surveillance of detectives. Alice had a notorious career. Twelve years earlier she had made a sensational appearance in Brooklyn as the plaintiff in a breach of promise suit against Henry Fleming, president of the Petroleum Exchange, placing her damages at $75,000. The trial lasted three days with the courtroom jammed every day. On the final day before an excited crowd she was declared to be the winner of the lawsuit and was awarded the full amount she had sought—$75,000. Legal maneuvers by Henry kept the case before the courts and a new trial was demanded. While no new trial was ever held the case dragged on for months and finally a compromise was reached by which, it was said, Alice received $7,500 in satisfaction of all her claims.

The story of the death of her mother, Eveline M. Bliss, was also sensational. Bliss lived at 397 St. Nicholas Avenue, New York City, and on August 30, 1895, the daughter Alice, it was alleged, sent her some chowder that was eaten by the older woman. Not long thereafter she was taken violently sick and died in agony. Circumstances were suspicious and police started an investigation. After Alice was arrested she was taken before coroner O'Meagher, who was inclined to release her on bail, but assistant district attorney Battle said she should not be released on bail as she was charged with a capital offense. She was, therefore, committed to the Tombs (the New York City prison), where she gave her age as 29. Searching for a motive the police learned Alice would come into $300,000 upon her mother's death. All the checks for food ordered in the restaurant in the Colonial Hotel on August 30 were investigated by the police. One was for an order of chowder, which had been sent to Alice's room. All orders for food served to guests in their rooms had to be signed and that particular order was signed by Alice's little daughter, Grace. The chowder was sent to her room shortly after 3:00 P.M.; Alice sent it on to Bliss.[10]

The lawsuit mentioned earlier was launched by Alice around 1882. She listed herself therein as Mary Alice Almont Livingstone. Her suit alleged that she was an infant under the age of 21 and went on to say that on June 22, 1881, in New York City, Fleming had promised to marry her, that on the strength of that promise he had "betrayed" her and that a child was born on January 19, 1882. She claimed Fleming was the father of the child. Fleming, in his defense, denied he ever promised to marry her and that Alice was a woman of the town and an inmate of a house of "questionable character." He did admit he had visited the house in question and had given Alice money at various times. The jury in that case deliberated for just one hour before finding in favor of Alice. When the verdict was announced in court, recalled John B. Byrnes, who was clerk of the court and present throughout the proceedings, "I never saw such a crowd or such excitement in any court before.... Alice was a pretty, attractive little thing of, I should say about 20 and she had the sympathy of everybody. The crowd cheered and yelled so enthusiastically when they learned the result that it was a minute before I could officially announce the verdict." Alice had three children: Walter, 13; Grace, 8; and Averill, 14 months.[11]

As she waited in jail for her trial, Alice spoke to a *New York Times* reporter to declare, "I want to deny that I smoke cigarettes or use tobacco in any form, and that to entrap me, a woman was placed in my cell."[12]

Her murder trial began in June 1896 and a reporter described her appearance in court: "Over her shoulder a thick mourning veil fell in a shower of black, and just once little quivering waves floating a-down the crepe betrayed the agitation of the wearer and, for an instant, her fan ceased its listless frou-frou to screen a vivid blush which went flitting over her face. Then the bowed head was lifted, the blush faded, the quiver died from her lips, and the woman's eyes resumed their level gaze." Read aloud in court as evidence was her private correspondence, such as old and juicy love letters. "The morbid curiosity which seems to spring eternal in the breast of many metropolitans led to the thronging of the passageway which leads to the courtroom long before the doors were opened. Curiosity shone in the faces of the crowd—nothing more," said an account.[13]

At the beginning of September, Alice was acquitted on the charge of murdering her mother. She had been charged with administering poison to Eveline Bliss in a dish of clam chowder on August 30, 1895—specifically the poison allegedly used was antimony and arsenic. It was a homicide and a murder trial that attracted a huge media coverage and great public interest. Reasons for her acquittal were thought to be the personality of the accused and the "array" of lawyers she hired. Alice's father was Robert Swift Livingstone, said to be "a man of taste and culture, who occupied a prominent place in society." He was a widower and at the age of 82 married a girl of 24 (Eveline) by whom he had one child—Alice. Eveline was said to be "very far beneath her husband's moral standing." Around 1886 Livingstone died and left $200,000 in trust for his daughter. Eveline married again, her second husband being Henry W. Bliss, a real estate man. All but $100,000 of that trust fund was lost in the financial panic of 1893 and it was in order to obtain control of that fund, it was alleged, that Alice murdered her mother.

Antedating the murder, the career of Alice was described as "bad" because she continued the life she had learned by observation of her mother, except that she intensified it. It was said to have been known that she became enamored of a coachman in her stepfather's employ. At a music hall she met Henry Fleming and their acquaintance ripened into intimacy. Fleming died not long after the legal dispute with Alice and thereafter she took to calling herself by his name—Mrs. Fleming—even though they had, of course, never married. Many of the news accounts of her murder trial referred to her as Mrs. Fleming although some chose not to, calling her Livingstone. High-priced lawyers on both sides were a feature of the murder trial, as well as the usual expert witnesses and scientists called in by both sides. Alice studied carefully the potential jurors as they were examined and told her counsel to reject those she did not like. A total of 1,100 talesmen were summoned and 609 were examined minutely in order to obtain a jury of 12 men. "It is due to her that each juryman had a nose of the same shape," remarked a courtroom observer, apparently seriously. "Mrs. Fleming was a known moral degenerate but she was not on trial for her morals. The accusation against her was murder, all the evidence was circumstantial," said a reporter. "Alice did want money and she had a motive and her mother was indeed poisoned. No one else had any motive and no one else was implicated even remotely."[14]

Augusta Styles

In Chicago on the afternoon of May 4, 1899, Mrs. Augusta Styles shot and killed her mother, Mrs. Catherine Schultz. The mother was to attend a meeting of a women's group in a Chicago hall and her daughter lay in wait for her near the building until she arrived for her meeting. At that point Styles revealed herself and fired five shots at Schultz, three finding the mark. Styles, 35, said she was driven to the act because her mother revealed a closed chapter in her early life to the 16-year-old daughter of Augusta. The child's parents had never been married and Schultz was said to have disclosed that fact to her granddaughter. Styles was arrested on the spot after the shooting.[15]

While the above account was presented in a straightforward manner, the story was featured in a different paper on the same day in a much more sensationalized and melodramatic fashion. "Goaded to frenzy and impelled by a tempestuous desire for vengeance against her own mother, Mrs. Augusta Styles planned and executed the murder of the aged woman yesterday, shooting her down deliberately as she entered a lodge hall at 183 North Avenue," went the story. The first shot caused the mother to fall "and as the old lady dropped to the floor on her hands and knees the daughter fired four more times at her mother, two of the bullets entering the woman's back and two bullets going wild. Then, waving the smoking pistol aloft, the daughter sprang into the hall crying hysterically: 'God forgive me; I had to do it! It is done! It is done.'" There were plenty of witnesses to the shooting, as other women were also arriving for the meeting. Schultz died in a minute or two and then, went the piece, Styles "now in the condition of a mad woman, was denouncing her from the speaker's platform."

Belle Styles was the 16-year-old in question; she lived with her mother and stepfather at 182 Sheffield Avenue and it was to that residence the grandmother had gone a few days earlier and revealed to the child the secrets that had been kept from her. "She told the girl things of which the latter never had dreamed, and which filled the child's heart with grief and hardened it toward her mother. Not until yesterday [the 4th] morning did Belle Styles summon the courage to tell her mother what the grandmother had told her." And, it was reported, "Mrs. Styles listened to the story of her daughter with growing anger and dismay. As the girl proceeded with her narrative of the revelations made by the grandmother the emotions of Mrs. Styles overcame her and she fell to the floor in a fit, and a physician had to be called to bring her back to consciousness."[16]

Several days later another newspaper related the story with the essential facts the same as in the other accounts, but with dramatically different details. In this account, Styles stepped forward to confront her mother, waving her gun and crying hysterically, "You have wrung my heart. You have betrayed my secret to my little daughter." Then Styles fired one shot, after which Schultz said to her, "'Gusta, you do not know what you are doing!.. Spectators of the thrilling scene were transfixed with horror. Mrs. Styles relentlessly pursued her murderous work. Shot after shot she deliberately fired into her mother's prostrate form until five were fired. Then she threw the revolver on the sidewalk and began to sob convulsively."[17]

Augusta Styles went on trial for murder in July 1899. After a trial that lasted one week and was said to be "full of hysterical episodes," the jury declared Augusta to be not guilty. When Belle took the stand she said when she told Augusta what Schultz had told her, Mrs. Styles "was frantic and, hunting for her mother, shot her down on sight." Said a reporter at the trial, "Much sympathy was excited for Mrs. Styles by the nature of the stories told to the child by her grandmother. When the verdict was announced Mrs. Styles was nearly frantic with delight and kissed her husband and daughter, her two attorneys and nearly everybody else she could reach."[18]

Even some of the jurors who had been impaneled to try Styles wept when the defendant became hysterical and fainted as she heard her attorney recount the circumstances leading up to the murder. When the attorney spoke of the poisoning of Belle's mind by the stories told her by Schultz, Styles threw herself forward on the table, sobbing convulsively, moaning and screaming. Court had to be adjourned until the next day.[19]

One of the witnesses at the trial, Mrs. William Meyers, who owned a hardware business, testified she sold a revolver on May 4 to Styles, who said it was for the purpose of frightening away burglars. A couple of medical people testified they thought Styles was mentally unbalanced and was prone to epileptic fits.[20]

At the trial the conduct of Schultz, in telling the slanderous tale to Belle, was presented by the defense as but the last in a series of lifelong abuses and defamations that Styles had received from her. Her defense was based on the plea of insanity, which manifested itself in epileptic fits. When the jury returned with its verdict after two hours of deliberation the courtroom, which was full of women, greeted it with a cheer and applause. "What show of a case did we have?" said assistant prosecuting attorney Olson. "The jurymen wept all the time, and the woman had an epileptic fit right in front of them." He added, "Popular sympathy was all with the defendant. She had an epileptic fit before the jurors, and it was easily proved that she was insane at times.... She might have been sent to an asylum, but I suppose the jurors thought she would be better off at home."[21]

9

Multiple Killers

Frank and Miriam Heath

The murder of Joshua Heath by his children in Dracut, Massachusetts, took place at the beginning of January 1858. Twenty-one-year-old son Frank had been in the house of correction for stealing, in the past, and daughter Miriam, 23, was reported to have had an illegitimate child. Joshua ran a blacksmith shop on the property where he resided; and when a neighbor by the name of Benjamin Kittredge called at the Heath place on a Monday to get some blacksmith work done, Miriam quickly confessed the murder to him. When Kittredge asked where Joshua was, Miriam confided to him—after a bit more questioning—that her brother had shot and killed their father and his body had been buried in the blacksmith shop. She asked Kittredge not to tell anybody. Kittredge went to the blacksmith shop, looked around, and discovered a patch of newly dug earth inside the earthen-floored shop that was about the size of a grave.

Leaving the property, Kittredge soon returned with three neighbors, one of whom was Jesse Heath, brother of the murdered man. Frank went into the shop with the men and Jesse asked about the patch of earth. Frank claimed it contained a dead horse that he had buried for meat for his dog. Even when the men offered to buy some of the meat at a very high price Frank refused to sell. At that point Jesse left the shop and went to talk to Miriam. Then he returned to confront Frank, saying Miriam had told him that Joshua's body was buried in the shop and that Miriam had given her father Apple of Peru tea, after which Frank had shot Joshua. Authorities were called in and the body was exhumed in the presence of the coroner and others. Joshua had been stripped of all his clothing before his body was buried and, in fact, Frank was wearing some of those clothes when he was confronted by Jesse and the neighbors. Various pieces of evidence were found linking the siblings to the murder and soon both had confessed. From the admissions made by the murderers, they first gave their father the poisonous tea and while he sat stupefied in his chair Frank loaded a gun, placed it within a few inches of his father's head, and shot him to death.[1]

Frank Heath said he had been born in Salem, New Hampshire; he was described as slender and slightly less than 5'4" in height. In the words of a reporter of the time, "He has a full, dark beard and though wearing a foolish look, is not very singular in appearance, till his hat, which he wears most of the time, is removed. Then his aspect is decidedly ludicrous, from a total deficiency of hair, which he says was lost by the salt rheum, and from the inferior shape of his head, which is, phrenologically, of a very unintellectual form." According to Frank's account he was always abused by his father, who was heavily addicted to alcohol and was mean when he was drunk. However, the son admitted Joshua was a good man when he was sober. Frank could not read or write and said his ignorance was due to his father's cruelty—never giving him any schooling but keeping him home to abuse him. Frank's mother had died when he was an infant and his elder brother, Frank's account continued, whom he could barely recall, left home due to their father's cruelty.

Frank did some farm work in the area for money, from time to time, but said his father took all his earnings from him so that the father could buy liquor. Miriam York Heath was described by the same reporter as "almost idiotic" in appearance and having a speech defect that rendered her speech almost unintelligible at times. She had a slight form and her hair grew "nearly to her eyes." Reportedly she was the mother of a three-month-old illegitimate child, fathered by a mulatto barber then long gone but once a resident of Lowell, Massachusetts. Miriam said she went to school "a little, once" and thought she could remember some of her letters from the alphabet. According to her, Frank was often drunk, and he bought the poisonous seeds, made the tea, and administered it to their father himself; she told her father what it was he was drinking, although by then he was too drugged to pay any attention to her warning. She added that Frank had long planned the murder. Not long before the murder he had asked Joshua what would poison a man quickest. Being told Apple of Peru seeds, Frank told Miriam he was going to procure some. He also planned, according to Miriam, that after their father was out of the way he would grow his own Apple of Peru seeds by the house, entice rich travelers to the house, poison them with the seeds and steal their valuables.[2]

The siblings were tried for the murder of Joshua Heath and convicted. Frank Heath was sentenced to a term of life imprisonment at the State Prison while Miriam Heath was sentenced to imprisonment for life, to be served in the House of Correction.[3]

Eugene and Max Wahrer

On a Sunday morning early in July 1872, a tragedy occurred at West Point, Lee County, Iowa, with the murder of Mrs. Wahrer. First reports indicated that Dr. Wahrer, his housekeeper Mrs. King, and his two sons, Eugene, 15 and Max, 11, all had a hand in the killing of their wife/employer /mother and were all under arrest. Mr. and Mrs. Wahrer had a stormy relationship that featured many quarrels and separations over the course of their 25 years of residence in West Point. However, during preliminary investigations and examinations, both Dr. Wahrer and Mrs. King were eliminated from the list of possible suspects.[4]

Mrs. Wahrer no longer resided at the family home at the time of her death but had been, said an account, "driven from home" and was employed at the reform school near Salem, where she also lived. Hearing of Dr. Wahrer's absence from home on that July day, she took the opportunity to go to her former home to see her children. She intended to return to the reform school that same day but Eugene pleaded with her to stay overnight, saying she could do so in perfect safety. However, that was apparently a ruse, as her body was found the next day concealed in the stable. She had been stabbed five times and a reporter described it as "certainly the most fiendish murder on record."[5]

Eugene and Max Wahrer were convicted in January 1873 in the district court of Des Moines, Iowa. A news account offered this thought: "Now if they could only hang it would be well." Judge Tracey, however, sentenced the brothers to a term of eight years each at hard labor in the state penitentiary. In his remarks during the sentencing Tracey said he had hoped that before time for pronouncing sentence came, some further light would have been thrown upon the case, for he was persuaded in his own mind that there was something back of it all, something that had not been disclosed. However, the boys insisted to the last they had told the truth and acted alone.[6]

On January 30, 1877, Eugene and Max received executive clemency and were pardoned as one of the last official acts of Iowa governor Kirkwood, a man contemptuously dismissed by one reporter as he "of fragrant memory." Kirkwood resigned to take his seat in the U.S. Senate. The brothers had been sent to the penitentiary from Lee County on February 4, 1873. The court record showed the mother quarreled often with the father and that after one of those quarrels Mrs. Wahrer left home and was gone for several months, that she returned to the family home one day while the father was absent and that during the ensuing night she got into difficulty with the two boys that resulted in her being killed. In granting the brothers a pardon, Kirkwood declared, "The crime of killing a mother is so abhorrent to all our better nature that at first I could hardly find consent to consider the case." But he did so because of the degree of punishment already suffered by the boys and because of the extreme youth of the offenders at the time the crime was committed.[7]

Thomas and James Goodwin

Dr. Prendergast informed the police in Jersey City, New Jersey, on the afternoon of October 4, 1875, that he had been summoned to attend an old man named Michael Goodwin, whom, he was told, was suffering from an attack of dropsy. When the physician arrived at the residence and examined the 70-year-old Michael he became suspicious because he found bruises and black marks all over the man's body. Michael died at about 4:00 P.M. that day. Prendergast refused to give the family a death certificate, although vigorously urged to do so by some of the family members. Police arrived and, upon inquiry, learned that some five days earlier Goodwin and some of his sons had been engaged in a drunken quarrel, during which the old man was badly kicked and beaten. Then the police arrested the dead man's three sons: Thomas, 27, James, 24, and Lawrence, 18. Some of the neighbors said the old man and his sons had been in the habit of quarreling frequently. Lawrence said that when he came home on the night in question he saw that a fight had taken place, as his father was bloodied, but that no further disturbance occurred after his arrival. Strongest suspicions, reportedly, pointed to Thomas, "who has a brutal, savage appearance, and has a very bad reputation."[8]

Early in January 1876, in Hudson County Court before Judge Knapp, James (27 in this account) and Thomas (21 herein) Goodwin went on trial for the murder of their father. At the time of the murder they lived with their parents and other siblings in a "notorious house" on Railroad Avenue in Jersey City, known as the "House of Blazes." On the evening of October 2, the daughter of the old man called at the office of Prendergast and informed him her father was near death. That sister had witnessed the beating administered to their father by her brothers James and Thomas. When the old man's condition deteriorated, one of the sons fled. However, both were soon arrested. At the trial the main witness against them was their sister. No outcome was reported.[9]

Charles and Albert Talbot

Late in January 1881 the Talbot (often Talbott) brothers, Charles and Albert, stood trial at Maryville, Missouri, accused of killing their father. On January 28, the jury returned a verdict of guilty of murder in the first degree against the pair.[10]

In due course they were sentenced to be executed together on June 24, 1881. As the date neared there was much speculation as to whether or not the governor would intervene. As well, a report surfaced that the brothers had offered to leave their interest in the estate left them by their father to an attorney if he would get a statement from a man named Wyatt, who turned state's evidence and became a chief witness against them. They wanted a statement from him that he, Wyatt, had sworn falsely at the trial. Additionally, another prominent witness against the accused men came forward to declare he had been offered $1,000 to contradict his testimony. Numerous telegrams had been sent to Governor Crittenden pleading for clemency for the boys. Both Charles and Albert asserted their innocence and complained bitterly of prejudice against them and of misrepresentation by the press. According to the brothers they were the victims of a conspiracy and would prove it. As the execution date neared they were housed in separate cells and no one was permitted to see them.[11]

On the morning of June 24, execution day, Crittenden granted the Talbots a reprieve to July 22. The state official claimed he had not been influenced by the petitions sent to him by clergymen, but had been governed by his own sense of right and justice. Before the reprieve was announced all the preparations for the double hanging had been completed and a great crowd of people had already arrived from the surrounding area and assembled to witness the execution. Albert, the eldest of the pair, had already had the farewell visit with his fiancée.[12]

As to the response from the crowd gathered for the execution, when they heard about the reprieve, a single newspaper account gave contradictory information. Two paragraphs, one after the other in a Decatur, Illinois, newspaper reported the following: The first paragraph was headlined "Saved," and datelined Maryville, Missouri. When the announcement of the reprieve was made to the assembled thousands, it said, "The crowd received it apparently good humouredly.... All is quiet at this time." On the other hand, the next paragraph, datelined Kansas City, Missouri, said, "[T]here is intense indignation and excitement over the reprieve.... It is feared an attempt will be made to lynch the Talbots. The armed guard about the jail has been doubled." According to this piece, 20,000—likely highly exaggerated—had assembled to witness the executions.[13]

During the reprieve a report was published that the brothers had made a confession to the murder of their father, Doctor Perry H. Talbot. Charles said he heard his mother's cries for help and upon going downstairs he had found her on the floor and his father kicking her. His father asked his son for a revolver and when Charles got a revolver he shot his father in the back. Continuing with the story, Charles said that his father—knowing he had received a fatal wound—told his sons, before he expired, to deny the shooting for the sake of their mother, and to say it was the work of an assassin.[14]

At 9:45 A.M. on July 21 the Talbot boys were brought to Maryville—site of the execution—from holding cells in St. Joseph. A large crowd was on hand to see them arrive. That night the brothers made another declaration in which they denied that either had anything to do with the shooting of their father. Charles told a reporter the other confession had been written for him by a man named Dawson and Charles only signed it on the promise that it would free them in five years. When the reporter asked them if there was anything they wanted done, Albert said, "For God's sake, telegraph the governor and beg him to stay the execution for only two weeks, and in that time we can prove that we had nothing to do with the murder." By this time both the brothers had embraced the Roman Catholic faith. Also on the 21st they were visited by their young brother Trump, who told them their mother and Zulea Lewis—the girl to whom Albert was engaged—were in town and would come to see them on that last day. "Miss Lewis is a tall and not particularly handsome woman who has already been married, but subsequently divorced," wrote a journalist. The pair was to have been married around the end of October. A strong guard was maintained over the prisoners at the Maryville jail; one guard was stationed in the cell with the brothers and a number of others were positioned inside the jail. Charles and Albert Talbot were hung on July 22, 1881.[15]

Facts of the crime were as follows: Doctor Perry H. Talbot was a leading physician and politician of Nodaway County, Missouri, who had a wife and 11 children, four sons and seven daughters. He had a large farm of 1,104 acres and was worth an estimated $40,000 to $50,000. Perry resided in the community of Arkoe, six miles south of Maryville. At the latter place he edited and published the *Greenback Standard*, a newspaper he had started to further his political aspirations. On Monday mornings he would go to Maryville and stay there for the week, returning to his home in Arkoe on Saturday evenings. On the evening of September 18, 1880, he was shot dead at about 9:00 while he was sitting in the family living room, his wife and a good part of the rest of his family being present at the time. It was believed that Charles or Albert had quietly drawn the curtains aside and the other one, standing outside the window, had shot Perry in the chest. Reportedly, he lived for several hours after the shooting and seemed to have discovered he had been shot by one of his own family. To conceal that fact, Perry told his listeners as he lay dying that he must have been killed by agents of the "gold bugs." With the police getting nowhere in the investigation an undercover detective entered the case and managed to get a job on the farm as a hired hand. One of the brothers became friendly with him and confessed to the killing of his father. "Dr. T. was a bad tempered man, harsh in his treatment of his family. He always kept his house full of fire-arms and his boys and girls were trained to shoot," said a reporter. "A harsh and murderous impulse was bred and trained into them. Apart from this hard and murderous instinct there seems to have been no reason for the murder, for Dr. T. does not seem to have been a worse husband and parent than thousands of other men. The mother was on the side of the boys and dead against her husband." During her last meeting with her boys before the execution the mother had a lengthy and very emotional time with them, not wanting to leave them and having to be almost dragged from the cell. As a result, the brothers begged the sheriff to telegraph the governor and tell him that their mother could not stand the execution, that hanging them would kill her.[16]

Perry was last seen in Maryville on Saturday the 18th at 6:00 P.M., after which hour he departed for his home, as was his custom. When he arrived home he found a neighbor farmer waiting for him to go to see a sick child. Dr. Talbot went and tended to the child and returned home around 9:00 P.M., according to the statement of Albert, about 24 years old. Perry sat down in a chair by the window and began to read. No sooner had he settled in than a shot rang out; the shot came through the open window from the outside and struck Dr. Talbot. Upon being shot, the father sprang up and cried, "Murder, I'm shot" and tried to reach a gun that was in the room. He could not and collapsed. Albert grabbed the gun and hurried to the door, where he heard footsteps rushing past by the front of the house. He opened the door and fired, without effect, at a retreating form, or so went the story told by the Talbot boys. Dr. Talbot was a Greenback speaker and writer of considerable prominence and during the previous two months had been editing the newspaper he had owned for a year.[17]

The death of Dr. Talbot caused consternation in the political faction opposed to Talbot and the Greenbacks. An editor with an Atchison, Kansas, newspaper briefly summarized the murder a couple of days after the event, noting that before he died Perry Talbot said he thought the person who shot him must have been a paid assassin of the national banks, "some enemy of the great cause which I represent." In response to that idea the editor asserted, "We regard this as ridiculous, and regret that a gentleman of the profession should leave such a foolish statement behind him."[18]

Five weeks later the same newspaper ran a follow-up editorial on the Talbot case, after the brothers had been taken into custody. Restating the situation, the editor said that as Talbot lay on his bed, dying, he was asked if he suspected anyone. He replied, "Some enemy of the great cause which I represent, or some enemy sent out by the National banks." Reminding the reader of the previous editorial, this one said, "At the time we stated that this insinuation was an absurdity and that Talbot's tragic death bed scene was a farce. It now turns out that he was killed by his own family for brutal treatment." Supposedly, it was then part of the neighborhood gossip that Dr. Talbot once brutally whipped his married daughter, Mrs. Mitchell, and that her husband and brothers swore vengeance. Concluded the editorial, "While the murder was a cruel one, Talbot must have been a mean man to induce it. We are glad that it had developed that it was not a banker who killed him, or an enemy of Greenbackism, as he was mean and silly enough to assert with his last breath. We have noticed that lots of men, who profess to die for their country, or for principle, are killed for entirely different reasons."[19]

One week later the same newspaper ran a third, and last, editorial on the obviously despised, by them, Talbot. It claimed he "was one of those dark-visaged, determined men, who believe in raising children by the hair. He hated his children, and they hated him; for the slightest offense he knocked them down with whatever came handy, and was a tyrant and brute in everything at home.... His sons very naturally despised him as a coward who insulted and beat them only because he was stronger than they.... When they grew up, they carried pistols and knives to protect themselves, and the result was that they finally assassinated him in his own house, while preparing to retire to his uneasy and dishonored bed."[20]

William and Mary Riley

Martin Riley, a farmer who lived eight miles north of Adrian, Minnesota, had been missing for about two weeks when his body was found at 3:00 P.M. in February 1884, in a straw pile, head downward and naked except for a gunnysack drawn down over his head and shoulders, saturated with blood, and frozen. An early report said there was "no doubt" he was murdered by his children, who had explained their father's absence by saying he had gone away for good and left them the farm. Various contradictory stories aroused suspicions and led eventually to a search for Martin.[21]

William Riley, the 15-year-old son of Martin, and 13-year-old Mary Riley, the deceased's daughter, were taken into custody right after the body was discovered. Reportedly, the girl had confessed and said her brother had been whipped by their father the previous night and he rose early the following morning and shot his father through the head as the elder Riley lay asleep in bed. The siblings left him dead in bed all that day until late at night when they dragged the body outside and along to the straw pile where they covered it up. Mary added that her brother had frequently prepared to kill their father with an axe but she dissuaded him, and that he had recently mixed poison in a glass of milk that the father drank. However, Martin Riley suffered no injury from that attempted poisoning.[22]

Three weeks later it was reported that William Riley had been indicted for murder in the first degree and would plead guilty, and that his lawyer was planning to make a statement as to the causes leading to the crime. Mary Riley had been indicted as an accessory after the fact. No disposition of the case was reported.[23]

Thomas, Rebecca, Caroline, and Jennie Morgan

John Morgan, a wealthy farmer, was fatally shot by his son Thomas, 23, on Thursday, August 18, 1892, at Carmichaels, Pennsylvania. As well, Thomas accidentally shot his younger sister while firing at his father. The scene of the tragedy was the Morgan family home, two miles southeast of Carmichaels. The shooting took place on the Thursday morning and was said to have been the result of trouble between John and his children over the attention the widower had been paying to Martha Walker of Morgantown. Some days prior to the shooting Walker had come to the Morgan home on a visit. The children objected to her further stay and made it quite unpleasant for their father; besides Thomas, the other children were three daughters, aged from 17 to 25. Thomas told his father he must send Walker away and that if John went home with her, he, Thomas, would kill John upon his eventual return home. Ignoring the warning, John went home with Walker and remained at her place for four days, returning home on the Wednesday evening before his death.

When he arrived home he found all the doors locked against him and the father ended up sleeping on the porch. On Thursday morning his daughter Callie (Caroline, 19) opened the door and as her father tried to squeeze by her she grabbed him as if to scuffle. Thomas was standing on the stairway inside with a revolver in his hand and as his sister seized their father, Thomas fired at him. The ball missed and struck Callie, inflicting, apparently, no serious injury. John fled the house and ran away, with his son in pursuit, firing his weapon. Struck once or twice, the father dragged himself to an outbuilding on the property, went inside, and bolted the door. Thomas fired through a window, hitting his father a couple more times. Next he piled some clothes and papers around the body in the shed and set fire to the pile. Leaving the shed he returned to the house, where he said to his sisters, "I have finished him now." However, John had, in the meantime, regained consciousness, crawled to the fire and extinguished it; his hands were said to have been burned "almost to a crisp."[24]

All that shooting on the Morgan property attracted neighbors to the scene. They took both shooting victims to a nearby home and got a doctor. John lingered until Saturday morning, in great agony, before he died. After the shooting Thomas barricaded himself in another outbuilding on the property and declared to the gathered neighbors that he would not be taken. The local sheriff was not notified about the crime until Friday morning, when he at once deputized a posse and went to the scene of the shooting. Morgan was advised the posse was there and to give himself up. He did. John Morgan was around 45 and described as a man "of a genial disposition and was well liked by all his acquaintances." After being arrested, and realizing the enormity of his crime, Thomas broke down completely. As the posse and the prisoner set off for jail he expressed a desire to go to his father and ask his forgiveness. His request was granted. It was said that the violent opposition of the children to their father's possible second marriage was borne of a fear that his property would pass away from them in the event of his death.[25]

On April 6, 1893, the Morgan murder cases were called to court in Waynesburg, Pennsylvania, and all were disposed of in less than two hours in total. Thomas Morgan was tried first, and alone, with the jury bringing in a verdict of guilty of murder in the second degree. Rebecca, Caroline, and Jennie were tried together, right after Thomas was dealt with. In that trial the verdicts returned were guilty of voluntary manslaughter against Jennie and guilty of murder in the second degree against Rebecca and Caroline. According to this item John Morgan was 55, and Thomas fired the first shot or shots at the command of one of his sisters. Sentences handed out to the Morgan siblings were as follows: Thomas, 12 years; Rebecca, 10 years; Caroline, 10 years; Jennie, three years.[26]

John and Ernest Swarthout

The murder and cremation of A.M. Swarthout, a wealthy farmer, on the evening of November 10, 1892, near Morrison, Illinois, created great excitement throughout the area. A couple of days later the man's two sons, John Swarthout and Ernest Swarthout, were arrested for the crime, and it was reported "it is feared that they will be lynched." Swarthout lived in Linden Township, eight miles south of Morrison. On November 10 he went to town but supposedly never came home. A search was begun and in the ashes of a straw pile on his farm his partly fire-consumed body was found. An examination showed he had been murdered, then his body stuffed into the straw pile and the pile set on fire. He was known to carry a large sum of money on his person and that was missing. However, evidence pointed to his two sons as the guilty parties.[27]

When another newspaper reported on the murder it declared it to be "One of the most atrocious crimes ever committed in Illinois.... For cold blooded brutality it is doubtful if it has an equal." Giving more detail, the account stated that Albert Swarthout drove to the city Thursday afternoon and after attending to some business matters started for home, arriving there at about 6:00 P.M. His two sons were engaged in work around the farm when their father returned but no words were exchanged between them. Swarthout unhitched the horse and put it in the stable. Then someone stepped up and shot him through the head. Next, his lifeless body was placed in a cart and wheeled a short distance to a straw pile, placed within it and then the straw set on fire. A daughter of the victim was the first to discover the fire and to give the alarm. John and Ernest responded by going to the pile but made no efforts to extinguish the flames. As well, the absence of their father did not seem to disturb his two sons, and it was not until a neighbor came and insisted on a search being made that they instituted one. When the ashes of the straw pile were examined portions of a charred body were found, including bones and part of a skull as well as metal pieces from clothing such as buttons and buckles. John and Ernest were quickly arrested; they denied all knowledge of the affair.[28]

Swarthout owned a farm that consisted of 200 to 300 acres of "fine land" and was considered to be one of the most well-to-do farmers in the county. After the fire had been extinguished, and before the body was discovered, the family went back to the house where the two sons asked where their father was. The other members of the household, Swarthout's daughter (their sister), and the wife of Ernest said they did not know. Then the four sat down for their meal without making a search for the absent man or showing any more interest in him. When neighbors called and inquired about Swarthout they were told he had probably gone to town and had not yet returned. Finally, though, some of the neighbors insisted on a search and the grim discovery of the body was made on Friday morning. A coroner's jury was called for an inquest but the jury could not determine what happened, nor could it deliver a satisfactory verdict. As a result, on Saturday morning the case was placed in the hands of the state attorney, who began a systematic investigation and soon discovered various clues that led to the sons being arrested as the killers. Clues uncovered included the finding of bloody clothing that belonged to John and Ernest hidden away in a shed, and so forth. At the time of death Swarthout had been carrying a valuable gold watch and "quite a sum of money," all of which remained missing. On Saturday evening the two sons were arrested. The fact that Swarthout intended to marry again was something that was said to be very displeasing to the children, as they worried it might interfere with their interest in the family property and force Ernest and his wife out of the farm.[29]

Three months later, in February 1873, John and Ernest remained in jail, indicted for murder and waiting for a trial date. "Prison life seems to agree with the young men. In the confinement of the cage they look exceedingly well. John, the older, has lost his pallor and is growing fat," noted an observer. "They maintain the demeanor observed on their arrest, a sang froid hardly deemed possible to anyone, innocent or guilty, of the heinous charge. They are not without callers, though few are admitted."[30]

At the end of April the pair were still in jail awaiting trial. The delay was reported to be due to the fact that John was in a "precarious physical condition." Jail physician Dr. A.J. Newton said that John Swarthout had consumption and that his lungs were badly affected. Newton was of the opinion that John could not recover. Six weeks later it was reported that John could live only for a short time. Speculation was rampant as to whether or not he might make a deathbed confession or statement about the murder of Albert.[31]

John Swarthout died in jail on July 10, 1893, after a lingering case of consumption. While the grand jury had returned an indictment of murder against him many months earlier, he had never been brought to trial because of his illness, as the authorities waited to see if he would recover or expire. As Ernest was to have been tried with John, the former remained in the same legal limbo pending the resolution of his brother's illness. It was rumored that John had made a statement with respect to the murder, just before he died, and that it was in the hands of lawyers and would be used at the trial of Ernest. John Swarthout was said to have been a graduate of a medical college in Chicago, but a graduate who had never practiced medicine.[32]

Ernest Swarthout's trial started in November 1893, wherein the prosecution asserted that an attempt had been made to destroy Albert's body in the fire but, failing in that, the face and other portions of the body were hacked to pieces by the brothers to prevent identification and those parts of the body were then hidden in a slough. The defense argued, in part, that the body found was not that of Albert. Said a courtroom observer "[Ernest] is a fine-looking young man of 24, with nothing of the criminal in his appearance." His wife, Libbie, sat by his side in court throughout the trial. Described as "but a girl," Libbie had married Ernest just six days before the murder of Albert Swarthout.[33]

The trial of Ernest Swarthout ended on November 17, the jury deliberations running to a total of 20 hours. On the first ballot the jury was equally divided as to the guilt of the prisoner. No agreement was reached until the 13th ballot, at which time the jury reached a verdict of guilty of murder. Ernest's sentence was set at 14 years in the state prison. At the trial it was revealed that Albert did intend to remarry. Also, there was little direct proof of the actual murder, with the boys arrested initially in the belief that one of them, at least, was guilty. John did leave a deathbed confession in which he said he alone fired the fatal shot and that Ernest had nothing whatsoever to do with the murder. "My brother knew nothing about the killing of father till after the fatal shot was fired. After I saw what I had done, of course I became anxious to dispose of the body and hide my crime," wrote John. "I went to my brother Ernest and told him what I had done and compelled him to aid me in getting the body of my father to the straw stack, and when that was done that ended entirely his doings concerning the matter. I fired the stack and made such disposition of the body as was afterward found by the officers of the law and the people." One piece of evidence against Ernest brought out at the trial was that he was heavily in debt to his father, who had required him to give a bill of sale of every dollar's worth of property he owned, and even the crops on his father's farm that he was working and the crop on his own farm of 20 acres.[34]

Grant and Edward Atterberry

David Atterberry, aged 62, a wealthy farmer of Penn Township, was shot dead on his wagon while he was on the public highway on his way home to his place near Shelbyville, Illinois. That murder took place on the night of November 28, 1891. George McClelland, who resided near where the body was found, heard a shot but paid no particular attention to it until he noticed a road cart dashing furiously up the road. Then he started out to the vicinity from where the shot had come. David had been killed while on his way home in a road cart. In returning home on that evening he went somewhat out of his way to visit the widow Nancy Denton, to whom he was said to be engaged. It was while driving north from her house to his place that the killing took place.

David had been shot in his cart from a distance of less than one foot. While the evidence was wholly circumstantial it was said to be very strong and pointed at David's two sons, Grant and Edward Atterberry. Just before the murder, the Atterberry brothers were seen in the area in a narrow tread wagon. It was the only narrow tread wagon in the area. McClelland saw the boys in the wagon, heard the shot, and found the corpse. It had rained during the day and traces of the road cart and narrow tread wagon were within 20 inches of each other, and the track of the narrow tread led directly to Edward's house. It was reported that much bitter feeling existed between the sons and their father and many threats had been made by them against him. A principal motive was thought to be the fact that David contemplated marriage to Denton. The sons were opposed to such a union, fearing it would do them out of their inheritance. The boys were arrested, given a preliminary hearing, and sent to jail, and then they were indicted for murder by a grand jury.[35]

Delays in the case then intervened. Edward became what was described as a "raving maniac" and was confined to the Kankakee Hospital, a lunatic asylum. That left Grant to stand trial alone after delays while the authorities tried to deal with the situation in regard to Edward's sanity. Finally, late in 1893, Grant came to trial and, on October 28, the jury at Shelbyville brought in a verdict of not guilty against Grant.[36]

Two days later Grant Atterberry and his family left Shelbyville and moved to Sullivan, Illinois. Said a reporter, "If ever men charged with crime played in big luck Grant Atterberry was one of them. His escape from conviction was a surprise to all, including the attorneys who defended him." One reason for the acquittal was thought to be the poor quality of the prosecution team. Three ballots were necessary for an acquittal to be registered. The first ballot was a tie, with six votes for guilty and six for not guilty; the second ballot was 10 votes to two in favor of acquittal.[37]

A little over two years later, excitement was said to have spread through the town of Sullivan near the end of January 1896 as a result of the assault committed on the person of Mrs. Roxy Atterberry (wife of Edward) on the 23rd of that month. She lived alone with her four children—boys ranging in age from four to 10 years. She was considered to have been the most important witness at Grant's trial, and a major reason for the not guilty verdict. Roxy had moved to Sullivan at the same time as Grant and his family. On the night of the assault two men broke into her house, bound her with rope, gagged her and threw a towel over her face; one of them then raped her. As the two men left one of them cursed her and said he now had his revenge. A search for the culprits was organized and bloodhounds were sent for. Also, a reward of $200 was posted. When those bloodhounds arrived they made a straight line to the house of Roxy's brother-in-law, Grant Atterberry. From the beginning he was regarded as a suspect because of a family feud between the pair. Edward remained insane and an inmate at Kankakee asylum. The prime catalyst for the feud was said to be the fact that a child had been born to Roxy at a time that Edward could not possibly have fathered it and Grant's wife thereafter refused to associate with Roxy. When the rapist left the victim's house he said she should now find herself in the same condition—that is, pregnant. When the dogs and the searchers arrived at Grant's house he defied the crowd and threatened to shoot any man or dog that came into his yard. However, the crowd soon overpowered him and took him to jail.[38]

Community feeling against Grant continued to mount in Sullivan and at 12:15 A.M. on January 26, a day after Grant was taken into custody, a mob of 150 gathered at the jail. Fifty of those men broke into the jail and went up the stairway to the cells. A lone deputy at the top of the stairs dispersed them. He told them to get out, and they did. Soon, the outside group also dispersed.[39]

A day later, in the wake of the abortive lynching attempt, a newspaper story appeared in which two paragraphs, one after the other, offered different versions of the mood of the town. One paragraph said only six men broke into the jail and "The excitement is abating and further trouble is scarcely anticipated." According to the following paragraph, the excitement had subsided somewhat, "yet it would take but little to arouse the people to the point of yet taking the law into their own hands." People continued to mill around the jail in a half-hearted way. Roxy refused to name Grant as her attacker, claiming she wasn't sure of the man's identity. But most people believed she was refusing to talk because she feared the Atterberry family.[40]

A crowd of 500 men milled around the jail on the night of January 31, but nothing was done in the way of an attempt to lynch Grant. By this time Roxy had named Grant as one of her attackers but she did not know who the other man was. A rope used to bind Roxy during the assault was identified as the rope Grant had used to tie his calf a few days before the assault.[41]

Then, in the vernacular of the day, Judge Lynch took over the case. At 1:00 A.M. on February 12, 1896, Grant was taken out of the Moultrie County Jail by 15 to 20 masked men and hanged to a tree in the courthouse yard. He was lynched in the presence of about 75 people, including some guests at the Eden House Hotel, directly across the street, who had been awakened by the noise. Grant died of strangulation. Sheriff Lansden was said to have been taken "by surprise" and had no extra guards at the jail. Atterberry's body was not cut down by the authorities until about 7:30 A.M. Reportedly, hundreds of people came by in the night to view the corpse. They used matches, torches, lanterns, and so forth, in order to get a better view. General sentiment among the citizens in the area was that he got what he deserved. When the mob attacked they were armed with guns and sledge-hammers and easily overpowered the sheriff, who was asleep with his family in the jail compound when the mob struck. There was not a single guard on duty at the jail when the mob arrived, at least not one who was awake. Early abortive efforts to lynch the prisoner had caused the sheriff to move the man to a jail in another city but he had been returned to Sullivan a couple of days before the mob struck because he was due in court on the assault charge. When the coroner's jury that investigated Grant's death returned its verdict it selected the one usually produced for such events: Grant came to his death by mob violence at the hands of parties unknown.[42]

With Grant dead, Roxy was rendered less fearful and she stated positively that Grant was her assailant. However, it was reported that another brother, Hinton Atterberry, had vowed to make her suffer for the lynching. She said her troubles with Grant had arisen over her husband's property, which Grant had been trying to get control over. In the wake of the rape a somewhat bizarre story had circulated widely that the second assailant was Grant's wife, dressed as a man. A warrant had been issued by the authorities for the arrest of the wife of Grant, charging her with being an accomplice of her husband in the assault. However, that warrant had not been served, and would not be, although no official reason was ever given as to why it was not served. With respect to the visits to see Grant's body after the lynching, one reporter commented, "The women who visited the scene contented themselves with a look from a distance, but the men gathered under the tree direct and discussed the affair with more or less levity. Not one word of regret, not one word of pity escaped from anybody." One who viewed the body—at the sheriff's office after it had been cut down—was Roxy. At the inquest into Grants' death, Sheriff Lansden and his adult son (also present during the mob attack) presented the specific names of three members of the mob whom they recognized from their clothing, voices, movements, and so on.[43]

A few months later, on May 5, a grand jury made its final report on the Atterberry lynching. They returned no true bills at all, that is, no one was indicted for the lynching of Grant. The fiction of "parties unknown" was maintained. Reportedly, what remained of the family of the deceased had left Sullivan permanently.[44]

Samuel and William Conrad

Samuel Conrad, 27, and his brother, William Conrad, 21, were in jail in Corydon, Indiana, in the middle of March 1893, charged with the murder of their father. Edward Conrad, the murdered man, was 68 years old and lived on a farm in Boone Township with his wife, two sons and widowed daughter. He owned a small tract of land but had no property of consequence. On Tuesday afternoon, March 14, he left his house to engage in making staves about a quarter of a mile from his house and that was the last seen of him until Wednesday morning when he was found lying in an unconscious condition on a pile of lumber where he had been at work. Lying near him was a sharp edged piece of lumber with hair and blood on it. Edward's clothing was badly torn and there was other evidence of a struggle. Edward had been badly battered and remained unconscious until he died Thursday morning. An inquest was held and it returned a verdict that Edward came to his death from wounds inflicted by Samuel Conrad and that William Conrad was an accessory to the crime. Numerous witnesses testified that the deceased had frequently been beaten and driven away from home by his sons and that they had at different times threatened to kill him. However, there was no apparent motive as to why they would want him dead except that he was getting old and could not work very much and the sons did not wish to support him. Samuel had been working for a neighbor that Tuesday and passed by where his father was at work on his way home. Around sunset, said neighbors, they heard the sound of someone crying, as if in distress, from that direction. And that was about all the evidence there was against the brothers. William was held as an accessory because on the Wednesday morning he was heard to say, with respect to his father, "We have fixed him."[45]

When the brothers stood trial for the murder in March they were both acquitted. It was not a surprising verdict considering the lack of evidence, even of a circumstantial nature. Detectives investigating the case had found no clues and came to the conclusion that it must have been the brothers who murdered the old man. Part of that reasoning seemed to be based on the frequent family quarrels that were a feature of the family. Nevertheless, the verdict was an unpopular one in the community and many residents continued to believe the brothers were guilty. Upon their release from custody the boys returned home and continued to work their farm as before.

Over the coming few months, the Conrad brothers received several notices from neighbors ordering them to leave the area. They paid no attention to those notices. On the night of August 5, 1893, a party of 100 or so men worked themselves into such a fury over the Conrad situation that they armed themselves with shotguns and pistols and in a body proceeded to the Conrad home intent on lynching the brothers. If the Conrad brothers had ignored the notices to leave they did pay attention to the threats to the extent of keeping their weapons and a stock of ammunition at the ready. When the mob discovered the Conrads were barricaded in their house and ready for any such mob attack, the leaders of the group called on them to surrender. When no answer was received the mob opened fire. The Conrads returned the fire, killing four members of the mob and seriously wounding a fifth. That caused the mob to quickly break up and run away. Returning later they found their dead and wounded comrades and also found that the Conrad brothers had disappeared from the scene. Posses were quickly formed to search for the young men but they were not found. Apparently the Conrad brothers were never captured.[46]

10

Multiple Victims

Benjamin D. White

According to one account, an "unnatural" crime was committed at Byron, Genesee County, New York, by a young man named Benjamin D. White and, as it appeared, "from the most singular motive which could influence a malignant heart." His father, also named Benjamin White, was said to be a man universally esteemed and possessed of some property. However, the son conceived a strong hatred for him for supposed ill treatment at his hands and "especially because he was a Christian." Father and son had many disputes on the subject of religion and several quarrels. Benjamin, 70, a deacon in the church and his son Benjamin D., 30, went into the woods near their home on March 16, 1842, to do some farm work. While there they had another dispute. Later in the day, as the pair made their way home after the day's work, the son drew a pistol as they neared the house and shot his father, the ball passing through his body. As his father staggered on trying to reach the house, young Benjamin stepped up to him and knocked him down with the butt of the pistol. Mrs. Benjamin, the boy's mother, had showed up in the doorway by this time and Ben shot at her but missed.

Young Ben then fled the scene but was soon pursued by neighbors and apprehended about eight miles from the scene of the crime. He was then taken to Batavia, New York, and jailed. One reporter observed, "The murderer has ever been unsteady in his habits and has caused his father much trouble. About a year and a half since he enlisted into the United States service, at Rochester, soon after which he deserted. He has a wife but, fortunately, no children." After Ben was tried and convicted on the charge of murder in the first degree he made a long and rambling address to the court in which he abused Christianity and his deceased father, whose murder he confessed. His father had recently bought a farm for him and stocked it. Nevertheless, Ben declared his act of murder was done for revenge, as he said, because his father had not given him a better education and more property. Ben manifested no penitence and was anxious only that a narrative in support of Deism should be published. Benjamin D. White was sentenced to be executed on April 29, 1843, although no account of the hanging, or a commutation of sentence, appears to have been published.[1]

J.R. Clements

In the town of Heath in Allegan County, Michigan, a man named J.R. Clements, about 35, killed his father, about 70, by striking repeated blows to his head with an axe, on March 2, 1854. Clements struck his father 13 blows with the weapon, and when he had finished killing his father he then attempted to kill his brother with the same weapon. When he was arrested Clements insisted he had done the deed in "perfectly cold blood" and would only be content when he had also destroyed his brother. Upon his conviction for the willful murder of his father, Clements was sent to the state prison for life. At the time there was no capital punishment in the state of Michigan.[2]

William Comstock

A "most atrocious" murder was committed on the night of January 10, 1858, at Poolville, four miles from Hamilton, New York. Jared Comstock and his wife, Clarissa Comstock, each over 70 years of age, were the victims, killed by their son William who, said a reporter, "has been for some time insane." Around 8:00 P.M. on the Sunday evening of January 10 he killed his father by knocking him down with an ax, and then he dispatched his mother with a skillet. Following the double murder he cut the hearts out of both of his victims, cut one of the bodies into pieces, roasted the other on the stove, and ate a portion of it. Reportedly, he also intended to kill his sister but she escaped.[3]

William, 37, was arrested around 5:00 A.M. on January 11, still wearing his blood-stained clothing. Unmarried, William had always resided with his parents and was well-known as having been a hard drinker for some time. After he was arrested he confessed to the murders. Calmly he explained to the authorities that for about four or five days something seemed to tell him that he must have a number of hearts, that someone who lived in Sherburne telegraphed him that he had to get those hearts. Three or four days earlier he said he planned to get his father's heart but the plan fell through. Then, earlier on the 10th he planned to kill his brother and sister-in-law for their hearts but did not find them at home. Returning home in the evening he found his parents quietly sitting in their living room, whereupon he attacked and killed them. "I got the axe and cut out their hearts and put them in the stove and burned them. The voice seemed to tell me that the hearts must be burned," he explained. After the murders he went to a neighbor's home, where his brother and sister-in-law chanced to be visiting. He told them he had some fresh meat up at father's place. Leaving there he went to another neighbor's, got a quart of cider and returned home without telling anyone about the murders. On arriving at home he lay down on the sofa near the bodies and slept until near morning. On awakening he left home but came upon several people coming towards the house. Still, he said he had no recollection of having told anyone about the murders. Those people asked him what he was doing and when he told them it was none of their business part of the group of men held him there while the others went on to the house to investigate; then he was arrested. The fact that he had apparently gone to various neighbors' houses wearing bloody clothing had, perhaps, aroused suspicions, if not open questioning. William added, "During the night after the deed I attempted to end my own life, and thus close the tragedy. I afterwards went to my brother's house to kill him and his wife. I knocked the panels of the door in, but they had gone away." No disposition of the case was apparently reported.[4]

John Stitesky

In the town of Caledonia, Racine County, Wisconsin, on Wednesday night, November 1, 1865, a young man named John Stitesky, the only son of a reputable Bohemian residing in the northern part of Caledonia, "committed one of the most atrocious and cold blooded acts of combined parricide and homicide that has ever been recorded in the annals of crime," remarked a reporter in exaggerated fashion. The father was a farmer in "excellent circumstances" who had been working in the woods during the day and had come in at nightfall for his supper. When the meal was prepared Mrs. Stitesky called her only son, John, 19, to come to the table. Suddenly a shot was fired from outside the house through the window, striking the farmer. Then a second shot was fired, which struck the mother. Then a third shot was fired but that one did not enter the house. The seriously wounded father staggered outside to find his son on the ground covered in blood and dying. Mr. Stitesky, over 60 years of age, and his wife were both alive at the press time of the earliest accounts but neither of them was expected to live. John, it was said, "was not sound in mind, though he had never been noticeably insane." A neighbor said the boy had never been crazy but had labored under a mental aberration at intervals although he had never been violent or considered to be dangerous.[5]

David Bevins

David F. Bevins killed his aged parents near Adrian, Michigan, in order to get their property. As well, he killed his young, pregnant wife so that he could marry his lover in Grafton, Ohio. After being convicted for the murders, Bevins was sentenced, in July 1865, to life imprisonment. At that time Michigan did not have the death penalty. According to a reporter, "His love of display did not desert him to the last," because he made a speech to the court requesting that whenever he died "they would bury him by the side of his mother, with his arm encircling her waist, as it did years ago." However, the judge was not impressed by that "filial fondness" and said to Bevins during the sentencing, "Go from among men into your solitary cell. The walls of your dungeon will yield you at least equal sympathy and commiseration to that exhibited by you to your victims. Mankind is entitled, by the verdict in your case, and the consequent protection of law, to be delivered from the danger of further depredations. You are sentenced to solitary confinement in the State Prison, at Jackson, during the period of your natural life."[6]

Albert Starkweather

On the morning of August 1, 1865, one of the residents of Manchester, Connecticut, was aroused by Albert Starkweather, who informed him that his mother and sister had been murdered and the house set on fire. Upon going to the residence, Mrs. Benjamin Starkweather and her daughter Ella were found dead; each had received several blows from an axe and had been stabbed repeatedly with a large knife. Albert had bruises and cuts on his body that he said were inflicted by the murderers in their struggle with him. Inconsistencies in his stories, along with the fact that no trace of the supposed murderers could be found, led to Albert's arrest that same day on suspicion of being the killer. Albert was said to have led a wild and extravagant lifestyle and had run up a large bill at a livery stable. He had unsuccessfully lobbied his mother to pay the bill for him. As well, he was engaged to marry Miss Campbell, a schoolteacher, shortly, but Campbell had put the wedding date off until Albert paid off his many outstanding debts. Mrs. Starkweather, a widow, had a farm of about 66 acres of good land, worth about $7,000. Mr. Starkweather had died some 10 years earlier. Albert was 22 at the time of the murders and was said to be not particularly bright. "He was addicted to practices then [in school], which may have had an unfortunate influence upon his subsequent career. His face betrays a certain weakness of character, if not of riotous passion," noted a journalist. "He maintained an assured and calm demeanor, that indicates either innocence of the awful crime with which he is charged, or an amount of hardihood and depravity seldom paralleled."[7]

Albert was indicted, tried and convicted of the two murders, and sentenced to death. Two days after the homicides Starkweather confessed to a friend, in secrecy, and the confession was not made public until after the trial. Prior to his engagement to Campbell he had several previous engagements to different women, all of which he broke. It was when Campbell put off the wedding that Albert decided he had to do something to show her he was a worthwhile and responsible suitor. During the week or so before the homicides Albert persuaded his mother to deed over some property to him, which he then put in the name of Campbell as a way of impressing her. Mrs. Starkweather severely censured her son for deeding away all he was worth and she took steps to negate Albert's transactions. With his hopes dashed, Albert brooded over the matter and, as he said later, for the next few days, "the idea of killing my mother did not leave my mind." The more he thought of the situation the angrier he grew. Then, toward morning on August 1, he took an axe and knife and proceeded to his mother's bedroom. When he struck his mother with the axe the sound woke his sister Ella, who was asleep in the same room. Although he had not intended to kill his sister, Albert dispatched his 14-year-old sister in the same fashion as he did his mother as she was the only witness. To make certain they were dead, Starkweather used the knife on each of the women, after he had finished attacking them with the axe. Next he set fire to the bedclothes in an effort to cover the crime and he battered his own head a little and cut his own clothing to try to lend credence to the idea that strangers had done the deed and that he had struggled with them. While he was in jail before his trial, he tried to bribe a jailer to let him escape by offering him all he expected to inherit from his mother. When that plan failed he devised another scheme but he made the mistake of telling another prisoner, who promptly informed on him. Albert Starkweather was executed by hanging at Hartford, Connecticut, on August 16, 1866.[8]

John Henry Salmon

From the initial reports it appeared that on the evening of November 4, 1869, John Henry Salmon, who lived near Stony Point, Virginia, went to his neighbor's place for a corn shucking and when he returned home in the early morning hours of the following day was surprised to find the front door of the family home standing open. He went to a neighbor and the pair of them returned to enter the Salmon residence together. There in the front room lay Mrs. Salmon, John Henry's mother, aged about 60, dead in a pool of blood. In the adjoining room lay John Henry's brother Luther, in the process of dying. Neighbors assessing the situation came to the conclusion a would-be robber entered the house after John Henry's departure, killed Luther by striking him on the head with a hatchet and then killed Mrs. Salmon with the same weapon. "The fiends then ransacked the house, breaking open all the drawers and scattering things in every direction," declared a news report, which got quite a few of the details wrong. "About twenty-five dollars in money was taken from Mrs. Salmon's pocket, and a small quantity of brandy is all that is missed from the house so far."[9]

Within a day or two the robber theory had been discarded and it was announced that John Henry had been arrested and was then in jail on murder charges. Several pieces of evidence linking him to the crime were discovered. As well, he was vocal in protesting the planned arrest—or worse—of a black man seen earlier at the house whom the neighbors had decided, on no evidence at all, was guilty and who, therefore, should perhaps even be lynched. Another piece of behavior exhibited by John Henry and which his neighbors found strange had to do with Luther. As the brother lay groaning, and dying, brandy was ordered to stimulate him. But John Henry refused to allow any stimulants to be given to Luther and stood in the doorway of the room to prevent anyone with stimulants from trying to enter the room. According to a reporter, "Salmon has heretofore borne a good character."[10]

Later in November a preliminary examination of the prisoner was conducted and John Henry was indicted for the murders of his mother and brother. "Public feeling was so shocked and incensed at the enormity and horrible barbarity of the crime that threats of summary vengeance were freely uttered should the perpetrator of the deed be found." Once John Henry was arrested for the crime it "occasioned additional and intense excitement and the people were only restrained from taking the law in their own hands by the counsel of some men of influence who yet entertained a doubt as to the guilt of John Henry Salmon. "To safeguard the prisoner, authorities moved the accused to the Charlottesville, Virginia, jail, but "there has been no abatement whatever of popular indignation, which is now centered upon the alleged criminal. So violent is this that if liberated the prisoner would pay the penalty of his crime at the hands of an out-raged community."[11]

The Salmon family was native Virginians and old residents of Albe-marle County, where they were reported to be "esteemed and respected" by all who knew them. Three years earlier, the father of the family had died, leaving a widow and two sons in comfortable though not affluent circumstances. They had a 100-acre farm located about eight miles from Charlottesville. As far as neighbors knew nothing but good feelings had existed in the family among the members since the death of the father. No one had ever heard of them quarreling. However, it was reported, John Henry, the eldest son, "had become, at the close of the [Civil] war, some-what dissolute in his habits, keeping low company and indulging in an extravagance altogether beyond his means, which soon involved him in debt." But it was not thought to be the subject of bad feeling or dissen-sion in the family. John Henry continued to live in that extravagant fash-ion until his credit was exhausted and he was threatened with lawsuits for recovery of the money he owed. There were no assets left for John Henry, except for the family farm, with which to satisfy his creditors. As he was part owner of the farm and worried his creditors might be able to seize it he made a deed of conveyance of his share to his brother Luther, to foil his creditors. That had happened 18 months earlier and while it had worked it was believed that John Henry regretted the transfer and coveted the entire farm. One month before the murders he consulted a lawyer named Bremond as to the disposition of the property in the event of the deaths of his mother and brother. Bremond assured John Henry he would become the sole owner.[12]

Evidence indicated John Henry killed the pair on the evening of November 4, before he went off to the corn shucking. His conduct there was not considered abnormal and the gathering broke up at about 11:00 P.M. An intoxicated John Henry rode home with a neighbor by the name of Alfred Herring. Upon reaching Herring's home that night—Salmon's home was little more than half a mile further along—John Henry expressed an unwillingness to return home that night. Herring let him stay at his place. Early on the morning of November 5 Salmon left for home but soon returned to announce that his mother and brother had been killed. Luther had died at around 1:00 P.M. on November 5. During the time that neighbors gathered at the Salmon residence on November 5 it was said that John Henry busied himself around the place but showed only indifference as to the fate of his people. In conversations with different people he suggested various reasons why the murders may have been committed, such as rumors the family had a large amount of money at home, and so forth. Nothing in the house had been disturbed. During that same day, John Henry made several efforts to sell the farm and in two or three other instances he tried to borrow money on it. No deal was made and many of those he approached in such a fashion turned away from him in disgust. When the funerals were held several days after the murders, John Henry tried to attend but was too intoxicated to do so. Evidence mounted against him and he told contradictory stories to the authorities. Finally, one day after the funerals, John Henry, 38 to 40 years old, was arrested; he continued to display "an indifference and callousness" to the situation. He hired the best lawyers available, making a deed of property for the farm over to them, in order to pay for their services.[13]

His trial was held in the summer of 1870, at which time John Henry Salmon was convicted of two counts of murder in the first degree. He was sentenced to be executed on November 4, 1870. "The sentence was received by the prisoner with unusual calmness, he not showing the least sign of excitement or confusion, but maintaining that stoical indifference which has characterized him ever since the crime was committed." No disposition of the case appears to have been reported.[14]

Silas Wilder

A February 1, 1876, report from East Lyndon, Vermont, stated that Silas Wilder, a 30-year-old well-to-do farmer residing in that town, had killed his father and mother that morning with an axe, as well as cutting his 22-year-old wife's throat. After all of that, he hung himself. Silas had been married for just one year. It was a marriage opposed by his parents, who went on to make his marital life very unpleasant. In an early account of the tragedy one newspaper ran its story with the following subhead: "Patricide, Matricide, Uxoricide, and Suicide committed by a passionate brute because his wife made his overalls too short." Actually, the wife of Silas was still alive at the press time of the earliest accounts and later reports never mentioned if she survived or died.[15]

A different account reasoned that Wilder had committed the killings because he was "laboring under temporary insanity superinduced by excessive excitement and passion." The father and mother were, respectively, 73 and 70 years of age. Immediate cause of the rampage was reported to have been an altercation with his wife, who, in altering a pair of his overalls, had made them too short. After angry words over her tailoring work, Silas started for the shed, saying he would get the axe and end the trouble. His wife followed him and seized the axe, but Silas draw a knife, slashed her with it and left her for dead. Then, taking up the axe, he started for his father, who was nearby, having come in response to the commotion. Silas struck his father a blow with the axe, crushing his head. Still infuriated, Silas sought out his mother and killed her with three blows to the head and chest with the axe. Leaving her in the front doorway of the house, Silas returned to the shed to find that his father had managed to crawl a short distance. He then struck him again with the axe, leaving it embedded in the old man's head. Then Silas cut his own throat, but that did not kill him, so he went into the barn, fastened a rope around his neck and jumped from a beam, breaking his neck and causing instant death. Both his parents died.[16]

An editorial, credited to the *Chicago Tribune* and reprinted in other newspapers, took a black-humored view of the tragedy: "The tragic and the comic are not infrequently combined in cases of crime. One of the instances of this rule is the low comedy and terrible tragedy of Tuesday at East Lyndon Vt. because Mrs. Silas Wilder made a pair of overalls too short...." The editor then summarized the events and said: "And all this because his overalls were too short. If he had scratched his finger he might have slaughtered all East Lyndon. If he had tumbled down on his knee-pan, Vermont might be an uninhabited wilderness today. And if a falling brick had crunched his crazy bone, there is no knowing but that he would have massacred all New England." The editor concluded: "If short overalls affect the rural mind in this manner in Vermont, the Legislature of that State should by all means make the production of a pair of abbreviated breeches cause for dissolving the marriage tie. Most women would prefer being divorced to being murdered."[17]

James Smith

A parricide/suicide occurred on the morning of July 24, 1878, at Rockford, Ontario, five miles from Jarvis. George Smith, 49, a well-to-do farmer, was roused at about 3:00 A.M. by his daughter Jane, who told him her brother James, 21, had been trying to steal money from the cash box. George went to his son's room and accused him of attempted theft. Heated words were exchanged between them, George finally declaring he would hitch up his horse and go to Simcoe for the police as he was tired of harboring a son who had systematically robbed him. George took a halter and started toward the field to get a horse for the trip just as dawn broke. James dressed and slipped out of the house after him. Coming upon his father near the barn, James picked up a cordwood log that was three feet long and beat his father murderously with it. Back in the house his daughters heard their father's cries: "Help, for God's sake, help! James is murdering me." One of them, 11 years old, ran outside in her nightclothes to see James raining blows on their father's head. After some minutes he stopped and said, "I guess I've finished the old bastard this time." Next he returned to the house, breaking off a pump handle on the way and taking it with him. James went to the bedroom occupied by two of his sisters, Jane, 18, and Eliza, 24. Breaking open their door he attacked them with the pump handle, inflicting several gashes. Leaving them he went downstairs and came upon his 11-year-old sister and knocked her unconscious with a blow from the handle. By this time his young brother Henry, 16, ran down the stairs and was charged by James. Henry picked up a kettle and threw it at his brother, striking James in the head and stunning him momentarily. Henry then ran to another room and returned with a loaded pistol. On seeing the pistol James fled outside and went to the barn, climbed onto the hay mower and hung himself to death from a beam with the halter his father had planned to use. Before doing that, however, he dragged his father's battered corpse 100 yards up a lane and stuck it into a haystack, where it was later found by neighbors.

The alarm was raised by Henry and neighbors quickly turned up in numbers. Jane and Eliza were both expected to survive but the youngest girl was more seriously hurt and it was not clear if she would live. Mrs. Smith, wife and mother to the family, had died a year earlier, reportedly, "heart broken at James' bad conduct and villainous habits." George's head had been "literally mashed into pulp." James died not from a broken neck from his suicide, but from slow strangulation. On the evening before the murder he told one of his sisters he was going to rob the cash box as he wanted money to go on a fraternal group's excursion on the following day. He also told her he had a club ready in case his father kicked up a fuss and he showed her the cordwood log with which he later committed the murder, but his sister thought James was joking.[18]

At the coroner's inquest it was revealed that sometime during the night of July 23-24 James slipped into his sister Jane's bedroom and stole the key to his father's money box from a string of keys that was wrapped around the girl's person. After he stole the money from the box he put the key back in the bed. But when Jane turned over in bed she felt the key, which awakened her. Since it was not in the right place, Jane suspected what had happened so she got up and awakened her father to tell him something was wrong, as the string of keys had been cut from her body. James Smith was to have been married on July 24, the day he killed his father. The coroner's jury returned a verdict that George Smith came to his death by wounds inflicted by his son James Smith "with a club, through malice aforethought" and that James came to his death by committing suicide.[19]

Joseph Sarver

The small, quiet village of West Lebanon, Pennsylvania, about 12 miles southwest of Indiana, was thrown into what was described as a "fever of excitement" on Saturday evening, November 10, 1883, when it was reported Joseph Sarver had shot his father and also attempted to kill a young lady who was making her home at his father's house. The victim was William Sarver, around 60 years old, whose wife had died a little over a year earlier. His sons Joseph and George no longer lived at home full time but did return occasionally. Belle Kelly, with her child, was the young woman who had been making her home with Sarver for the past three months. Joseph had spent most of the past two to three weeks living at the family home doing work for his father, who had been unwell for a time and unable to work. At the coroner's inquest Belle Kelly told the following story. Joseph came home from threshing at about 3:30 P.M. on that Saturday; his father had been to the store and bought some things about which Joseph was angry. He complained that William had no business going into debt to buy things that the family did not need. William replied that he had paid cash for most of the items he had bought and would soon pay off the balance. Getting angrier, Joseph said he would burn all the items that had been bought; William declared that he would go up to Squire Oliver's and have him arrested. When William left the house to go to do just that, Joseph went and took his revolver from the cupboard and followed him up the road. Belle heard the father say "let me alone" to the son, and then she followed the pair along the road. William continued walking toward Lebanon, declaring he would have his son arrested. Joseph called him back and was able to calm his father down somewhat. William crawled into a nearby haystack for a nap, staying there until about 5:00 P.M. Kelly and Joseph returned to the farmhouse where Belle started to prepare the evening meal. A little later, when she went to get William for supper, he told her he was afraid for his life, that Joseph would kill the both of them. However, as he was both wet and cold he went back to the house for supper.[20]

After supper Joseph went out while William sat by the fire. Over the next little while Joseph was in and out of the house several times. On the last occasion when he came in he blew out the lamp and fired off his revolver in the house but had not aimed at anything. William then got the cat and took it outside; Joseph followed him. The pair was outside for some time during which Kelly heard the sound of a gunshot. Right after that, Joseph entered the house and said to Kelly, "I have shot my father and will shoot you"; he had a revolver in his hand and then shot her in the arm. She ran outside screaming and he shot her again. Joseph then fled the scene while Belle staggered to a neighbor's place to get help. Just before she reached the neighbor's door she came across the dead body of William, with the neighbors and the doctor gathered around. Mrs. Jane Foster was the neighbor. She testified that at about 7:00 P.M. she heard a pistol shot outside but near her front door. When she went to investigate she found William lying on the ground, almost at her front porch. The coroner's jury reached a verdict that William came to his death by a bullet discharged from a pistol in the hands of his son Joseph Sarver. Word of the tragedy spread rapidly and on Sunday morning a great many citizens in the area were out hunting for Joseph. He was arrested on Sunday evening and taken to jail. "The parricide is said to be of rather weak mind, but with a very violent temper, especially when under the influence of liquor," said a reporter. "He was known several times last summer, when in town and under the influence of bad whiskey, to draw a razor and make threatening demonstrations."[21]

In another early account of the situation one newspaper told its readers, somewhat grandly, "Without intending to write a sensational and fanciful description of the lamentable occurrence, so highly derogatory to our county, we intend to give the facts as near as they can be obtained from persons in the neighborhood. It is not possible to get to all the details as the stories of all whom we have seen to obtain reliable information very materially differ." Herein William was described as "an industrious but careless man of quick temper." Until August of 1882 the family consisted of William, his wife and two sons, Joseph (the eldest) and George. Both sons had married and had families, although Joseph had not lived with his wife and children for several years, his wife having left him on account of neglect and cruel treatment. Occasionally, each of the sons returned to the family home to stay for a time. William owned six acres of land on which stood a two-story log house; the land and house appraised at a total of $72. Since leaving home, Joseph had worked at a variety of places and traveled throughout the area. From July 1882 onward he had been working for a farmer near Livermore by the name of Long. From his own statement Joseph described himself as about 38 years old, 5'6" and 140 pounds. "He has a quick and keen glance and is ready to talk. He takes his arrest and imprisonment with as much unconcern as if he were entirely innocent, and occupies his time in smoking, joking and playing cards with his prison companions, occasionally attempting a dance," said a journalist. "He appears to be totally devoid of moral principle and as it appears to the writer, is a cool, calculating villain, and bright and smart in conversation." William Sarver was said herein to be about 66 years of age.[22]

While he was in jail Joseph said they would never hang him as he was a Democrat, as was Pennsylvania governor Pattison. "He is a good deal of a fool, but not insane," wrote another journalist. "There was much excitement in town and country Monday night, but no threats of lynching were made and no extra guards were placed about the jail as it was not necessary." Sarver confessed to the crime while incarcerated. On the Friday evening he said he had a little tiff with his father and Kelly. Then on Saturday he went off and worked for one neighbor in the morning and for a different one in the afternoon, before returning home. From that point on Joseph's confession matched the statement Kelly had made.[23]

The trial of Joseph Sarver concluded at 10:00 P.M. on March 8, 1884, with the jury returning a verdict of guilty of murder in the first degree. That verdict was reached after six hours of deliberation. When it was delivered Sarver "never winced or changed color. A slight throbbing in the neck was the only outward evidence that he appreciated the import of the verdict," noted a courtroom observer. "When remanded to jail to await sentence he accompanied the Sheriff with a steady step and a smile on his face. Soon after being placed in his cell he went to bed and was soon enjoying a sound and refreshing sleep." First ballot by the jury was 11 votes for guilty of murder in the first degree and one vote for acquittal on the ground of insanity. According to an account, "The condemned man had neither money nor friends and the crime was so atrocious that the feeling in the community was all against him. The case was well conducted on both sides and the attorneys for the prosecution and the defense can have no regrets."[24]

After a motion for a new trial was rejected in May 1884, Judge John P. Blair sentenced Sarver. "You seem to have give unbridled license to your evil passions," Blair told him. "The evidence against you did not present a case of ordinary killing. Your crime was most unnatural—the murder of a parent. It was an awful violation of the Divine command to honor your father. Instead of honoring him you slew him. It is not to such persons that length of days is promised. I do not remind you of the horrible character of your sin for the purpose of distressing you, but to move and incite you to a true and thorough repentance." Blair told Sarver not to hold out any hope for relief from any more legal maneuverings or from applications for a pardon or commutation from the state. "In any event, and in every aspect to the case, it will be better for you not to indulge the pleasing thought of freedom and exemption from punishment; but to contemplate the worst and by deep sorrow and penitence, seek to prepare yourself for it. Though every earthly prospect should fail, there remains even for you, the hopes and consolation of the Christian religion. Great as your sin may be, it is not too great for a compassion that is infinite." Blair pointed out the evidence was clearly against him and, as to Joseph's plea of insanity, Blair said it "is often resorted to when others fail; but nevertheless a good defense or excuse when satisfactorily established. This defense was properly and fairly submitted to the jury by the Court and they found against you. I cannot disapprove of their finding.... I can have no sympathy with the philosophy which would resolve all crimes into species of insanity ... let no one who contemplates the commission of a crime cherish the delusion that it will be easy to escape responsibility upon specious but doubtful and unsatisfactory evidence of mental unsoundness." He was sentenced to be executed by hanging.[25]

Toward the end of August 1884, the Pennsylvania governor issued the death warrant that directed Sheriff M.F. Jamison to execute Joseph Sarver by hanging on September 23. A lawyer took his case to the Pardon Board of the State of Pennsylvania, looking to have the sentence commuted to life imprisonment, but the request was refused. In the last week of his life Sarver turned to religion and sent for Reverend Father Brown (Roman Catholic) with whom he then spent much of his remaining time. A woman who claimed to have been engaged to him paid him frequent visits, also, and was with him on the 22nd. When Father Brown arrived at the jail on the 22nd and found the woman, Lizzie, visiting Sarver, he asked them whether they were married. Upon receiving a negative answer the priest ordered her out of the room. "His last night on earth ought to have been one sad reflection on the errors and crimes of a misspent life, but we fear that he was as stolid and insensible as ever," remarked a reporter. He ascended the scaffold steps firmly and died virtually instantly from a broken neck. Joseph Sarver was executed at 11:30 A.M. on Tuesday, September 23, 1884. "Since his confinement in prison he has been unconcerned and at times even in a jolly mood, seemingly to have no sense of moral responsibility or the enormity of his crime," commented another observer.[26]

Notwithstanding the pressure brought to bear on him for tickets of admission to the execution enclosure, it was said Sheriff Jamison kept the number to within the limits of the law. The crowd was estimated at 500 to 600 spectators. "Thus has been expiated one of the most fearful crimes ever committed in this county," concluded a journalist. "The criminal deserved the full extent of the law and justice is vindicated. 'Thou shalt not kill,' is the lesson to be learned." Sarver made the following written statement to his spiritual advisor (Brown) on September 19. "I, Joseph Sarver, finding myself now standing on the brink of eternity and knowing full well that in a few short hours I must stand before the Judge of the living and the dead, do most sincerely and humbly beg pardon of god for all my sins and offenses against his Divine Majesty, and I hereby ask pardon from all whom I may have injured or offended." And, after thanking his lawyers, the sheriff, his family and Father Brown, Sarver concluded his statement by saying, "I willingly offer up my life in atonement for my sins and die a true, though unworthy, member of the Roman Catholic Church. May god have mercy on my soul."[27]

Wesley Elkins

A farmer named John Elkins and his wife lived seven miles northeast of Edgewood, Iowa, and were murdered on their property on a night late in July 1889. Their bodies were found the following morning, dead, in their room, the man with a rifle ball through the head and the woman with her head and face "pounded to jelly." Early reports believed the man was killed instantly and was the first to die. Mrs. Elkins was awakened by the gunshot and then engaged in a desperate struggle with the killer as the walls, bedclothes, and even the ceiling of the room were splashed with the blood and brains of the victim. A little girl, aged 18 months, was sleeping between her parents in the same bed and was unharmed. The only other occupant of the farm was Wesley Elkins, the 14-year-old son of John, who was sleeping in the barn and was also awakened by the shot. He was terrified by the noise and the sounds of a struggle in the house and he did nothing for a time, waiting for it to get quiet before he dared to go into the house. When he finally went in and saw the carnage, he took his baby sister and went to a neighbor's place, where he gave the alarm. At that point there were said to be no clues as to the killer's identity.[28]

A few days later a different story emerged when it was reported that Wesley Elkins, 11, had killed his father and his stepmother. Wesley's age varied from report to report and was given, variously, as 11, 12, 13, or 14. On July 26 Wesley confessed his crime to Judge Hatch. The boy had some difficulty with his father and on the night of the murder he slept in the barn. Between 2:00 and 3:00 A.M. Wesley got up, went into the house, took down the rifle hanging in the kitchen, loaded it, and went into the room where the three members of his family slept. "I placed the muzzle of the rifle to my father's head," he said, "and sent a bullet through his brain." That caused his stepmother to awaken, whereupon Wesley got a club from the kitchen and beat her to death. After some 30 minutes he took the baby into the next room, changed its blood-stained clothes, and went to a neighbor's place to raise the alarm.[29]

When he went to the neighbor he told him he had discovered his parents murdered and fled the area to preserve his own life and the life of his baby sister. In his confession he stated he "went to a neighbor's and related the crime that had been committed, but shielded myself. I am guilty of the crime."[30]

John Elkins was 45, and his wife, Hattie Elkins, was 22. At first, suspicion rested upon a cousin as the killer, based primarily on evidence given before the coroner's jury by Wesley before he confessed. Said a reporter, "The boy-murderer bears an intelligent look and many, notwithstanding the confession, believe that the story is told to shield some one else."[31]

An indictment for murder against Wesley was found, despite the fact there was said to be no evidence against him except his own confession. In that statement, though, he said, "Nobody helped me in any way nor told me to kill them. I did it all alone." The statement also related that after Wesley got the club and his stepmother was bending over his father Wesley said, "I struck her on the head as she was stooping and she straightened up and fell backward on the bed over father. I then got up on the bed and struck her a great many times on the head until I thought she was dead. Then I heard father make a noise in his throat and I struck him two blows on the head that smashed the skull." According to this account, "The boy is a very intelligent little fellow, weighing only 78 pounds, and is very frail looking."[32]

Wesley was indicted for both murders but was tried only for the murder of his father. In court in January 1890, he pled guilty to murder in the first degree and was sentenced on January 11 to imprisonment for life, with hard labor, at the state penitentiary. When he was sentenced Wesley was said to have shown "no feeling." The judge ordered the boy's confession should not be released to the public owing to its "sensational character." However, it was a little late for that, as portions of the confession had by then been published by many newspapers. Because he pled guilty to the charge of murdering his father he was not tried for the murder of his stepmother. As far as the motive for the slayings went, all Wesley had said was that he desired to leave home and shift for himself but his parents had objected to such an idea.[33]

While on a visit to Anamosa Penitentiary in Iowa in February 1890 the Reverend S.S. Hunting, president of the Iowa Prisoners' Aid Association, held a conversation with the 12-year-old Wesley. Hunting said the boy told him that his father had been very cruel to him and at the foot of the bed where the boy slept hung a loaded rifle and that Wesley would lie in bed and meditate on killing his father until he lost control and actually committed the crime; and then he killed his stepmother for fear she would tell on him. Hunting believed that a boy as young as Wesley should not have been sent to a penitentiary, where he was constantly in the company of criminals. Rather, one so young should be reformed and Wesley should have been sent to a reform school.[34]

Several years later, in December 1890, an editorial appeared in an Iowa newspaper on the supposed "rush" of applications for pardons that had been sent to the governor. He could grant pardons to convicts, except those serving out sentences for capital offenses—in such a case the application had to be acted upon by the legislature. Since Wesley was in prison for a capital offense, only the Iowa legislature could grant him a pardon, not the governor acting alone. With respect to an application pending for Wesley, the editor declared, "The deed was an exceedingly cold-blooded one and the fact that the boy was only about eleven years of age when the crime was committed, and his subsequent action, marks him as a frightful example of juvenile depravity.... For some reason a number of tender hearted individuals whose sympathy has warped their judgment and whose knowledge of the case is limited, have undertaken to influence the legislature to grant him a pardon." The "tender hearted individuals" were trying to do that by writing lots of letters to the press, pointing to Wesley's extreme youth and to the fact he was being kept in the penitentiary with hardened criminals. While the editor thought such arguments could be used in a general sense to perhaps improve the system whereby juvenile offenders were handled, he concluded, "In the case of Wesley Elkins, however, there is a good deal of wasted sympathy being aired just now and we hardly think that the legislature will feel like releasing him when the facts in the case are fully understood."[35]

With respect to the pardon application for Wesley, an editor with a different Iowa newspaper asserted, "He was only 11 years old at the time he committed the awful crime, and it was deliberately carried out, seemingly with the only idea of killing. The penitentiary is still a pretty good place for him."[36]

Reverend E.J. Lockwood served as a minister at Edgewood from 1886 to 1890, his church being located near the Elkins residence, and he used to see them at church occasionally. According to Lockwood, the boy ran away from home once. When his grandfather learned where he was he told Wesley's father and the latter went after him and brought him home. A few mornings after that, the boy rose early one morning and committed the murders. The family physician and the neighbors thought him to be two years older than the age the boy stated. At the funeral for his parents, Wesley showed no emotion and Lockwood speculated, "In multitudes of ways he gave evidence of an utter absence of moral consciousness. He seemed to have no capacity to discern that his deed was in any way wrong. Men who attended the trial asserted that when the boy heard his sentence he said there was just one other person he would like to kill before he went, and that was his grandfather." A former teacher of Wesley told Lockwood that she used to be compelled to keep him in school until the other children were well on their way home as he was liable at some slight provocation to assault any of them in "the most vicious manner." Reverend Lockwood concluded that all the evidence he could obtain pointed to Wesley "as a thorough degenerate, utterly abnormal in his make-up, the moral faculty entirely wanting."[37]

The application to pardon Wesley failed in 1895 but another one was on file in 1898. An editorial with respect to that application declared, in direct contradiction to Lockwood's statements. "It appears that the lad, undersized and rather effeminate, had no previous record of cruel or malicious disposition, having been regarded as a good, quiet boy.... But after his father's re-marriage, little attention seems to have been paid to him at home, until there was a baby for him to take care of, to which duty he was quite closely confined. He ran away once to avoid it."[38]

Nor was a pardon granted to Wesley at the session of the Iowa legislature that ended in March 1898. His application, though, had occasioned what was described as a "memorable fight" between the proponents and the opponents. That application had been "backed by a great number of philanthropists and humanitarians all over the county and a flood of letters had poured into the legislature in his favor." However, the backers of the petition withdrew it at the last minute, before it was put to a vote, because they feared that a formal vote of rejection would hurt his future chances for a pardon; hence it was withdrawn.[39]

Yet another application for a pardon was in the works in the early months of 1902. The main proponent of the application at that time was Professor Harlan of Mount Vernon, Iowa, who stood ready to take personal responsibility for Wesley. Iowa senator Bishop (who hailed from the area where the crime took place) remained opposed to leniency and regarded the boy as a "degenerate." Times and opinions had changed, though. In April 1902 the Iowa legislature granted a pardon to Wesley Elkins. It had certain conditions attached to it and today we would call it a parole. On April 19, 1902, Wesley Elkins walked out of Anamosa at 8:30 A.M. after an imprisonment of 12 years, three months, and five days. He was met by Professor Harlan of Cornell College, Mount Vernon, who drove him over to Mount Vernon. He was to stay with Professor and Mrs. Harlan for a time. When released he was given a new dark blue serge suit and $5. Upon his release Wesley was probably about 25 years old.[40]

Some six years later a brief item was published that noted Wesley had by then been employed in the land department of the Northern Pacific Railroad, at St. Paul and was "making good," as he had been promoted several times. After attendance at Harlan's college for a time Wesley Elkins went out to make his own way in the world.[41]

Walter Shaw

On the night of March 30, 1892, in Houston, announced a news report, "[O]ne of the most foul murders that ever darkened the history of this city was committed…. Two ladies were found dead in their house with their throats cut from ear to ear and the city stands aghast and appalled at the atrocity of the deed." Dr. A.D. Burroughs went to the house with the police at around 10:00 A.M. on March 31 in response to a call. When the group arrived they found the bodies of Mrs. Belle Johnson and Mrs. Anna Shaw, and a bloody razor was recovered from the floor that was covered in blood. The women had lived in a single-story house with five rooms. Mrs. Shaw was thought to be 55 to 60 years old, while Mrs. Johnson, her sister, was estimated to be 40 to 45 years of age. A neighbor by the name of Mr. Jones was in the habit of stopping at the house each day to see how the women were doing, as Johnson was described as an invalid. He found them dead on the floor the morning of March 31, with their throats cut from ear to ear. A different neighbor had been in the house at dusk on the day before and had spoken to both women. She said the older woman's son, Walter Shaw, had been home then. She had not actually seen him but heard him coughing in another room. It was believed the murder had occurred at about 9:00 P.M. When the bodies were discovered Walter was absent. Robbery was not believed to be the motive as items of value remained untouched in the house, all in plain sight. Walter, nephew of Johnson, had not been seen since the night of the murder. Walter lived in the house with the two women and was seen on the evening of the 30th in an intoxicated state. According to neighbors, Walter had lived there with his mother and aunt for many years and "nothing combative has ever cropped up in his nature, but at home his character is said to be entirely different." He was about 35 years old. As news of the murders spread around the area people began to gather around the house, and by noon some 500 curious people had assembled near the murder house, speculating and swapping rumors.[42]

Police sent out bulletins to other regions and began the search for Walter Shaw. It was discovered that the son had been arrested in Galveston by a beat cop in an intoxicated condition and taken to jail as an unknown, a John Doe. However, the description sent around by the Houston police was received in Galveston and the authorities then realized who they had in custody. When questioned, Walter was still under the influence and talked incoherently. He had reached Galveston near midnight and was seen by several people frequenting saloons. When he was searched in jail blood was found on his underclothing. From neighbors it was also learned that twice before he had attempted to kill his mother and his aunt and once would have succeeded with a knife; but because he was very drunk the two women were able to overpower him and take the weapon away from him. Walter had been born in Texas and lived for most of his life in Houston; he had relatives in both Houston and Galveston. As a boy he had worked at a freight office. Since that time he had worked as a railroad clerk at Houston and other points until his drinking problem got so bad that he could no longer obtain employment. When he was arrested in Galveston he had only 50 cents on his person. When it was learned Walter Shaw was in custody, a reporter commented, "Lynching has been freely talked of, but burning has the greater number of advocates. It is not likely that either will be attempted, as the sheriff would resist it to death."[43]

Shaw was in court in Houston on April 7 to have a trial date set for the double murder and, observed a reporter, "The prisoner was handcuffed and showed no remorse, regret or sorrow, but was perfectly cool and free of trouble. He took his seat by a table and enjoyed his usual cigarette." When he was asked about a lawyer, the prisoner said he did not have one and did not want one; he wanted to conduct his own defense. Nevertheless, the judge appointed a lawyer for him.[44]

On April 19, 1892, Walter Shaw stood trial for the murder of his mother; it was a trial that lasted for one day. One day later he was tried for the murder of his aunt. During the trials the prisoner took a hand in the questioning of witnesses and also spoke to the jury. Long before the 10:00 A.M. start of the trial crowds of people hovered around the courthouse hoping to get seats. However, due to the size of the crowd most of the people did not get in. Evidence at the trial indicated that Walter had done little or nothing to earn his own living over the previous 12 to 18 months and that he was completely dependent on his mother for financial support. With respect to the motive for the killings, all the prosecution brought forward was the idea that Walter had killed for $42, a sum of money Mrs. Shaw had received a week or so earlier and had stashed away in the house for emergencies. Trunks in the house had been ransacked and linen disturbed. In his summation District Attorney Gillespie stated, "The murder was committed by her son, one of her own flesh and blood. It was done for filthy lucre, and two lives were taken for $42.50. The money had been laid away to provide for the family. He took the money and spent it for liquor.... He had never done any work and murdered his poor old mother for her hard earned money.... [H]e killed those poor old women for their money. One who stands nearer to the heart of anyone in the civilized world—the mother." After being out for 75 minutes the jury returned with a verdict against Walter Shaw of guilty of murder in the first degree in the death of his mother.[45]

Shaw was found guilty a day later of murder in the first degree with respect to the death of his aunt, and was then sentenced to death. However, an appeal was made by his lawyer that Walter's "irrational and insane" actions and behavior at the trials had prevented his counsel from mounting a full defense. After it heard that argument the higher court granted Shaw's motion for a new trial.[46]

At his trial in December 1892, a statement from Walter, over the protest of his attorney, was read out at the start of the proceedings: "I was sober and I can prove it, and wish to waive an examination. I know that I did that God damned deed and ought to be hanged for it."[47]

Convicted again and sentenced again to be executed, more legal maneuvers delayed the fixing of the execution date for a period of time. On the morning of June 23, 1893, in Houston, Shaw was brought before the criminal court, at which time Judge E.D. Cavin sentenced him to be executed by hanging on July 28. Before being sentenced Walter gave a long and rambling discourse to the effect that he was ill served by his lawyers and should have been allowed to represent himself as he had requested from the start and for that reason he should get a new trial. He also argued he had medical evidence to the effect he was insane. Judge Cavin dismissed such arguments and passed the death sentence, after which Shaw said, "I am glad you omitted the 'God have mercy on your soul' [from the sentencing speech] for that would be sarcasm but, judge, I wish the court would instruct that I shall be furnished writing material, as I wish to write a novel, for which northern publishers have already offered me a good sum." Cavin said he had no jurisdiction over such matters. As Walter left the courtroom his final comment was "Kangarooed, by God."[48]

Two days before his slated execution Shaw sold title to his body to Dr. George Lankford. To make it legal a formal agreement was drawn up, witnessed and signed. The agreement read as follows: "This memorandum witnesseth that I, Walter E. Shaw, for and in consideration of the sum of $200, to me in hand paid by Dr. Geo. A. Lankford, the receipt whereof is hereby acknowledged, do bargain and sell to the said Dr. Lankford my remains, which is to be delivered after my official execution by the sheriff of Harris County, and I do hereby authorize and empower the said Dr Lankford to demand and receive from the sheriff of Harris County my remains. The intention of this sale being in the interest of science and upon the condition that the said Dr. Lankford shall give my remains Christian and decent burial in Glenwood cemetery in the lot formerly owned by Mrs. Isabella C. Johnson." That agreement was entered into on July 26. Lankford planned to study Shaw's brain.[49]

On July 28 at 10:00 A.M. in Houston, just one hour before the scheduled execution, a telegram was received from Texas governor Hogg granting a reprieve of one week in order that an examination could be conducted into Shaw's mental condition. When the prisoner was informed of the last minute stay of execution he shrugged his shoulders and remarked, "That's too bad, and I am disappointed."[50]

As far as the public reaction to the stay went, one reporter remarked it was not talked about all that much, "although when spoken of it is condemned, and in very bitter terms, by many." Asked about the reprieve, Dr. Lankford stated, "Well, really, I felt there was a sudden suspension of a business transaction caused by the interference of his excellency, in which the saw, scalpel and microscope, in the interest of medical science, would have very soon begun to play an important part."[51]

Within a few days of the reprieve a petition against any further executive interference in the execution was circulated and then forwarded to Governor J.S. Hogg. It did not appear that any formal investigation into Shaw's sanity was actually held during the one week stay. A petition in favor of a further reprieve or a commutation of sentence was started by one F.N. Gray and left in the courthouse for people to sign. After two days, though, it contained no signatures at all, apart from Gray's. Instead of some type of formal investigation into the prisoner's mental state, all that took place was that Hogg "reviewed" all the papers in the case. On August 3, Hogg let it be known there would be no more interference in the case from his office. Reportedly, Shaw had recently posted an ad: "NOTICE—The public and all journals are hereby warned not to purchase or trade for any private letters or papers of mine after my death as the same will have acquired a money value, and have been disposed of by will. (Signed) Walter E. Shaw." By his own request his last supper consisted of tenderloin trout broiled, lettuce salad, mayonnaise potatoes, light bread and port wine.[52]

Early on August 4, 1893, Walter Shaw looked out from his death cell in Houston on his execution day. "As he gazed into the mystic future he did not have the appearance of a man who was about to ascend the gallows. His expression was not one of horror and neither was it one of fright. No tear dimmed his eye and not a sob shook his slender frame," declared an observer. "As silent as the grave which was soon to environ him, he lingered at the small window and calmly reflected. Now and then different expressions would flit across his careworn and bearded face. One moment he would smile with the innocence of childhood—the next he would frown in a somber way and assume the look of dark devilish defiance." He was executed at 11:35 A.M. and died from a broken neck. As soon as the rope was cut to remove the body, several men rushed up with knives to cut off pieces of the hanging rope to save as souvenirs. Soon there was a mad rush by others and the rope was quickly sectioned into pieces and was gone. Many were disappointed not to be able to claim a small piece of the rope. Meanwhile, Lankford took possession of the body and immediately examined it. Revealed was the fact that Shaw had a brain that weighed 42 ounces; average weight of a man's brain was said to be 49.5 ounces, 44 ounces for a woman's brain. Shaw's liver was found to be enlarged and "clearly alcoholic. It was simply gigantic in its dimensions."[53]

In the summary of the crime, given in the story that covered the execution, it was said to embrace "the account of a double murder of the most atrocious character, and the act of a human being, who by many is believed to be insane, but by a large majority of well informed people to be an incarnate monster of the most hideous proportions." When all the facts became known, "The atrocious deeds of Jack the Ripper had been eclipsed. They had paled to insignificance compared with the black deeds that appalled this community on that beautiful April day." Herein it said Walter was 37 and was born on Galveston Island. He graduated from the high schools of New Orleans when he was a little over 14. His aunt was teaching school there and his high school years were the only ones he spent outside of Texas. His father died three months before he was born and he was raised by his widowed mother and her three sisters. It was said that "He was considered bright in a literary way but he threw himself away several years ago [from alcohol], since which he has been worthless to himself and every one." Motive was again said to be the $42. When the women refused to give him the money, he decided to take it and that resulted in the death of his mother and aunt. He had no money at all before that night when he took the train to Galveston but he was seen with a fair amount of money just before taking the train, and when he paid his fare to the conductor.[54]

Before he was executed, Shaw entered into a contract with J.H. Weiner giving Weiner the exclusive rights to Shaw's dictated statement or biography. In return Weiner agreed to pay the cost ($35) of disinterring the bodies of Walter's two victims and reburying them in Glenwood cemetery with his own remains. His mother and aunt had initially been buried in the German cemetery. That agreement declared: "I, J.H. Weiner, do hereby bind myself, for and in consideration of receiving from Walter E. Shaw a dictated statement or biography, to which he gives me sole right of publication and ownership to perform the following service, to wit: I agree to have the bodies of Mrs. A.C. Shaw and Mrs. I.C. Johnson, at present interred in German cemetery, removed and interred in a lot owned by Mrs. Isabelle C. Johnson in Glenwood cemetery, provided that said service shall be performed in decent and respectable manner. (Signed) J.H. Weiner."[55]

Lizzie Borden

Of all the patricides and matricides outlined in this book, the one that generated the most public interest and media coverage, by far, was the case involving Lizzie Borden. The slayings, the subsequent trial, and the never-ending trial by media turned the story into a lasting and enduring piece of Americana, with the fame of the event enshrined in American popular culture and criminology. Well over a century after the event, the Borden case still generated much debate and still garnered media interest.

It all began on the morning of August 4, 1892, when Lizzie's father,

Andrew Jackson Borden, and her stepmother, Abby Durfee Borden, were murdered by an axe in the family home at Fall River, Massachusetts. The Borden family consisted of the father, 70, the stepmother, 64, a servant named Bridget Sullivan, and Mr. Borden's two daughters, Lizzie, 32, and Emma, 41. Emma was at the time visiting friends in a nearby city and had been for some days. At 8:00 on the morning of the murder Mrs. Borden left the house to visit a friend and soon afterward her husband followed and walked down the street to a bank. Andrew returned at 10:30 A.M. and stretched out on the sofa for a rest. Bridget passed through the room a few moments later and the pair exchanged a few words. Within half an hour both Andrew and Abby were dead, brutally murdered.

There had been no outcry and as far as the authorities could determine, no one was seen to enter or leave the house between 10:30 and 11:00 A.M. It was Lizzie who found the body of Mr. Borden, shortly after 11:00 A.M. Lizzie called to Bridget, who was then in her room on the third floor of the house, saying someone had killed her father. Shortly thereafter, while Lizzie was being comforted and tended by neighbors and the family doctor, Bridget discovered the body of Mrs. Borden upstairs in the guest bedroom. Both victims had been killed by multiple blows to the head from an axe. According to Lizzie she was out in the barn at around 11:00 A.M. when she thought she heard a cry of distress from the house and, running back to the house, found her murdered father. Police made exhaustive searches but the murder weapon was never found, nor was any other clue. Nothing of value was missing from the house, which seemed to rule out robbers. Finally, the police theorized the homicides must have been the work of Lizzie in an effort to secure a half interest in the estate, valued at around $500,000. Lizzie was arrested on August 11 and in December 1892 the grand jury indicted her for the murders with 20 jurors voting in favor of indictment, and one voting against it.[56]

Over a period of some years after the death of the first Mrs. Borden, relations between the parents and children had deteriorated. The front of the second floor of the house was the domain of the Borden sisters, while their father and stepmother controlled the rear section. Family meals were not always taken together. An important conflict between the father and his daughters revolved around his decision to divide up valuable property among relatives before his death. Shortly before the murders a heated argument had taken place over that issue and had resulted in Lizzie and Emma both leaving home on extended "vacations." Lizzie, though, decided to cut her trip short and she returned to the family home early. Not long before the murders Lizzie tried to buy some prussic acid (cyanide) from a local druggist, telling him she wanted it to clean a sealskin coat. The druggist refused her request.

Lizzie's trial began in New Bedford, Massachusetts, in June 1893. While Lizzie's stories were inconsistent and her behavior suspect, the prosecution had no strong evidence. There was no murder weapon or blood-stained clothing. A few days after the murder Borden tore apart and burned a light blue dress in the kitchen stove, claiming she had brushed against fresh baseboard paint that had smeared on the dress. Despite some incriminating evidence Lizzie Borden was acquitted by the jury after 90 minutes of deliberations. Solidly behind the verdict was an editor with the *New York Times*, who wrote, "The acquittal of this most unfortunate and cruelly persecuted woman was, by this promptness, in effect, a condemnation of the police authorities of Fall River and of the legal officers who secured the indictment and have conducted the trial. It was a declaration not only that the prisoner was guiltless, but that there never was any serious reason to suppose that she was guilty." He added he was not surprised the Fall River police should have attached their suspicions on Lizzie: "The town is not a large one. The police are of the usual inept and stupid and muddle-headed sort that such towns manage to get for themselves. There is nothing more merciless than the vanity of ignorant and untrained men charged with the detection of crime, in the face of a mystery that they cannot solve, and for the solution of which they feel themselves responsible. The Fall River police needed a victim ... and the daughter was the nearest and most helpless. They pounced on her."[57]

Lizzie Borden died of pneumonia on June 1, 1927, in Fall River, Massachusetts. Nine days later, on June 10, her sister, Emma, from whom Lizzie was then estranged, died from a fall in Newmarket, New Hampshire. To this day there is a widespread belief that Lizzie was guilty. No one else was ever arrested or tried. Speculation as to the identity of the killer or killers remained rampant.[58]

Thomas Rodgers

In a tragedy that took place in Chester, Pennsylvania, on the afternoon of January 14, 1893, Thomas Rodgers (21, or perhaps 24) killed both of his parents, Thomas Rodgers, about 60, and Martha Rodgers, also about 60 years old. As well, he shot his married sister, Mrs. William Kildey. It all started when the father reprimanded his son that day for laziness and told the young man he had to go to work. "You can't put me out," answered his son and going upstairs he took his brother-in-law's revolver and went back downstairs to confront his father. Both his mother and sister were in the room and attempted to save the elder man but the son deliberately fired two shots into his father. After the older man had fallen to the floor the son kicked him in the face. As Mrs. Rodgers attempted to flee to the cellar her son shot her in the back. Then his sister tried to flee the house but Thomas also shot her in the back. Mrs. Kildey survived. Thomas then ran up the street to an alderman's office and entered, locking the door against the large crowd that had gathered at the noise of the gunshots and then followed the young man. Police were called and they quickly arrested him. Thomas told them the attack was the result of a family row and that he intended to kill the old man. However, he gave no reasons for the attacks on his mother and sister. "There is much excitement in the community and extra precautions are taken by the police to guard against lynching," said an account.[59]

The mayor of Chester, Pennsylvania, took an antemortem statement from the two dying parents later on the fourteenth, shortly before each expired. The father said his son had frequently threatened his life when he had pressed the young man to go to work. On several occasions Mr. Rodgers had secured the arrest of his son but withdrew the charges on promises from his son of good behavior. Both parents believed their son intended to kill his father, and said he had not been drinking. The four children of Mrs. Kildey were present in the house at the time of the shooting.[60]

Kildey said her father was a "quiet industrious workman" and she described her mother as an "amiable old lady." According to one reporter, "Thomas Rodgers, who did the shooting, has been known as a worthless character, and much of his time was spent in loafing upon his father's support. Recently he had been arrested, charged with beating and abusing his old mother, but when the time came for the trial the old lady would not appear against him, and the case was dropped, the mother being held for the costs."[61]

Thomas Rodgers was convicted of murder and sentenced to a term of 24 years in prison. While in jail in Media, Pennsylvania, Rodgers died, on June 28, 1894, after being incarcerated for a year or so. No cause of death was reported although the news account summarized that Rodgers had shot three people and attempted suicide. No time frame was given for the suicide attempt.[62]

William Gipp

Without provocation, it was said, William Gipp shot his mother to death on the morning of November 2, 1894, at Buffalo, New York, and seriously wounded his father. At first it was felt that Mr. Gipp would die from the gunshot he had received, but he did survive. William was employed as a railway car inspector who worked the night shift. Upon returning home from work on the morning of November 2 he drew a revolver and without uttering a word he fired twice at his mother, killing her instantly. Hearing the shots, his father entered the room, whereupon the son fired twice at him. At that point other sons entered the room and grappled with William. However, he broke away and escaped. His freedom was short lived as he was captured in a barn on the night of November 2. "He is a raving maniac and it required the combined strength of eight strapping big fellows to hold him at police headquarters," remarked a reporter. Another journalist remarked, "Gipp is undoubtedly insane, as he had no trouble with his parents." He was 20 years old and was employed by the Lehigh Valley Railroad. In his statement to the coroner the father said the couple heard a noise at 2:00 A.M. of someone tapping at the window and his wife asked who was there. William identified himself and explained he had left work to come home and get his overcoat. When Mrs. Gipp got up and opened the door William rushed in and shot her. Mr. Gipp entered the room and struggled with his son but William broke free and shot his father.[63]

When William was taken into custody the authorities thought he was demented. Not long after he arrived at police headquarters in Buffalo he fell into what was called a "trance." He was removed to the state mental hospital in Buffalo, where he remained in a state of coma. Food was administered to him by hospital attendants. Then, suddenly and unexpectedly, after being in a coma for about three years and two months, William surprised his keeper one Saturday morning early in January 1898 by arising from his bed and walking across the room. When he was spoken to by attendants he had great difficulty in framing answers to queries, but improved as the day wore on. So much improved was he that a reporter commented that he was "now apparently on the road to complete recovery." No other outcome was reported.[64]

William Foley

Mrs. Foley, a 65-year-old widow, and her unmarried daughter Fanny Foley, 40, were found murdered in their home near Liberty, Missouri, on

November 18, 1896. No motive for the crime was known. William Foley, the 25-year-old son and brother of the deceased women, had visited a neighbor on November 17 and returned home after midnight, at which point he discovered the dead bodies. Each woman was found dead in her separate bedroom, dressed in her nightgown and covered with blood. Both had been shot, the mother through the head and the daughter through the back. William gave the alarm to the neighbors and a number of people were soon gathered who went off to search the area in the hope of finding the culprits. Finding no clues, though, they rode to Kansas City, Missouri, 15 miles distant from the murder scene and reported the killings to the local police. Detectives were immediately sent to Liberty.[65]

More details were released wherein the son indicated that when he arrived home after midnight he found the gates to the farm were open and the cattle and horses loose, as well as the front door to the house being ajar. It was claimed that investigations showed it had been "a cold blooded murder, for the sole purpose of robbery." Robbers, it was surmised, had killed the women and ransacked the house. Missing from the house and presumably stolen was the sum of $50.[66]

A day later the coroner held an inquest but his jury met in secret, with the participants sworn to secrecy. "There is a strong sentiment against the son and brother, William Foley, who first reported the murder, and though he has heretofore borne an excellent reputation he is being closely watched," noted a reporter. One rumor had it that there had long been friction in the family over Mrs. Foley's persistent refusal to divide the family estate among her three children. The murdered daughter was said to have sided with her mother in those family dissensions.[67]

Later in November, the coroner's jury delivered its verdict in the murders and William was promptly arrested and charged with both killings. "Excitement is intense and a lynching is threatened. Officers will take Foley to Kansas City," remarked a newsman. In jail in Kansas City, Foley was said to have broken down and wept when informed the feeling of his neighbors was against him.[68]

Foley was tried in July 1897 but the jury could not agree on a verdict. So it was back to a cell in Liberty for him to await a second trial. On the night of October 21, 1897, shortly after midnight, a mob of about 100 masked and armed men attempted to enter the county jail in Liberty for the purpose of lynching Foley, and a man named Frank Kade, who was also awaiting his own murder trial. The sheriff assembled some deputies and with a show of arms managed to cause the mob to desist and disperse. Several shots were fired during the confrontation but nobody was hit.[69]

On the afternoon of January 1, 1898, the jury trying Foley for the two murders returned a verdict of guilty of murder in the first degree against him. Judge Broaddus sentenced Foley to be hanged on February 18, 1898. The jury was out for two hours and 40 minutes. In passing the hanging sentence, Broaddus said he had grave doubts about Foley's guilt at the first trial but that those doubts were swept away in the second trial. "The evidence has shown you to be guilty. While it looks incredible, the chain of circumstantial evidence is complete. I cannot conceive why you should murder your mother and sister," said Broaddus. "You must be one of the most depraved human beings that ever walked the earth. I can not think you murdered them for any motive. You and your God know why you stained your hands with the blood of those it was your duty to love and protect."[70]

However, on appeal Foley was granted a new trial. And, on February 24, 1899, William Foley was acquitted on the charge of murdering his mother. He had been tried on just one court of murder in his third trial and remained under indictment for the murder of his sister. But it was understood that he would never be tried on that charge, as the legal proceedings against Foley came to an end at this point. Some 10 weeks later a brief item noted that Foley was working in a livery stable at Plattsburgh, Missouri.[71]

Eli Shaw

Mrs. Emma Zane, 78, and her daughter, Mrs. Sara Shaw, 42, were killed by what were thought to be burglars who were presumed to have entered the women's residence at 242 Line Street in Camden, New Jersey, at around 4:00 A.M. on October 12, 1897. At least that was the tale told by Eli Shaw, 22 (son of Sarah, grandson of Emma), who said he witnessed the shooting of his mother and grandmother. Police from both Camden and Philadelphia were involved in investigating the case. Both women had died from a single gunshot to the head. Eli was "vigorously" examined by the police later in the day on October 12 but in the end he was not detained. The glass of one of the kitchen windows had apparently been smashed by the burglars in gaining entrance to the house but, as the police discovered, that window had been broken from the inside.

Mrs. Zane had lived with her daughter and grandson in a three-story house she owned. Eli's story was that at about 4:00 A.M. he was disturbed in his sleep; he thought he heard a noise downstairs. But it was not repeated so he did not go downstairs to investigate. All three people slept on the second floor, in separate rooms. He lay awake for a few minutes and then went to get a drink of water. His noise woke the two women and all three were up and in the hallway when Eli suddenly saw two strange men downstairs in the house and called to the women. Then he ran to a window to call to the outside for help. At the same time, two shots rang out and the women screamed. Then all was quiet. Police soon arrived and found the bodies of the two women on the second floor, each in her room; Zane was dead and Shaw would die a few minutes later. On the lower floor police found the silverware packed in a bundle; everything of value on the ground floor of the house had been collected. During the afternoon of October 12, the mayor of Camden offered a reward of $500 for the arrest and conviction of the murderers.[72]

While Eli Shaw was not initially detained by the police he was kept under surveillance and in Camden, on the afternoon of October 15, Shaw was arrested and charged with the murder of his mother and grandmother. On that day, police found a revolver hidden in the chimney of his room and upon that evidence he was taken into custody. He had been questioned a number of times and had never been able to make his stories match. He had claimed he had gone downstairs and thus the burglars must have passed him going up in order to shoot the women. And if that was the case, why had they not shot him? As to his claim that he yelled out for help only moments before the women were killed, it was also proven to be false. A doctor arrived very soon after the yell, with the police, and the doctor found the blood had already coagulated when he arrived— meaning the women had been shot some time before the yell was issued. Also, when the police entered they found no fresh blood visible nor did they find traces of smoke or gunpowder in the air. Meanwhile, a policeman was locked into the cell with Eli, to prevent a suicide attempt. Still, after many hours of questioning the police did not have a confession. Prosecutor Jenkins declared, "We are sure we have the right man. There is no doubt about it."[73]

Both women were buried on October 17. Eli was allowed to attend the funeral. "Shaw acted like a drunken man. He staggered up the front steps of the house with the police at his side, and he reeled as he made his way to the parlor, where the bodies of the two women were," said an observer.

"Standing between the caskets, young Shaw called to God to witness his innocence of the charges against him." The police hoped Eli might confess when he saw the faces of the dead women, but they were disappointed. With Shaw was his fiancée, Maybelle Neilson, who was described as "hysterical."[74]

Much media coverage and general interest was generated by the Shaw case. The motive for the murders was thought to be money, as Eli had been scheduled to be married November 16 and the inheritance from the two women would start him off right. Maybelle Neilson and her family declared a week after his arrest that Eli was innocent and that they were determined to spend their entire fortune—$10,000—to save him.[75]

Everyone thought that Eli would be tried for the two murders together but prosecutor Wilson Jenkins of Camden County surprised people when he announced that Eli would be tried first only for the murder of his grandmother. Jenkins explained that if the jury acquitted him on that charge he would immediately be placed on trial for the murder of his mother.[76]

More drama occurred in the case a day after the announcement from Jenkins. In the Camden County jail, Eli was the recipient, in the mail on January 1, 1898, of a supposed "infernal machine"—a bomb. The package was received at the jail at noon and was addressed to "Eli Shaw, Camden jail." Shaw was reportedly suspicious of it at once as it seemed heavy. After he had removed the wrapping paper Shaw carefully attempted to open the lid. As he did so there was a hiss and a sputter and a puff of smoke. The box itself was pasteboard, about 6" long and 3" wide, and "stained with some substance resembling nitroglycerine." Packed in the paper were four brass cylinders connected by fine copper wires and with a wire running to the lid of the box. Some of the jail officials regarded the matter as a practical joke; others took a more serious view.[77]

Upon examination by authorities the bomb proved to be harmless, not at bomb at all. Contents of the package were shown to be a common dry battery stuffed with manganese of oxide and sal ammoniac, a harmless combination. Jenkins declared it was his belief that the package had been sent to arouse public sympathy for Shaw, as the package had been received just a few days in advance of the start of his trial. Also, Jenkins said he had no doubt Shaw expected the package and merely pretended to be greatly frightened.[78]

As his trial began, on January 4, 1898, it was revealed that Eli stood to inherit between $3,000 and $4,000. The bodies of the two women were found on the second floor, each on the floor of her own bedroom. Neighbors arrived on the scene mere moments after Shaw yelled out from the window "Murder" and "Police." They searched the place but could find no sign of intruders despite the fact Eli told them the two burglars were still inside the house.[79]

On the morning of January 4, on the day it began, the trial of Eli for the murder of his grandmother was brought to a sudden and unexpected termination. Judge Garrison announced the case would be tried at the April term of the court. As to the reason for the sudden termination of the trial, the only explanation made by the court was that the defendant asked that a juror be withdrawn and, after consulting with both sides, the court agreed to the request. It was understood the objection was made against one of the jurors who, it was said, was a member of the Camden Lodge of the Junior Order of American Mechanics, of which Eli Shaw was also a member. That lodge had recently voted an appropriation of money to assist in the defense of Shaw and adopted a resolution expressing a belief in his innocence. When interviewed by the press that afternoon the juror in question said he had withdrawn from the lodge 18 months earlier and had not been to any of its meetings since. No one believed that was the real reason for terminating the trial and a rumor circulated persistently that the real reason for the mistrial was that one or more jurors had been approached in an effort to induce them to vote in a certain way when it came time to case their vote for a verdict.[80]

An allegation of bribery was indeed the underlying reason for the mistrial. Within a few weeks a grand jury was investigating the accusation of "embracery" in connection with the Shaw trial. On January 29 it presented seven true bills of indictment. One was against Harry S. Scovel, the senior counsel for Shaw. Another indictment was against Camden police chief Johnson, and one was against John Meshaw, a man who had been in the panel for the Shaw trial but was not selected as one of the jurors. Scovel's bail of $2,500 was immediately posted by ex–Judge Carrow who, with ex–Judge Westcott, were retained by Scovel as his counsel in the case.[81]

Harry Scovel was charged with embracery in having given Meshaw $20 and also with attempted embracery in having promised Meshaw a much larger amount in case Meshaw was later drawn on the Shaw jury. Samuel Johnson, the chief of police, was charged with approaching a juror named Schiller.[82]

When Scovel stood trial on the bribery charges in April it was also alleged he had offered Jacob Schiller the sum of $100 in exchange for a verdict favorable to his client. Edward Enterken, the county jailer, swore that after the jury was selected, Scovel came to him in the county jail and, calling his attention to the jury list, asked "if Schiller was all right." Enterken said he thought he was. Scovel then told the witness to tell Schiller there was $100 in it for him if he was "all right." When the mistrial was announced, Scovel came to him, testified Enterken, and asked him to never say anything about the $100. Eli Shaw was brought from his cell to testify at Scovel's trial but all he had to say was that he knew nothing about any attempts to bribe people. Scovel was acquitted.[83]

Eli's second trial for the murder of his grandmother started in Camden on April 25. On the morning of April 30, the jury returned with a verdict of not guilty. "Shaw broke down when the verdict was announced, and fell from his chair weeping. The verdict was greeted by applause, and a number of persons in the courtroom were arrested for attempting a demonstration," said an observer. One of those who testified for Shaw was his fiancée, Maybelle Neilson. She said that Eli had no need of money as she planned to buy the house in which the couple would live and to furnish it completely, all with her own money.[84]

Shaw was placed on trial for the third time on a murder charge, on October 4, 1898. That time it was on a charge of having murdered his mother, Mrs. Sarah Shaw. Scovel remained Eli's chief counsel in all his trials. On the morning of October 8, the jury returned with a verdict of not guilty. Later that day he was released from custody, after an incarceration that had lasted about one year. It was reported that "thousands" of people had gathered outside the courtroom hoping, unsuccessfully, to gain access to the courtroom. When the jury's verdict reached the street it "was greeted with cheers by the assemblage."[85]

Upon hearing the verdict, Eli had "a sobbing fit." Scovel sent a telegram to Maybelle Neilson with the verdict and when she received the wire she promptly fainted. She continued to stand behind him and visited him on the evening he was set free. Maybelle had been called the "principal witness" in her fiancé's behalf at the trials and it was understood she had paid for some of his defense.[86]

Soon, though, the couple split up. A formal announcement was made on December 17, 1898, that Maybelle had broken her engagement to Eli and that she never wanted to see him again. Since his release Shaw had made his home at the Neilson mansion in Woodbury, New Jersey. "I realized that all my former friends were cutting my acquaintance because of my association with Eli, and I decided long ago that I could never marry him," Maybelle explained. "But we still harbored him. My sister would not sleep under the same roof with him, and I gave him my final decision yesterday when

I notified him he must leave our house, never to return, as I never wanted to see him again." She continued: "Shaw left last night, taking with him all his belongings. Now I feel a liberty unknown to me for a long time. We took a great deal of interest in the unfortunate young man and did all we could to free him of the horrible charge that hung over him, but our interest ended with his acquittal.... My associations with him in Woodbury have made everything unpleasant for me. Friends would not visit the house."[87]

Less than one year later, in October 1899, Mrs. Eva R. Wood, mother of 19-year-old Eva Wood, both of Camden, declared her daughter was the victim of hypnotic suggestion held over her by Eli. The daughter had met Shaw in the Camden county jail and ever since that time when she gazed upon him behind the bars, for the first time, she had cared for him, complained her mother. Mrs. Neilson (mother of Maybelle) had written to Mrs. Wood warning her against Eli. Mrs. Wood had forbidden Eli to enter her home, she explained, because "for some time past I have regarded him as I would a Svengali. Eva is hypnotized beyond a doubt."[88]

Six months later, in March 1900, William H. Hay and Howard K. Sloan, formerly reporters for a Philadelphia newspaper, were on trial on a charge of conspiring to injure the reputation of Eugene J. Darnell. It was argued the two defendants caused to be published a confession alleged to have been made to them by Eli Shaw in which he had admitted to killing his mother and grandmother and which implicated Darnell as an accessory after the fact. Darnell was arrested but was released and exonerated after his alibi held up. Shaw repudiated the story and Darnell caused the two reporters to be arrested on the charge of conspiracy. As well, Eva Wood—by this time described as Shaw's former fiancée—testified that on the day of the publication of the article containing his supposed confession, Shaw told her that every word of the story was true. Called to the stand, Eli denied the testimony of his former fiancée.[89]

One month after that, at the end of April, Eva Wood came forward to change her story. She said she would now make an affidavit to the effect that the story she told of Eli's confession being true, which she told in court under oath in the Hay/Sloan trial, was false.[90]

Mrs. George Treider

Following a family quarrel on July 16, 1899, in Libertyville, Illinois, Mrs. George Treider shot and killed her mother, Mrs. Christian Foss, wounded her husband, and then killed herself. Treider was shot three times but was expected to recover. Apparently the quarrel was precipitated by longstanding family troubles. During that quarrel Mrs. Treider stepped into a back room and reappeared a moment later with a revolver and opened fire on her mother. The first shot was fatal to Foss and when Treider sprang forward to disarm his wife she shot him three times. He staggered from the house and when he was outside he heard two more shots, the ones that killed his wife. Heated words had been exchanged that morning between Foss and her daughter and Treider was also involved. Things then settled down and the trouble seemed to be over when, after dinner, it broke out anew. Foss was said to be 80 years old and Mrs. Treider was 35; she left two children, seven and five years old.[91]

Chapter Notes

Chapter 1

1. "Parricide in Illinois." *New York Times,* October 21, 1866, p. 3.
2. *Ibid.*
3. *Ibid.*
4. "New York." *Daily Register Call* [Colorado], June 4, 1873, p. 2.
5. "A terrible parricide." *New York Times,* June 4, 1873, p. 8.
6. *Ibid.*
7. *Ibid.*
8. "Illinois." *Georgetown Daily Colorado Miner,* June 7, 1873, p. 2.
9. "The New York tragedy." *Liberty (MO) Weekly Tribune,* July 4, 1873, p. 2.
10. "Mr. Charles O'Connor on parricide." *New York Times,* July 3, 1874, p. 4.
11. "The case of Walworth the parricide." *New York Times,* August 6, 1874, p. 3.
12. "Noted lunatics." *St. Louis Globe Democrat,* October 3, 1875, p. 9.
13. "The boy who killed his father." *Washington Post,* August 27, 1879, p. 2.
14. "Sunday tragedies." *New York Times,* July 19, 1875, p. 8.
15. *Ibid.*
16. "Parricide." *Brooklyn Eagle,* July 19, 1875, p. 2.
17. "The Bailey parricide." *New York Times,* July 22, 1875, p. 8.
18. "The parricide." *Ogden (UT) Standard Examiner,* August 13, 1879, p. 2.
19. "A beaten boy shoots his father." *Reno Weekly Gazette,* August 21, 1879, p. 8.
20. "Another increase." *Salt Lake Tribune,* August 13, 1880.
21. "A thirteen year old boy shoots his father." *Newark (Ohio) Daily Advocate,* July 7, 1882, p. 1.
22. "A son's terrible crime." *Janesville (WI) Daily Gazette,* July 8, 1882, p. 1.
23. No title. *Decatur (IL) Daily Republican,* July 8, 1882, p. 2.
24. "Found guilty of murder." *Fort Wayne (IN) Daily Gazette,* July 30, 1882, p. 4.
25. No title. *Hancock (IA) Herald,* August 12, 1882, p. 2; "Local." *Liberty (MO) Weekly Tribune,* November 24, 1882, p. 3.
26. "Story Co. tragedy." *Perry (IA) Chief,* February 23, 1883, p. 3.
27. "Murdered." *Indiana (PA) Progress,* August 24, 1887, p. 3.
28. "Additional local." *Indiana (PA) Weekly Messenger,* September 21, 1887, p. 2.
29. "Deed of two sons." *Racine (WI) Daily Journal,* November 13, 1893, p. 3.
30. "Butchered his father." *Marshfield (WI) Times,* November 17, 1893, p. 1.
31. "Are let off easy." *Oshkosh (WI) Daily Northwestern,* December 9, 1893, p. 1.
32. "Joins his brother in jail." *Centralia (WI) Enterprise and Tribune,* December 29, 1894, p. 11.
33. "Will January convicted." *Quincy (IL) Journal,* October 12, 1896, p. 1.

Chapter 2

1. "Intemperance and parricide." *Brooklyn Eagle,* April 9, 1846, p. 2.
2. "Parricide and attempted suicide." *New York Times,* October 15, 1851, p. 3.
3. "Murderer convicted." *New York Times,* September 10, 1852, p. 2; "Movements for pardons," *New York Times,* November 1852, p.3

New York Times, November 18, 1852, p. 3.
4. "Shot dead by his son." *Fort Wayne (IN) Daily Gazette,* February 12, 1884, p. 7.
5. "Another murder in Fayette County." *Indiana (PA) Weekly Messenger,* February 13, 1884, p. 2.

6. "Sentences and other business." *Connellsville (PA) Keystone Courier,* June 13, 1884, p. 4.

7. "Charged with parricide." *New York Times,* June 7, 1888, p. 1.

8. "How did Patrick McDermitt die?" *New York Times,* January 23, 1889, p. 8.

9. "City and suburban news." *New York Times,* March 30, 1889, p. 3.

Chapter 3

1. "Parricide." *Brooklyn Eagle,* July 26, 1842, p. 2.

2. "Further particulars of the murder in Watertown, Wis." *Janesville (WI) Gazette,* April 19, 1867, p. 2.

3. *Ibid.*

4. "Trial of a young man in Wisconsin for parricide." *New York Times,* December 10, 1867, p. 2.

5. "Ware's execution yesterday." *New York Times,* December 16, 1871, p. 2; "The New Jersey matricide." *New York Times,* August 19, 1870, p. 2.

6. "The Camden parricide." *New York Times,* January 29, 1871, p. 8, and February 1, 1871, p. 8; "From Philadelphia." *Brooklyn Eagle,* February 1, 1871, p. 3.

7. No title. *Brooklyn Eagle,* February 4, 1871, p. 2; "Interview with Ware." *New York Times,* February 11, 1871, p. 2.

8. "The Camden parricide respited." *New York Herald,* April 8, 1871, p. 10; "The frequency of parricide." *New York Times,* May 2, 1871, p. 4; "The Ware murder." *New York Herald,* July 19, 1871, p. 5.

9. "Waiting for death." *New York Herald,* November 2, 1871, p. 5; "Sentenced to be hanged." *Brooklyn Eagle,* November 2, 1871, p. 3.

10. "Ware to be hanged today." *New York Times,* December 15, 1871, p. 2.

11. "Ware's execution yesterday." *New York Times,* December 16, 1871, p. 2.

12. "A parricide hanged." *New York Herald,* December 16, 1871, p. 2.

13. "A murderer hung." *Indiana (PA) Progress,* January 4, 1872, p. 2.

14. "A lesson from the gallows." *Indiana (PA) Progress,* February 15, 1872, p. 3.

15. No title. *Fitchburg (MA) Daily Sentinel,* September 30, 1878, p. 3.

16. "Crime and criminals." *New York Times,* March 14, 1879, p. 2.

17. "Varied aspects of crime." *New York Times,* March 15, 1879, p. 2.

18. "Connecticut." *Titusville (PA) Herald,* May 12, 1880, p. 1.

19. "The death of a parricide." *New York Times,* May 14, 1880, p. 5.

20. "Murdered and disfigured." *New York Times,* September 27, 1879, p. 2.

21. *Ibid.*

22. No title. *Fitchburg (MA) Daily Sentinel,* October 15, 1879, p. 2.

23. "A destroying angel." *Helena (MT) Independent,* June 26, 1881, p. 2.

24. *Ibid.*

25. "A parricide pardoned." *Las Cruces (NM) Rio Grande Republican,* March 26, 1887, p. 2.

26. "Startling development about the patricide." *Newark (OH) Daily Advocate,* May 22, 1882, p. 1; No title. *Decatur (IL) Daily Republican,* May 22, 1882, p. 2.

27. "Iowa items." *Perry (IA) Chief,* February 2, 1883, p. 6.

28. "May result in his hanging." *Lincoln Nebraska State Journal,* September 14, 1893, p. 2.

29. "Believed to be dead." *Lincoln (NB) Evening News,* September 15, 1897, p. 3; "Parricide hunted to Death." *Traverse (MI) Morning Record,* September 16, 1897, p. 4.

30. "Sacrificed father." *Washington Post,* June 19, 1898, p. 4.

31. *Ibid.*

32. "Topeka patricide trial." *New York Times,* December 9, 1898, p. 7.

33. "Kansas patricide convicted." *New York Times,* December 25, 1898, p. 2.

34. No title. *Aspen (CO) Tribune,* December 29, 1898, p. 2.

35. "Kansas patricide pleads innocence." *New York Times,* March 28, 1899, p. 8.

36. "John Collins now behind prison walls." *Lincoln (NB) Evening News and Daily Call,* April 6, 1899, p. 1.

37. "Son kills father." *Oshkosh (WI) Daily Northwestern,* November 13, 1899, p. 1.

38. "Cigarette fiend shoots his father." *Quincy (IL) Daily Whig,* November 18, 1899, p. 3.

Chapter 4

1. "Probably fatal stabbing affray." *Brooklyn Eagle,* August 20, 1860, p. 2; "The parricide in Williamsburgh." *Brooklyn Eagle,* September 1, 1860, p. 3.

2. "The parricide case." *Brooklyn Eagle,* November 21, 1860, p. 7.

3. "The end of a parricide." *Brooklyn Eagle,* December 14, 1863, p. 2.

4. "The parricide at Concord." *Chicago Tribune,* February 27, 1865, p. 2.

5. "Parricide in Mayfield." *Elyria (OH) Independent Democrat,* November 28, 1866, p. 2.

6. "Horrible parricide." *Chicago Tribune,* November 24, 1866, p. 2.

7. "The parricide in Maine." *New York Times,* May 10, 1874, p. 7.

8. No title. *Toronto Globe and Mail,* December 2, 1875, p. 3.

9. "A hunchback parricide." *New York Times,* January 28, 1878, p. 3.

10. "Killed by his son." *New York Times,* January 23, 1879, p. 2; "A parricide arrested." *New York Times,* January 24, 1879, p. 5; "Sentenced for parricide." *Brooklyn Eagle,* February 15, 1879, p. 4.

11. "Suspected of parricide." *New York Times,* January 14, 1881, p. 2.

12. *Ibid.*

13. "Rooney killed by his son." *New York Times,* January 15, 1881, p. 8.

14. "Fooling the police." *Brooklyn Eagle,* July 13, 1887, p. 4.

15. "A parricide hunted for thirteen years." *New York Times,* October 13, 1893, p. 5.

16. "A terrible tragedy." *Indiana (PA) Democrat,* June 24, 1880, p. 2.

17. *Ibid.*

18. "The execution of Allison." *Indiana (PA) Democrat,* February 11, 1882, p. 3.

19. "Hanging a parricide." *New York Times,* February 18, 1882, p. 2.

20. "Official notice." *Indiana (PA) Weekly Messenger,* March 1, 1882, p. 2.

21. "Parricide." *Cambridge (OH) Jeffersonian,* October 27, 1881, p. 3.

22. "A shocking history." *Chicago Tribune,* November 9, 1881, p. 5.

23. "Parricide." *Toronto Globe and Mail,* May 15, 1883, p. 2.

24. "Like the Allison case." *Indiana (PA) Weekly Messenger,* August 8, 1883, p. 3.

25. "A parricide found guilty." *Newark (OH) Daily Advocate,* February 29, 1884, p. 1.

26. "Parricide." *Manitoba (Winnipeg) Free Press,* January 3, 1884, p. 1.

27. "Trial of Stanley Griffith." *East Liverpool (OH) Saturday Review,* December 6, 1884, p. 2; "From Wednesday's daily." *East Liverpool (OH) Saturday Review,* December 11, 1886, p. 8.

28. "A parricide." *Brooklyn Eagle,* April 29, 1884, p. 4.

29. "A wicked conspiracy." *Atlanta Constitution,* April 30, 1884, p. 4.

30. "A demoniacal deed." *Williamsport (PA) Daily Gazette and Bulletin,* May 1, 1884, p. 1.

31. "A harmless old man dragged from his bed and hanged." *Lowell (PA) Sun,* May 5, 1884, p. 8.

32. "Cold blooded murder." *Waterloo Iowa State Reporter,* May 8, 1884, p. 9.

33. "Parricides lynched." *Quincy (IL) Daily Journal,* February 25, 1885, p. 1.

34. "A terrible nemesis." *Titusville (PA) Herald,* February 5, 1885, p. 1.

35. "Mob law in Iowa." *Decatur (IL) Morning Review,* February 6, 1885, p. 1.

36. "Lynched." *Marshfield (WI) Times and Gazette,* February 14, 1885, p. 4.

37. "Patricide." *Ogden (UT) Standard Examiner,* July 28, 1887; "A parricide will probably be lynched." *Washington Post,* July 28, 1887, p. 3; "Pointed paragraphs." *Massillon (OH) Independent,* March 30, 1888, p. 1.

38. "A father murdered by his son." *Washington Post,* August 7, 1888, p. 7.

39. "General news." *Gettysburg (PA) Star and Sentinel,* August 14, 1888, p. 3.

40. "Sentenced to be hanged." *New York Times,* November 11, 1888, p. 9.

41. "Successfully executed." *Reno Evening Gazette,* January 3, 1889, p. 2.

42. "Met his fate bravely." *Washington Post,* January 4, 1889, p. 2.

43. "Parricide hanged." *Dunkirk (NY) Observer-Journal,* January 4, 1889, p. 1.

44. "Suicide and parricide." *Ogden (UT) Standard Examiner,* November 30, 1889.

45. "A diabolical deed." *Salt Lake Tribune,* December 16, 1890.

46. "The boy who killed his father." *New York Times,* December 17, 1890, p. 3.

47. "Horrible tragedy in Chicago." *Olean (NY) Democrat,* December 18, 1890, p. 1; "Condensed Telegrams." *Cedar Rapids (IA) Evening Gazette,* May 9, 1891, p. 1.

48. "The Carpenter murder." *Middletown (NY) Daily News,* December 14, 1893, p. 1.

49. "Parricide hung." *Davenport (IA) Daily Leader,* June 14, 1894, p. 1.

50. "Shrouded in mystery." *Titusville (PA) Herald,* November 18, 1899, p. 1.

51. "Son confesses patricide." *New York Times,* November 22, 1899, p. 8; "Parricide sentenced to death." *Tyrone (PA) Daily Herald,* March 30, 1900, p. 1.

Chapter 5

1. "The murder in Springfield." *New York Times,* December 16, 1867, p. 2.
2. "Sentence of a matricide at Springfield, Mass." *New York Times,* May 27, 1868, p. 5.
3. "Shocking matricide." *New York Herald,* December 30, 1869, p. 7.
4. "Mead the matricide." *Brooklyn Eagle,* February 23, 1870, p. 3.
5. "A probable matricide." *New York Times,* August 21, 1872, p. 8; "The Dykes matricide case." *New York Herald,* August 28, 1872, p. 8.
6. "A brutal son—manslaughter in the fourth degree." *New York Times,* October 26, 1872, p. 4.
7. "Execution of a matricide." *New York Herald,* September 7, 1872, p. 7.
8. *Ibid.*
9. *Ibid.*
10. "The extreme penalty." *New York Times,* September 7, 1892, p. 4.
11. "Sunday crime." *New York Times,* August 30, 1875, p. 8.
12. *Ibid.*
13. "The Callaghan matricide." *New York Times,* September 3, 1875, p. 8.
14. "An alleged matricide." *New York Times,* October 22, 1875, p. 8.
15. "The trial of Thomas Callaghan." *Brooklyn Eagle,* October 22, 1875, p. 4.
16. "The Callaghan matricide." *New York Times,* October 23, 1875, p. 3.
17. "Kills his mother at Rockford, Ill." *Chicago Tribune,* April 30, 1893, p. 5.
18. "Burke a monster in crime." *Monroe (WI) Evening Times,* May 6, 1893, p. 4.
19. "Given a life term." *Iowa City (IA) Daily Citizen,* May 20, 1893, p. 1.
20. "Parrott hanged." *Toronto Globe and Mail,* June 24, 1899, p. 23.

Chapter 6

1. "Matricide." *New York Times,* January 15, 1874, p. 8.
2. "The Bergen matricide." *New York Times,* January 16, 1874, p. 5.
3. "The Jersey City matricide." *New York Times,* January 16, 1874, p. 4.
4. "The Freeman matricide." *New York Times,* March 12, 1874, p. 2.
5. "The Freeman matricide." *New York Times,* March 15, 1874, p. 8.
6. "The work of criminals." *New York Times,* January 7, 1883, p. 7.
7. No title. *Janesville (WI) Daily Gazette,* February 22, 1883, p. 4.
8. "A matricide's suicide." *Chicago Tribune,* July 13, 1882, p. 11.
9. "Killed his mother." *Cedar Rapids (IA) Evening Gazette,* April 23, 1888, p. 1.
10. "Tragedy near Sioux City." *Waterloo (IA) Courier,* April 25, 1888, p. 1.
11. "The Eaton murder." *Hamilton (OH) Daily Democrat,* January 14, 1889, p. 3.
12. "Confessed his crime." *Newark (OH) Daily Advocate,* January 15, 1889, p. 1.
13. *Ibid.*
14. "He was not lynched." *Newark (OH) Daily Advocate,* January 16, 1889, p. 1.
15. "Convicted." *Newark (OH) Daily Advocate,* May 3, 1889, p. 1.
16. "Murderer Sharkey reprieved." *New Philadelphia Ohio Democrat,* September 25, 1890, p. 6.
17. "A double execution." *Sandusky (OH) Daily Register,* December 19, 1890, p. 1.
18. "Singular property suit." *New York Times,* October 23, 1892, p. 13.
19. "A woman murdered." *New York Times,* January 26, 1889, p. 5.
20. "The Latimer examination." *Marshall (MI) Daily Chronicle,* February 1, 1889, p. 1.
21. "Silly women petting a matricide." *Frederick (MD) News,* February 4, 1889, p. 1.
22. "Murdered his mother." *Hawarden (IA) Independent,* April 11, 1889, p. 6.
23. "Latimer found guilty." *Janesville (WI) Daily Gazette,* May 7, 1889, p. 2; "General news of the week." *Athens (OH) Messenger,* May 16, 1889, p. 1
24. "Insane or a good actor." *Indiana (PA) Progress,* July 24, 1889, p. 6.
25. "Deep prison plot." *Winnipeg (Manitoba) Free Press,* August 27, 1889, p. 1.
26. "Brevities." *Marshall (MI) Daily Chronicle,* April 16, 1890, p. 3.
27. "Brevities." *Marshall (MI) Daily Chronicle,* February 13, 1891, p. 3.
28. "Escaped murdered." *Aspen (CO) Daily Chronicle,* March 17, 1893, p. 1.
29. "Poisoned the guards." *Brooklyn Eagle,* March 27, 1893, p. 1.
30. "Drugged the guard." *Davenport (IA) Tribune,* March 28, 1893, p. 3.
31. "A conspiracy." *Cedar Rapids (IA) Evening Gazette,* March 29, 1893, p. 1.
32. "Murderer Latimer captured." *Cedar*

Rapids (IA) Evening Gazette, March 29, 1893, p. 1.

33. "The triple murderer." *Ogden (UT) Standard,* March 30, 1893, p. 1.

34. "Murders in Michigan." *Washington Post,* March 31, 1893, p. 4.

35. "The Haight inquest." *Decatur (IL) Daily Review,* April 1, 1893, p. 7.

36. *Ibid.*

37. "Irving Latimer out." *Marshall (MI) Daily Chronicle,* October 27, 1893, p. 1.

Chapter 7

1. "Matricide." *Liberty (MO) Weekly Tribune,* May 25, 1849, p. 1.

2. "Execution of a matricide." *New York Times,* November 5, 1860, p. 5.

3. "Matricide in Willett Street." *New York Times,* June 13, 1860, p. 8; "Law reports." *New York Times,* October 1, 1860, p. 2.

4. "Horrible murder of a mother by her son." *New York Times,* December 9, 1861, p. 8.

5. "The matricide in First Avenue." *New York Times,* December 10, 1861, p. 8.

6. "Case of the matricide McGill." *New York Times,* December 14, 1861, p. 5.

7. "The Shawangunk murderer." *Port Jervis (NY) Evening Gazette,* April 15, 1871, p. 1.

8. "Current events." *Brooklyn Eagle,* February 28, 1881, p. 2.

9. "A perfect monster." *Bangor (ME) Daily Whig and Courier,* March 11, 1881, p. 3.

10. "Local and state news." *Augusta (ME) Daily Kennebec Journal,* May 11, 1881, p. 3.

11. "Local and state news." *Augusta (ME) Daily Kennebec Journal,* May 12, 1881, p. 3.

12. "Local and state news." *Augusta (ME) Daily Kennebec Journal,* May 13, 1881, p. 3.

13. No title. *Augusta (ME) Daily Kennebec Journal,* May 14, 1881, p. 2.

14. "An alleged matricide." *Brooklyn Eagle,* December 7, 1884, p. 1.

15. "Later." *New Phildelphia Ohio Democrat,* December 11, 1884, p. 2.

16. "Hangman's day." *Galveston Daily News,* June 20, 1885, p. 2.

17. *Ibid.*

18. "An unnatural murder." *Syracuse (NY) Daily Standard,* October 4, 1887, p. 1.

19. "Slain by her own son." *New York Times,* October 4, 1887, p. 2.

20. *Ibid.*

21. "Asbury Hawkins's crime." *New York Times,* October 5, 1887, p. 8.

22. "Hawkins assigns his property." *Brooklyn Eagle,* January 8, 1888, p. 9.

23. "Found in time." *Brooklyn Eagle,* April 17, 1888, p. 6.

24. "A matricide sentenced." *New York Times,* October 23, 1888, p. 8.

25. "Murdered his mother." *Fitchburg (MA) Sentinel,* December 11, 1888, p. 4.

26. Another murderer gone." *Titusville (PA) Herald,* December 12, 1888, p. 1; "Death of a matricide." *New York Times,* December 12, 1888, p. 3.

27. "Brief mention." *Frederick (MD) News,* December 14, 1888, p. 1.

28. "A son kills his mother." *Washington Post,* July 4, 1889, p. 2.

29. *Ibid.*

30. "Herman Probst may recover." *New York Times,* July 5, 1889, p. 8; "The Probst matricide." *New York Times,* July 6, 1889, p. 8; "Condensed telegrams." *Cedar Rapids (IA) Evening Gazette,* July 15, 1889, p. 1.

31. "A matricide captured." *New York Times,* September 29, 1891, p. 2.

32. "That improbable son." *Boulder (CO) Daily Camera,* September 29, 1891, p. 1.

33. "Telegraphic brevities." *Boise Idaho Daily Statesman,* November 29, 1891, p. 4.

34. "A matricide." *Cranbury (NJ) Press,* May 25, 1894, p. 4.

Chapter 8

1. "Horrible matricide in New York." *Chicago Tribune,* February 11, 1859, p. 2; No title. *Gettysburg (PA) Adams Sentinel,* February 14, 1859, p. 2.

2. "A female parricide." *Janesville (WI) Daily Gazette,* October 18, 1884, p. 3.

3. "A strange crime." *Davenport (IA) Morning Tribune,* December 2, 1888, p. 3.

4. "Killed her mother." *Fitchburg (MA) Sentinel,* October 31, 1892, p. 1.

5. "Murdered her mother." *Decatur (IL) Daily Republican,* November 1, 1892, p. 1.

6. "Chapter of crimes." *Lima (OH) Daily Times,* November 1, 1892, p. 1; "Mrs. Marean is insane." *Trenton (NJ) Times,* November 18, 1892, p. 3.

7. "John Roessler's death." *North Adams (MA) Transcript,* November 21, 1895, p. 4.

8. "The Roessler mystery." *North Adams (MA) Transcript,* November 22, 1895, p. 4.

9. "Lost his life." *Oakland Tribune,* February 20, 1895, p. 1; "A baby parricide." *Portsmouth (OH) Daily Times,* February 26, 1895, p. 2.

10. "The Bliss poisoning case." *Brooklyn Eagle,* September 4, 1895, p. 1.

11. *Ibid.*

12. "No more arrests made." *New York Times,* September 8, 1895, p. 8.

13. "Mrs. Fleming's letters." *New York Times,* June 16, 1896, p. 6.

14. "The Fleming case." *Manti (UT) Messenger,* September 4, 1896.

15. "Two fair homicides." *Waterloo (IA) Daily Reporter,* May 5, 1899, p. 2.

16. "Murdered her mother." *Fort Wayne (IN) News,* May 5, 1899, p. 2.

17. "She killed her mother." *Quincy (IL) Weekly Whig,* May 11, 1899, p. 3.

18. "Mrs. Styles acquitted." *Lima (OH) Daily News,* July 26, 1899, p. 1.

19. "Jury weeps for Mrs. Styles." *Chicago Tribune,* July 21, 1899, p. 12.

20. Mrs. Styles defense begins." *Chicago Tribune,* July 22, 1899, p. 9.

21. "Mrs. Styles goes free." *Chicago Tribune,* July 26, 1899, p. 8.

Chapter 9

1. "The case of parricide in Dracut—terrible depravity." *New York Times,* January 7, 1858, p. 5.

2. *Ibid.*

3. "Miscellaneous." *New York Times,* June 22, 1859, p. 3.

4. No title. *Waterloo Iowa State Reporter,* July 10, 1872, p. 1.

5. No title. *Centerville (IA) Citizen,* July 27, 1872, p. 1.

6. No title. *Dubuque (IA) Herald,* January 28, 1873, p. 1; No title. *Centerville (IA) Citizen,* February 8, 1873, p. 2.

7. No title. *Waterloo (IA) Daily Courier,* January 29, 1898, p. 1.

8. "An old man's mysterious death." *New York Times,* October 5, 1875, p. 7.

9. "On trial for parricide." *New York Times,* January 6, 1876, p. 6.

10. "Convicted of parricide." *New York Times,* January 30, 1881, p. 7.

11. "The doomed parricides." *Fort Wayne (IN) Daily Gazette,* June 25, 1881, p. 1.

12. "Alleged murderers respited." *Fort Wayne (IN) Daily Gazette,* June 25, 1881, p. 1.

13. "Respite granted." *Decatur (IL) Daily Review,* June 25, 1881, p. 1.

14. "Confessing to parricide." *New York Times,* July 7, 1881, p. 2.

15. No title. *Decatur (IL) Daily Republican,* July 22, 1881, p. 2.

16. "The Talbott murder." *Waterloo Iowa State Reporter,* August 10, 1881, p. 6.

17. "The shooting of Dr. Talbott." *Galveston Daily News,* September 21, 1880, p. 1.

18. No title. *Atchison (KS) Globe,* September 21, 1880, p. 4.

19. No title. *Atchison (KS) Globe,* October 27, 1880, p. 4.

20. No title. *Atchison (KS) Globe,* November 2, 1880, p. 4.

21. "Butchered by babes." *Calliope (IA) Independent,* February 21, 1884, p. 1.

22. "Horrible parricide." *Manitoba (Winnipeg) Daily Free Press,* February 16, 1884, p. 1.

23. "Young criminals." *Fort Wayne (IN) Daily Gazette,* March 10, 1884, p. 10.

24. "A brutal parricide." *Connellsville (PA) Courier,* August 19, 1892, p. 1.

25. *Ibid.*

26. "Convicted of killing their father." *New York Times,* April 7, 1893, p. 2; "The East." *Maquoketa (IA) Jackson Sentinel,* April 20, 1893, p. 2.

27. "Arrested for patricide." *Quincy (IL) Daily Whig,* November 15, 1892, p. 5.

28. "Accused of their father's murder." *Brooklyn Eagle,* November 15, 1892, p. 1.

29. "Slain by his sons." *Racine (WI) Daily Journal,* November 15, 1892, p. 3.

30. "Brevities." *Davenport (IA) Tribune,* February 10, 1893, p. 4.

31. "The Lyndon murder." *Davenport (IA) Daily Leader,* April 10, 1893, p. 7, and "Will never squeal." *Davenport (IA) Weekly Leader,* June 14, 1893, p. 5.

32. "Accused of his father's murder." *Brooklyn Eagle,* July 20, 1893, p. 5.

33. "Says he killed his father." *Janesville (WI) Gazette,* November 7, 1893, p. 1.

34. "Fourteen years for Swarthout." *Racine (WI) Daily Journal,* November 17, 1893, p. 3.

35. "They regret it." *Decatur (IL) Daily Republican,* February 13, 1896, p. 8.

36. "On trial at last." *Decatur (IL) Daily Republican,* October 20, 1893, p. 3, and "Not guilty." October 28, 1893, p. 4.

37. "In big luck." *Decatur (IL) Daily Republican,* October 30, 1893, p. 3.

38. "The Sullivan outrage." *Decatur (IL) Daily Republican,* January 25, 1896, p. 8.

39. "Will lynch Atterberry." *Decatur (IL) Daily Review,* January 26, 1896, p. 1.
40. "Mob spirit." *Decatur (IL) Daily Republican,* January 28, 1896, p. 4.
41. "A woman in the case." *Decatur (IL) Bulletin-Sentinel,* February 1, 1896, p. 1.
42. "Judge Lynch." *Decatur (IL) Daily Republican,* February 12, 1896, p. 8.
43. "Lynching echoes." *Decatur (IL) Daily Republican,* February 14, 1896, p. 3.
44. "Lynchers go free." *Decatur (IL) Daily Republican,* May 6, 1896, p. 8.
45. "Held for murdering their father." *Chicago Tribune,* March 15, 1893, p. 6.
46. "Shot and killed four men." *New York Times,* August 7, 1893, p. 5.

Chapter 10

1. "Murder and parricide." *Canton (OH) Repository,* April 7, 1842, p. 3; "Murder in Genesee Co. N.Y." *Milwaukee Sentinel and Farmer,* April 9, 1842, p. 2; "A parricide." *Brooklyn Eagle,* March 17, 1843, p. 2.
2. "Horrid murder." *New York Times,* March 22, 1854, p. 2; "A parricide sentenced." *Brooklyn Eagle,* November 3, 1854, p. 1.
3. "Horrible murder." *Brooklyn Eagle,* January 12, 1858, p. 2.
4. "Horrible murder at Poolville, N.Y." *Brooklyn Eagle,* January 14, 1858, p. 2.
5. "Terrible crime in Racine Co." *Janesville (WI) Gazette,* April 19, 1867, p. 2.
6. "Sentence of Bevins the Michigan parricide." *Chicago Tribune,* July 12, 1865, p. 3.
7. "The murder in Connecticut." *New York Times,* August 4, 1865, p. 2.
8. "Starkweather." *New York Times,* August 18, 1866, p. 8.
9. "A mother and her son murdered for gain." *New York Herald,* November 9, 1869, p. 4.
10. "Virginia." *New York Herald,* November 9, 1869, p. 20.
11. "A Virginia horror." *New York Herald,* November 24, 1869, p. 22.
12. *Ibid.*
13. *Ibid.*
14. "A monster sentenced to death." *New York Times,* August 5, 1870, p. 5.
15. A quadruple tragedy." *Atlanta Constitution,* February 6, 1876.
16. "A horrible butchery." *Dubuque (IA) Herald,* February 2, 1876, p. 1.
17. "Overalls and murder." *Fitchburg (MA) Sentinel,* February 10, 1876, p. 1.
18. "Parricide and suicide." *Elyria (OH) Weekly Republican,* August 1, 1878, p. 8.
19. "Tragedy at Rockford." *Toronto Globe and Mail,* July 25, 1878, p. 1; and "The Rockford tragedy." July 26, 1878, p. 1.
20. "A son murders his father." *Indiana (PA) Progress,* November 15, 183, p. 3.
21. *Ibid.*
22. "A terrible crime." *Indiana (PA) Democrat,* November 15, 1883, p. 3.
23. "Joe Sarver, the parricide." *Indiana (PA) Weekly Messenger,* November 21, 1883, p. 3.
24. "The verdict of the jury in the Sarver trial." *Indiana (PA) Democrat,* March 13, 1884, p. 3.
25. "The sentence of Sarver." *Indiana (PA) Democrat,* May 8, 1884, p. 3.
26. "The gallows." *Indiana (PA) Democrat,* September 25, 1884, p. 3.
27. *Ibid.*
28. "Murder at Edgewood." *Waterloo (IA) Courier,* July 24, 1889, p. 1.
29. "A youthful murderer." *Sandusky (OH) Daily Register,* July 27, 1889, p. 1.
30. "A boy's terrible crime." *New York Times,* July 28, 1889, p. 16.
31. "A parricide's story." *Oxford Junction (IA) Oxford Mirror,* August 1, 1889, p. 4.
32. No title. *Oelwein (IA) Register,* October 24, 1889, p. 5.
33. "A young life criminal." *New York Times,* January 13, 1890, p. 5; No title. *Tyrone (PA) Herald,* January 30, 1890, p. 7.
34. "Ought to go to the reform school." *Orange City (IA) Sioux County Herald,* February 27, 1890, p. 5.
35. "All want pardon." *Waterloo (IA) Daily Courier,* December 9, 1895, p. 4.
36. No title. *Waterloo Iowa State Reporter,* December 12, 1895, p. 5.
37. "A pathetic letter." *Semi-Weekly Cedar Falls (IA) Gazette,* February 9, 1897, p. 1.
38. No title. *Waterloo (IA) Daily Courier,* January 29, 1898, p. 1.
39. "No pardon for Elkins." *Hawarden (IA) Independent,* March 17, 1898, p. 2.
40. "Wesley Elkins is free." *Des Moines Daily Leader,* April 20, 1902, p. 18.
41. No title. *Oxford Junction (IA) Oxford Mirror,* July 23, 1908, p. 1.
42. "A demon's deed." *Galveston Daily News,* April 1, 1892, p. 3.
43. *Ibid.*

44. "Shaw soon to be tried." *Galveston Daily News,* April 8, 1892, p. 3.

45. "Shaw must die." *Galveston Daily News,* April 20, 1892, p. 3.

46. "Another trial for Shaw." *Galveston Daily News,* June 25, 1892, p. 3.

47. "Walter Shaw on trial." *Galveston Daily News,* December 13, 1892, p. 2.

48. "The Houston murderer." *Galveston Daily News,* June 24, 1893, p. 3.

49. "A title to Shaw's body." *Galveston Daily News,* July 27, 1893, p. 3.

50. "Shaw disappointed by reprieve." *New York Times,* July 29, 1893, p. 9.

51. "Inebrity and crime." *Galveston Daily News,* July 30, 1893, p. 3.

52. "Shaw will be hanged." *Galveston Daily News,* August 4, 1893, p. 3.

53. "Justice is done." *Galveston Daily News,* August 5, 1893, p. 3.

54. *Ibid.*

55. "Shaw contract settled." *Galveston Daily News,* August 8, 1893, p. 3.

56. "Story of the double crime." *New York Times,* June 6, 1893, p. 2.

57. "The acquittal of Miss Borden." *New York Times,* June 21, 1893, p. 4.

58. "Bequest for tomb of slain father." *New York Times,* June 8, 1927, p. 20.

59. "Hanging is too good for him." *Ogden (UT) Standard Examiner,* January 15, 1893.

60. "Work of a brutal son." *Brooklyn Eagle,* January 15, 1893, p. 20.

61. "An idler's crime." *Frederick (MD) News,* January 16, 1893, p. 1.

62. "Young patricide dies in prison." *Washington Post,* June 29, 1894, p. 6.

63. "Killed his father and mother." *Oshkosh (WI) Daily Northwestern,* November 2, 1894, p. 1; "A Buffalo parricide." *Middletown (NY) Daily Argus,* November 3, 1894, p. 1; "Shot his father and mother." *New York Times,* November 3, 1894, p. 9.

64. "Recovers from trance." *Waukesha (WI) Freeman,* January 13, 1898, p. 6.

65. "Double murder." *Fort Wayne (IN) Sentinel,* November 18, 1896, p. 1.

66. "Horrible murder." *Reno Evening Gazette,* November 18, 1896, p. 1.

67. "The son is being watched." *Waterloo (IA) Daily Reporter,* November 19, 1896, p. 1.

68. "Lynching threatened." *Trenton (NJ) Evening Times,* November 23, 1896, p. 4.

69. "Sheriff disperses a mob." *Alton (IL) Evening Telegraph,* October 21, 1897, p. 4.

70. "Sentenced to hang." *Galveston Daily News,* January 2, 18908, p. 1.

71. "Acquitted of matricide." *Washington Post,* February 25, 1899, p. 11; "Missouri matters." *Moberly (MO) Weekly Monitor,* May 5, 1899, p. 4.

72. "Camden women murdered." *New York Times,* October 13, 1897, p. 4.

73. "Eli Shaw under arrest." *New York Times,* October 16, 1897, p. 4.

74. "Camden victims buried." *New York Times,* October 17, 1897, p. 17.

75. "Camden murder mystery." *Washington Post,* October 21, 1897, p. 9.

76. "Eli Shaw's murder trial." *New York Times,* January 1, 1898, p. 5.

77. "Attempt to kill Eli Shaw." *Washington Post,* January 2, 1898, p. 9.

78. "Eli Shaw's bomb harmless." *New York Times,* January 3, 1898, p. 2.

79. "Shaw placed on trial." *Washington Post,* January 4, 1898, p. 3.

80. "Eli Shaw's trial stopped." *New York Times,* January 5, 1898, p. 4.

81. "The Shaw jury case." *New York Times,* January 30, 1898, p. 2.

82. "The Camden embracery charges." *New York Times,* February 1, 1898, p. 3.

83. "Lawyer Scovel on trial." *New York Times,* April 7, 1898, p. 4.

84. "Eli Shaw not guilty." *Washington Post,* May 1, 1898, p. 14.

85. "Eli Shaw acquitted." *Washington Post,* October 9, 1898, p. 2.

86. "Eli Shaw a free man." *New York Times,* October 9, 1898, p. 3.

87. "Eli Shaw jilted." *Trenton (NJ) Evening Times,* December 17, 1898, p. 1.

88. "Says girl is hypnotized." *Athens (OH) Messenger and Herald,* October 5, 1899, p. 2.

89. "The Eli Shaw confession." *Waterloo (IA) Daily Reporter,* March 28, 1900, p. 2.

90. "That Eli Shaw business." *Waterloo (IA) Daily Reporter,* April 26, 1900, p. 2.

91. "Killer mother and herself." *North Adams (MA) Transcript,* July 17, 1899, p. 6; "A fatal family row." *New York Times,* July 17, 1899, p. 2.

Bibliography

"Accused of his father's murder." *Brooklyn Eagle,* July 20, 1893, p. 5.

"Accused of their father's murder." *Brooklyn Eagle,* November 15, 1892, p. 1.

"Acquittal of matricide." *Washington Post,* February 25, 1899, p. 11.

"The acquittal of Miss Borden." *New York Times,* June 21, 1893, p. 4.

"Additional local." *Indiana (PA) Weekly Messenger,* September 21, 1887, p. 2.

"All want pardon." *Waterloo (IA) Daily Courier,* December 9, 1895, p. 4.

"An alleged matricide." *New York Times,* October 22, 1875, p. 2.

"An alleged matricide." *Brooklyn Eagle,* December 7, 1884, p. 1.

"Alleged murderers respited." *Fort Wayne (IN) Daily Gazette,* June 25, 1881, p. 1.

"Another increase." *Salt Lake Tribune,* August 13, 1880.

"Another murder in Fayette County." *Indiana (PA) Weekly Messenger,* February 13, 1884, p. 2.

"Another murderer gone." *Titusville (PA) Herald,* December 12, 1888, p. 1.

"Another trial for Shaw." *Galveston Daily News,* June 25, 1892, p. 3.

"Are let off easy." *Oshkosh (WI) Daily Northwestern,* December 9, 1893, p. 1.

"Arrested for patricide." *Quincy (IL) Daily Whig,* November 15, 1892, p. 5.

"Asbury Hawkins's crime." *New York Times,* October 5, 1887, p. 8.

Aspen (CO) Tribune, December 29, 1898, p. 2,

Atchison (KS) Globe, November 2, 1880, p. 4 [no title].

Atchison (KS) Globe, October 27, 1880, p. 4 [no title].

Atchison (KS) Globe, September 21, 1880, p. 4 [no title].

"Attempt to kill Eli Shaw." *Washington Post,* January 2, 1898, p. 9.

Augusta Daily (ME) Kennebec Journal, May 14, 1881, p. 2 [no title].

"A baby parricide." *Portsmouth (OH) Daily Times,* February 26, 1895, p. 2.

"The Bailey parricide." *New York Times,* July 22, 1875, p. 8.

"A beaten boy shoots his father." *Reno Weekly Gazette,* August 21, 1879, p. 8.

"Believed to be dead." *Lincoln (NB) Evening News,* September 15, 1897, p. 3.

"Bequest for tomb of slain father." *New York Times,* June 8, 1927, p. 20.

"The Bergen matricide." *New York Times,* January 16, 1874, p. 5.

"The Bliss poisoning case." *Brooklyn Eagle,* September 4, 1895, p. 1.

"The boy who killed his father." *Washington Post,* August 27, 1879, p. 2.

"The boy who killed his father." *New York Times,* December 17, 1890, p. 3.

"A boy's terrible crime." *New York Times,* July 28, 1889, p. 16.

"Brevities." *Marshall (MI) Daily Chronicle,* April 16, 1890, p. 3.

"Brevities." *Marshall (MI) Daily Chronicle,* February 13, 1891, p. 3.

"Brevities. *Davenport (IA) Tribune,* February 10, 1893, p. 4.

"Brief mention." *Frederick (MD) News,* December 14, 1888, p. 1.

Brooklyn Eagle, February 4, 1871, p. 2 [no title].

"A brutal parricide." *Connellsville (PA) Courier,* August 19, 1892, p. 1.

"A brutal son-manslaughter in the fourth degree." *New York Times,* October 26, 1872, p. 4.

"A Buffalo parricide." *Middletown (NY) Daily Argus,* November 3, 1894, p. 1.

"Burke a monster in crime." *Monroe (WI) Evening Times,* May 6, 1893, p. 4.

"Butchered by babes." *Calliope (IA) Independent,* February 21, 1884, p. 1.

"Butchered his father." *Marshfield (WI) Times,* November 17, 1893, p. 1.

"The Callaghan matricide." *New York Times,* September 3, 1875, p. 8.

"The Callaghan matricide." *New York Times,* October 23, 1875, p. 3.

"The Camden embracery charges." *New York Times,* February 1, 1898, p. 3.

"Camden murder mystery." *Washington Post,* October 21, 1897, p. 9.

"The Camden parricide." *New York Times,* January 29, 1871, p. 8.

"The Camden parricide." *New York Times,* February 1, 1871, p. 8.

"The Camden parricide respited." *New York Herald,* April 8, 1871, p. 10.

"Camden victims buried." *New York Times,* October 17, 1897, p. 17.

"Camden women murdered." *New York Times,* October 13, 1897, p. 4.

"The Carpenter murder." *Middletown (NY) Daily News,* December 14, 1893, p. 1.

"The case of parricide in Dracut—terrible depravity." *New York Times,* January 7, 1858, p. 5.

"Case of the matricide McGill." *New York Times,* December 14, 1861, p. 5.

"The case of Walworth the parricide." *New York Times,* August 6, 1874, p. 3.

Centerville (IA) Citizen, February 8, 1873, p. 2 [no title].

Centerville (IA) Citizen, July 27, 1872, p. 1 [no title].

"Chapter of crimes." *Lima (OH) Daily Times,* November 1, 1892, p. 1.

"Charged with parricide." *New York Times,* June 7, 1888, p. 1.

"Cigarette fiend shoots his father." *Quincy (IL) Daily Whig,* November 18, 1899, p. 3.

"City and suburban news." *New York Times,* March 30, 1889, p. 3.

"Cold blooded murder." *Waterloo Iowa State Reporter,* May 8, 1884, p. 9.

"Condensed telegrams." *Cedar Rapids (IA) Evening Gazette,* July 15, 1889, p. 1.

"Condensed telegrams." *Cedar Rapids (IA) Evening Gazette,* May 9, 1891, p. 1.

"Confessed his crime." *Newark (OH) Daily Advocate,* January 15, 1889, p. 1.

"Confessing to parricide." *New York Times,* July 7, 1881, p. 2.

"Connecticut." *Titusville (PA) Herald,* May 12, 1880, p. 1.

"A conspiracy." *Cedar Rapids (IA) Evening Gazette,* March 29, 1893, p. 1.

"Convicted." *Newark (OH) Daily Advocate,* May 3, 1889, p. 1.

"Convicted of killing their father." *New York Times,* April 7, 1893, p. 2.

"Convicted of parricide." *New York Times,* January 30, 1881, p. 7.

"Crime and criminals." *New York Times,* March 14, 1879, p. 2.

"Current events." *Brooklyn Eagle,* February 28, 1881, p. 2.

"Death of a matricide." *New York Times,* December 12, 1888, p. 3.

"The death of a parricide." *New York Times,* May 14, 1880, p. 5.

Decatur (IL) Daily Republican, July 8, 1882, p. 2 [no title].

Decatur (IL) Daily Republican, July 22, 1881, p. 2 [no title].

Decatur (IL) Daily Republican, May 22, 1882, p. 2 [no title].

"Deed of two sons." *Racine (WI) Daily Journal,* November 13, 1893, p. 3.

"Deep prison plot." *Winnipeg Free Press,* August 27, 1889, p. 1.

"A demoniacal deed." *Williamsport (PA) Daily Gazette and Bulletin,* May 1, 1884, p. 1.

"A demon's deed." *Galveston Daily News,* April 1, 1892, p. 3.

"A destroying angel." *Helena (MT) Independent,* June 26, 1881, p. 2.

"A diabolical deed." *Salt Lake Tribune,* December 16, 1890.

"The doomed parricide." *Fort Wayne (IN) Daily Sentinel,* June 24, 1881, p. 1.

"A double execution." *Sandusky (OH) Daily Register,* December 19, 1890, p. 1.

"Double murder." *Fort Wayne (IN) Sentinel,* November 18, 1896, p. 1.

"Drugged the guard." *Davenport (IA) Tribune,* March 28, 1893, p. 3.

Dubuque (IA) Herald, January 28, 1873, p. 1 [no title].

"The Dykes matricide case." *New York Herald,* August 28, 1872, p. 8.

"The east." *Marquoketa (IA) Jackson Sentinel,* April 20, 1893, p. 2.

"The Eaton murder." *Hamilton (OH) Daily Democrat,* January 14, 1889, p. 3.

"Eli Shaw a free man." *New York Times,* October 9, 1898, p. 3.

"Eli Shaw acquitted." *Washington Post,* October 9, 1898, p. 2.

"The Eli Shaw confession." *Waterloo (IA) Daily Reporter,* March 28, 1900, p. 2.

"Eli Shaw jilted." *Trenton (NJ) Evening Times,* December 17, 1898, p. 1.

"Eli Shaw not guilty." *Washington Post,* May 1, 1898, p. 14.

"Eli Shaw under arrest." *New York Times,* October 16, 1897, p. 4.

"Eli Shaw's bomb harmless." *New York Times,* January 3, 1898, p. 2.

"Eli Shaw's murder trial." *New York Times,* January 1, 1898, p. 5.

"Eli Shaw's trial stopped." *New York Times,* January 5, 1898, p. 4.

"The end of a parricide." *Brooklyn Eagle,* December 14, 1863, p. 2.

"Escaped murderer." *Aspen (CO) Daily Chronicle,* March 27, 1893, p. 1.

"Execution of a matricide." *New York Times,* November 5, 1860, p. 5.

"Execution of a matricide." *New York Herald,* September 7, 1872, p. 7.

"The execution of Allison." *Indiana (PA) Democrat,* February 11, 1882, p. 3.

"The extreme penalty." *New York Times,* September 7, 1892, p. 4.

"A fatal family row." *New York Times,* July 17, 1899, p. 2.

"A father murdered by his son." *Washington Post,* August 7, 1888, p. 7.

"A female parricide." *Janesville (WI) Daily Gazette,* October 18, 1884, p. 3.

Fitchburg (MA) Daily Sentinel, October 15, 1879, p. 2 [no title].

Fitchburg (MA) Daily Sentinel, September 30, 1878, p. 3 [no title].

"The Fleming case." *Manti (UT) Messenger,* September 4, 1896.

"Fooling the police." *Brooklyn Eagle,* July 13, 1887, p. 4.

"Found guilty of murder." *Fort Wayne (IN) Daily Gazette,* July 30, 1882, p. 4.

"Found in time." *Brooklyn Eagle,* April 17, 1888, p. 9.

"Fourteen years for Swarthout." *Racine (WI) Daily Journal,* November 17, 1893, p. 3.

"The Freeman matricide." *New York Times,* March 12, 1874, p. 2.

"The Freeman matricide." *New York Times,* March 15, 1874, p. 8.

"The frequency of parricide." *New York Times,* May 2, 1871, p. 4.

"From Philadelphia." *Brooklyn Eagle,* February 1, 1871, p. 3.

"From Wednesday's daily." *East Liverpool (OH) Saturday Review,* December 11, 1886, p. 8.

"Further particulars of the murder in Watertown, Wis." *Janesville (WI) Daily Gazette,* April 19, 1867, p. 2.

"The gallows." *Indiana (PA) Democrat,* September 25, 1884, p. 3.

"General news." *Gettysburg (PA) Star and Sentinel,* August 14, 1888, p. 3.

"General news of the week." *Athens (OH) Messenger,* May 16, 1889, p. 1.

Gettysburg (PA) Adams Sentinel, February 14, 1859, p. 2 [no title].

"Given a life term." *Iowa City (IA) Daily Citizen,* May 20, 1893, p. 1.

"The Haight inquest." *Decatur (IL) Daily Review,* April 1, 1893, p. 7.

Hancock (IA) Herald, August 12, 1882, p. 2 [no title].

"Hanging a parricide." *New York Times,* February 18, 1882, p. 2.

"Hanging is too good for him." *Ogden (UT) Standard Examiner,* January 15, 1893.

"Hangman's day." *Galveston Daily News,* June 20, 1885, p. 2.

"A harmless old man dragged from his bed and hanged." *Lowell (MA) Sun,* May 5, 1884, p. 8.

"Hawkins assigns his property." *Brooklyn Eagle,* January 8, 1888, p. 9.

"He was not lynched." *Newark (OH) Daily Advocate,* January 16, 1889, p. 1.

"Held for murdering their father." *Chicago Tribune,* March 15, 1893, p. 6.

"Herman Probst may recover." *New York Times,* July 5, 1889, p. 8.

"A horrible butchery." *Dubuque (IA) Herald,* February 2, 1876, p. 1.

"Horrible matricide in New York." *Chicago Tribune,* February 11, 1859, p. 2.

"Horrible murder." *Brooklyn Eagle,* January 12, 1858, p. 2.

"Horrible murder." *Reno Evening Gazette,* November 18, 1896, p. 1.

"Horrible murder at Poolville, N.Y." *Brooklyn Eagle,* January 14, 1858, p. 2.

"Horrible murder of a mother by her son." *New York Times,* December 9, 1861, p. 8.

"Horrible parricide." *Manitoba (Winnipeg) Daily Free Press,* February 16, 1884, p. 1.

"Horrible tragedy in Chicago." *Olean (NY) Democrat,* December 18, 1890, p. 1.

"Horrid murder." *New York Times,* March 22, 1854, p. 2.

"The Houston murderer." *Galveston Daily News,* June 24, 1893, p. 3.

"How did Patrick McDermott die?" *New York Times,* January 23, 1889, p. 8.

"A hunchback parricide." *New York Times,* January 28, 1878, p. 3.

"An idler's crime." *Frederick (MD) News,* January 16, 1893, p. 1.

"Illinois." *Georgetown Daily Colorado Miner,* June 7, 1873, p. 2.

"In big luck." *Decatur (IL) Daily Republican,* October 30, 1893, p. 3.

"Inebriety and crime." *Galveston Daily News,* July 30, 1893, p. 3.

"Insane or a good actor." *Indiana (PA) Progress,* July 24, 1889, p. 6.

"Intemperance and parricide." *Brooklyn Eagle,* April 9, 1846, p. 2.

"Interview with Ware." *New York Times,* February 11, 1871, p. 2.

"Iowa items." *Perry (IA) Chief,* February 2, 1883, p. 6.

"Irving Latimer out." *Marshall (MI) Daily Chronicle,* October 27, 1893, p. 1.

Janesville (WI) Daily Gazette, February 22, 1883, p. 4 [no title].

"The Jersey City matricide." *New York Times,* January 16, 1874, p. 2.

"Joe Sarver, the parricide." *Indiana (PA) Weekly Messenger,* November 21, 1883, p. 3.

"John Collins now behind prison walls." *Lincoln (NB) Evening News and Daily Call,* April 6, 1899, p. 1.

"John Roessler's death." *North Adams (MA) Transcript,* November 21, 1895, p. 4.

"Joins his brother in jail." *Centralia (WI) Enterprise and Tribune,* December 29, 1894, p. 11.

"Judge Lynch." *Decatur Daily (IL) Republican,* February 12, 1896, p. 8.

"Jury weeps for Mrs. Styles." *Chicago Tribune,* July 21, 1899, p. 12.

"Justice is done." *Galveston Daily News,* August 5, 1893, p. 3.

"Kansas patricide convicted." *New York Times,* December 25, 1898, p. 2.

"Kansas patricide pleads innocence." *New York Times,* March 28, 1899, p. 8.

"Killed by his son." *New York Times,* January 23, 1879, p. 2.

"Killed her mother." *Fitchburg (MA) Sentinel,* October 31, 1892, p. 2.

"Killed his father and mother." *Oshkosh (WI) Daily Northwestern,* November 2, 1894, p. 1.

"Killed his mother." *Cedar Rapids (IA) Evening Gazette,* April 23, 1888, p. 1.

"Killed mother and herself." *North Adams (MA) Transcript,* July 17, 1899, p. 6.

"Kills his mother at Rockford, Ill." *Chicago Tribune,* April 30, 1893, p. 5.

"Later." *New Philadelphia Ohio Democrat,* December 11, 1884, p. 2.

"The Latimer examination." *Marshall (MI) Daily Chronicle,* February 1, 1889, p. 1.

"Latimer found guilty." *Janesville (WI) Daily Gazette,* May 7, 1889, p. 2.

"Law reports." *New York Times,* October 1, 1860, p. 2.

"Lawyer Scovel on trial." *New York Times,* April 7, 1898, p. 4.

"A lesson from the gallows." *Indiana (PA) Progress,* February 15, 1872, p. 3.

"Like the Allison case." *Indiana (PA) Weekly Messenger,* August 8, 1883, p. 3.

"Local." *Liberty (MO) Weekly Tribune,* November 24, 1882, p. 3.

"Local and state news." *Augusta (ME) Daily Kennebec Journal,* May 11, 1881, p. 3.

"Local and state news." *Augusta (ME) Daily Kennebec Journal,* May 12, 1881, p. 3.

"Local and state news." *Augusta (ME) Daily Kennebec Journal,* May 13, 1881, p. 3.

"Lost his life." *Oakland (CA),* February 20, 1895, p. 1.

"Lynched." *Marshfield (WI) Times and Gazette,* February 14, 1885, p. 4.

"Lynchers go free." *Decatur (IL) Daily Republican,* May 6, 1896, p. 8.

"Lynching echoes." *Decatur (IL) Daily Republican,* February 14, 1896, p. 3.

"Lynching threatened." *Trenton (NJ) Evening Times,* November 23, 1896, p. 4.

"The Lyndon murder." *Davenport (IA) Daily Leader,* April 10, 1893, p. 7.

"Matricide." *Liberty (MO) Weekly Tribune,* May 25, 1849, p. 1.

"Matricide." *New York Times,* January 15, 1874, p. 8.

"A matricide." *Cranbury (NJ) Press,* May 25, 1894, p. 4.

"A matricide captured." *New York Times,* September 29, 1891, p. 2.

"The matricide in First Avenue." *New York Times,* December 10, 1861, p. 8.

"Matricide in Willett Street." *New York Times,* June 13, 1860, p. 8.

"A matricide resentenced." *New York Times,* October 23, 1888, p. 8.

"A matricide's suicide." *Chicago Tribune,* July 13, 1882, p. 11.

"May result in his hanging." *Lincoln Nebraska State Journal,* September 14, 1893, p. 2.

"Mead the matricide." *Brooklyn Eagle,* February 23, 1870, p. 3.

"Met his fate bravely." *Washington Post,* January 4, 1889, p. 2.

"Miscellaneous." *New York Times,* June 22, 1859, p. 3.

"Missouri matters." *Moberly (MO) Weekly Monitor,* May 5, 1899, p. 4.

"Mob law in Iowa." *Decatur (IL) Morning Review,* February 6, 1885, p. 1.

"Mob spirit." *Decatur (IL) Daily Republican,* January 28, 1896, p. 4.

"A mother and her son murdered for gain." *New York Herald,* November 9, 1869, p. 4.

"A mother sentenced to death." *New York Times,* August 5, 1870, p. 5.

"Movements for pardons." *New York Times,* November 18, 1852, p. 3.

"Mr. Charles O'Connor on parricide." *New York Times,* July 3, 1873, p. 4.

"Mrs. Fleming's letters." *New York Times,* June 16, 1896, p. 6.

"Mrs. Marean is insane." *Trenton (NJ) Times,* November 18, 1892, p. 3.

"Mrs. Styles acquitted." *Lima (OH) Daily News,* July 26, 1899, p. 1.

"Mrs. Styles defense begins." *Chicago Tribune,* July 22, 1899, p. 9.

"Mrs. Styles goes free." *Chicago Tribune,* July 26, 1899, p. 8.

"Murder and parricide." *Canton (OH) Repository,* April 7, 1842, p. 3.

"Murder at Edgewood." *Waterloo (IA) Courier,* July 24, 1889, p. 1.

"The murder in Connecticut." *New York Times,* August 4, 1865, p. 2.

"Murder in Genesee Co. N. Y." *Milwaukee Sentinel and Farmer,* April 9, 1842, p. 2.

"The murder in Springfield." *New York Times,* December 16, 1867, p. 2.

"Murdered." *Indiana (PA) Progress,* August 24, 1887, p. 3.

"Murdered and disfigured." *New York Times,* September 27, 1879, p. 2.

"Murdered her mother." *Decatur (IL) Daily Republican,* November 1, 1892, p. 1.

"Murdered her mother." *Fort Wayne (IN) News,* May 5, 1899, p. 2.

"Murdered his mother." *Fitchburg (MA) Sentinel,* December 11, 1888, p. 4.

"Murdered his mother." *Hawarden (IA) Independent,* April 11, 1889, p. 6.

"Murderer convicted." *New York Times,* September 10, 1852, p. 2.

"A murderer hung." *Indiana (PA) Progress,* January 4, 1872, p. 2.

"Murderer Latimer captured." *Cedar Rapids (IA) Evening Gazette,* March 29, 1893, p. 1.

"Murderer Sharkey reprieved." *New Philadelphia Ohio Democrat,* September 25, 1890, p. 6.

"Murders in Michigan." *Washington Post,* March 31, 1893, p. 4.

"The New Jersey matricide." *New York Times,* August 19, 1870, p. 2.

"New York." *Daily Register Call* [Colorado], June 4, 1873, p. 2.

"The New York tragedy." *Liberty (MO) Weekly Tribune,* July 4, 1873, p. 2.

"No more arrests made." *New York Times,* September 8, 1895, p. 8

"No pardons for Elkins." *Hawarden (IA) Independent,* March 17, 1898, p. 2.

"Not guilty." *Decatur (IL) Daily Republican,* October 28, 1893, p. 4.

"Noted lunatics." *St. Louis Globe Democrat,* October 3, 1875, p. 9.

Oelwein (IA) Register, October 24, 1889, p. 5 [no title].

"Official notice." *Indiana (PA) Weekly Messenger,* March 1, 1882, p. 2.

"An old man's mysterious death." *New York Times,* October 5, 1875, p. 7.

"On trial at last." *Decatur (IL) Daily Republican,* October 20, 1893, p. 3.

"On trial for parricide." *New York Times,* January 6, 1876, p. 6.

"Ought to go to the reform school." *Orange City (IA) Sioux County Herald,* February 27, 1890, p. 5.

"Overalls and murder." *Fitchburg (MA) Sentinel,* February 10, 1876, p. 1.

Oxford Junction (IA) Oxford Mirror, July 23, 1908, p. 1 [no title].

"A parricide." *Brooklyn Eagle,* April 29, 1884, p. 4.

"A parricide." *Brooklyn Eagle,* March 17, 1843, p. 2.

"Parricide." *Brooklyn Eagle,* July 19, 1875, p. 2.

"Parricide." *Brooklyn Eagle,* July 26, 1842, p. 2.

"Parricide." *Cambridge (OH) Jeffersonian,* October 27, 1881, p. 3.

"Parricide." *Manitoba (Winnipeg) Free Press,* January 3, 1884, p. 1.

"The parricide." *Ogden (UT) Standard Examiner,* August 13, 1879, p. 2.

"Parricide." *Toronto Globe and Mail,* May 15, 1883, p. 2.

"Parricide and attempted suicide." *New York Times,* October 15, 1851, p. 3.

"Parricide and suicide." *Elyria (OH) Weekly Republican,* August 1, 1878, p. 8.

"A parricide arrested." *New York Times,* January 24, 1879, p. 5.

"The parricide at Concord." *Chicago Tribune,* February 27, 1865, p. 2.

"The parricide case." *Brooklyn Eagle,* November 21, 1860, p. 7.

"A parricide found guilty." *Newark (OH) Daily Advocate,* February 29, 1884, p. 1.

"A parricide hanged." *New York Herald,* December 16, 1871, p. 2.

"Parricide hanged." *Dunkirk (NY) Observer-Journal,* January 4, 1889, p. 1.

"Parricide hung." *Davenport (IA) Daily Leader,* June 14, 1894, p. 1.

"A parricide hunted for thirteen years." *New York Times,* October 13, 1893, p. 5.

"Parricide hunted to death." *Traverse City (MI) Morning Record,* September 16, 1897, p. 4.

"Parricide in Illinois." *New York Times,* October 21, 1866, p. 3.

"The parricide in Maine." *New York Times,* May 10, 1874, p. 7.

"Parricide in Mayfield." *Elyria (OH) Independent Democrat,* November 28, 1866, p. 2.

"The parricide in Williamsburg." *Brooklyn Eagle,* September 1, 1860, p. 3.

"A parricide pardoned." *Las Cruces (NM) Rio Grande Republican,* March 26, 1887, p. 2.

"A parricide sentenced." *Brooklyn Eagle,* November 3, 1854, p. 1.

"Parricide sentenced to death." *Tyrone (PA) Daily Herald,* March 30, 1900, p. 1.

"A parricide will probably be lynched." *Washington Post,* July 28, 1887, p. 3.

"Parricides lynched." *Quincy (IL) Daily Journal,* February 25, 1885, p. 1.

"A parricide's story." *Oxford Junction (IA) Oxford Mirror,* August 1, 1889, p. 4.

"Parrott hanged." *Toronto Globe and Mail,* June 24, 1899, p. 23.

"A pathetic letter." *Semi-Weekly Cedar Falls (IA) Gazette,* February 9, 1897, p. 1.

"Patricide." *Ogden (UT) Standard Examiner,* July 28, 1887.

"A perfect monster." *Bangor (ME) Daily Whig and Courier,* March 11, 1881, p. 3.

"Pointed paragraphs." *Massillon (OH) Independent,* March 30, 1888, p. 1.

"Poisoned the guards." *Brooklyn Eagle,* March 27, 1893, p. 1.

"A probable matricide." *New York Times,* August 21, 1872, p. 8.

"Probably fatal stabbing affray." *Brooklyn Eagle,* August 20, 1860, p. 2.

"The Probst matricide." *New York Times,* July 26, 1889, p. 8.

"A quadruple tragedy." *Atlanta Constitution,* February 6, 1876.

"Recovers from trance." *Waukesha (WI) Freeman,* January 13, 1898, p. 6.

"Respite granted." *Decatur Decatur (IL) Daily Review,* June 25, 1881, p. 1.

"The Rockford tragedy." *Toronto Globe and Mail,* July 26, 1878, p. 1.

"The Roessler mystery." *North Adams (MA) Transcript,* November 22, 1895, p. 4.

"Rooney killed by his son." *New York Times,* January 15, 1881, p. 8.

"Sacrificed father." *Washington Post,* June 19, 1898, p. 4.

"Says girl is hypnotized." *Athens (OH) Messenger and Herald,* October 5, 1899, p. 2.

"Says he killed his father." *Janesville (WI) Daily Gazette,* November 7, 1893, p. 1.

"Sentence of a matricide at Springfield, Mass." *New York Times,* May 27, 1868, p. 5.

"Sentence of Bevins the Michigan parricide." *Chicago Tribune,* July 12, 1865, p. 3.

"The sentence of Sarver." *Indiana (PA) Democrat,* May 8, 1884, p. 3.

"Sentenced for parricide." *Brooklyn Eagle,* February 15, 1879, p. 4.

"Sentenced to be hanged." *Brooklyn Eagle,* November 2, 1871, p. 3.

"Sentenced to be hanged." *New York Times,* November 11, 1888, p. 9.

"Sentenced to hang." *Galveston Daily News,* January 2, 1898, p. 1.

"Sentences and other business." *Connellsville (PA) Keystone Courier,* July 13, 1884, p. 4.

"Shaw contract settled." *Galveston Daily News,* August 8, 1893, p. 3.

"Shaw disappointed by reprieve." *New York Times,* July 29, 1893, p. 9.

"The Shaw jury case." *New York Times,* January 30, 1898, p. 2.

"Shaw must die." *Galveston Daily News,* April 20, 1892, p. 3.

"Shaw placed on trial." *Washington Post,* January 4, 1898, p. 3.

"Shaw soon to be tried." *Galveston Daily News,* April 8, 1892, p. 3.

"Shaw will be hanged." *Galveston Daily News,* August 4, 1893, p. 3.

"The Shawangunk murderer." *Port Jervis (NY) Evening Gazette,* April 15, 1871, p. 1.

"She killed her mother." *Quincy (IL) Weekly Whig,* May 11, 1899, p. 3.

"Sheriff disperses a mob." *Alton (IL) Evening Telegraph,* October 21, 1897, p. 4.

"A shocking history." *Chicago Tribune,* November 9, 1881, p. 5.

"Shocking matricide." *New York Herald,* December 30, 1869, p. 7.

"The shooting of Dr. Talbott." *Galveston Daily News,* September 21, 1880, p. 1.

"Shot and killed four men." *New York Times,* August 7, 1893, p. 5.

"Shot dead by his son." *Fort Wayne (IN) Daily Gazette,* February 12, 1884, p. 7.

"Shot his father and mother." *New York Times,* November 3, 1894, p. 9.

"Shrouded in mystery." *Titusville (PA) Herald,* November 18, 1899, p. 1.

"Silly women petting a matricide." *Frederick (MD) News,* February 4, 1889, p. 1.

"Singular property suit." *New York Times,* October 23, 1892, p. 13.

"Slain by her own son." *New York Times,* October 4, 1887, p. 2.

"Slain by his sons." *Racine (WI) Daily Journal,* November 15, 1892, p. 3.

"Son confesses patricide." *New York Times,* November 22, 1899, p. 8.

"The son is being watched." *Waterloo (IA) Daily Reporter,* November 19, 1896, p. 1.

"Son kills father." *Oshkosh (WI) Daily Northwestern,* November 13, 1899, p. 1.

"A son kills his mother." *Washington Post,* July 4, 1889, p. 2.

"A son murders his father." *Indiana (PA) Progress,* November 15, 1883, p. 3.

"A son's terrible crime." *Janesville (WI) Daily Gazette,* July 8, 1882, p. 1.

"Starkweather." *New York Times,* August 18, 1866, p. 8.

"Startling development about the patricide." *Newark (OH) Daily Advocate,* May 22, 1882, p. 1.

"Story Co. tragedy." *Perry (IA) Chief,* February 23, 1883, p. 3.

"Story of the double crime." *New York Times,* June 6, 1893, p. 2.

"A strange crime." *Davenport (IA) Morning Tribune,* December 2, 1888, p. 3.

"Successfully executed." *Reno Evening Gazette,* January 3, 1889, p. 2.

"Suicide and parricide." *Ogden (UT) Standard Examiner,* November 30, 1889.

"The Sullivan outrage." *Decatur (IL) Daily Republican,* January 25, 1896, p. 8.

"Sunday crime." *New York Times,* August 30, 1875, p. 8.

"Sunday tragedies." *New York Times,* July 19, 1875, p. 8.

"Suspected of parricide." *New York Times,* January 14, 1881, p. 2.

"The Talbott murder." *Waterloo Iowa State Reporter,* August 10, 1881, p. 6.

"Telegraphic brevities." *Boise Idaho Daily Statesman,* November 29, 1891, p. 4.

"A terrible crime." *Indiana (PA) Democrat,* November 15, 1883, p. 3.

"Terrible crime in Racine Co." *Janesville (WI) Daily Gazette,* November 8, 1865, p. 4.

"A terrible nemesis." *Titusville (PA) Herald,* February 5, 1885, p. 1.

"A terrible parricide." *New York Times,* June 4, 1873, p. 8.

"A terrible tragedy." *Indiana (PA) Democrat,* February 11, 1882, p. 3.

"That Eli Shaw business." *Waterloo (IA) Daily Reporter,* April 26, 1900, p. 2.

"That improbable son." *Boulder (CO) Daily Camera,* September 29, 1891, p. 1.

"They regret it." *Decatur (IL) Daily Republican,* February 13, 1896, p. 8.

"A thirteen year old boy shoots his father." *Newark (OH) Daily Advocate,* July 7, 1882, p. 1.

"A title to Shaw's body." *Galveston Daily News,* July 27, 1893, p. 3.

"Topeka patricide trial." *New York Times,* December 9, 1898, p. 7.

Toronto Globe and Mail, December 2, 1875, p. 3 [no title].

"Tragedy at Rockford." *Toronto Globe and Mail,* July 25, 1878, p. 1.

"Tragedy near Sioux City." *Waterloo (IA) Courier,* April 25, 1888, p. 1.

"Trial of a young man in Wisconsin for parricide." *New York Times,* December 10, 1867, p. 2.

"Trial of Stanley Griffith." *East Liverpool (OH) Saturday Review,* December 6, 1884, p. 2.

"The trial of Thomas Callaghan." *Brooklyn Eagle,* October 22, 1875, p. 4.

"The triple murderer." *Ogden (UT) Standard Examiner,* March 30, 1893, p. 1.

"Two fair homicides." *Waterloo (IA) Daily Reporter,* May 5, 1899, p. 2.

Tyrone (PA) Daily Herald, January 30, 1890, p. 7 [no title].

"An unnatural murder." *Syracuse (NY) Daily Standard,* October 4, 1887, p. 1.

"Various aspects of crime." *New York Times,* March 15, 1879, p. 2.

"The verdict of the jury in the Sarver trial." *Indiana (PA) Democrat,* March 13, 1884, p. 3.

"Virginia." *New York Herald,* November 9, 1869, p. 20.

"A Virginia horror." *New York Herald,* November 24, 1869, p. 22.

"Waiting for death." *New York Herald,* November 2, 1871, p. 5.

"Walter Shaw on trial." *Galveston Daily News,* December 13, 1892, p. 2.

"The Ware murder." *New York Herald,* July 19, 1871, p. 5.

"Ware to be hanged today." *New York Times,* December 15, 1871, p. 2.

"Ware's execution yesterday." *New York Times,* December 16, 1871, p. 2.

Waterloo (IA) Daily Courier, January 29, 1898, p. 1 [no title].

Waterloo Iowa State Reporter, December 12, 1895, p. 5 [no title].

Waterloo Iowa State Reporter, July 10, 1872, p. 1 [no title].

"Wesley Elkins is free." *Des Moines Daily Leader,* April 20, 1902, p. 18.

"A wicked conspiracy." *Atlanta Constitution,* April 30, 1884, p. 4.

"Will January convicted." *Quincy (IL) Journal,* October 12, 1896, p. 1.

"Will lynch Atterberry." *Decatur (IL) Daily Review,* January 26, 1896, p. 1.

"Will never squeal." *Davenport (IA) Weekly Leader,* June 14, 1893, p. 5.

"A woman in the case." *Decatur (IL) Bulletin-Sentinel,* February 1, 1896, p. 1.

"A woman murdered." *New York Times,* January 26, 1889, p. 5.

"Work of a brutal son." *Brooklyn Eagle,* January 15, 1893, p. 20.

"The work of criminals." *New York Times,* January 7, 1883, p. 7.

"Young criminals." *Fort Wayne (IN) Daily Gazette,* March 10, 1884, p. 10.

"A young life criminal." *New York Times,* January 13, 1890, p. 5.

"Young patricide dies in prison." *Washington Post,* June 29, 1894, p. 6.

"A youthful murderer." *Sandusky (OH) Daily Register,* July 27, 1889, p. 1.

Index